Extra-Ordinary

The Touch That Marked Eternity

"Who are these men that have turned the world upside down?"

D.N.H III

ISBN 978-1-0980-4047-5 (paperback)
ISBN 978-1-0980-4048-2 (digital)

Christian Faith Publishing, Inc.
832 Park Avenue
Meadville, PA 16335
www.christianfaithpublishing.com

Printed in the United States of America

PREFACE

In 2004, I began a journey in Mexico that would forever change my life. I was nineteen years old and never imagined what was about to unravel. What was supposed to be a two-week trip marked me too deep to forget, and a year later, I returned to Mexico. In September of 2005, there was a small voice in my heart that I tried to hide from that said, *These will be ten years of preparation for you for something great.* From two weeks through the next ten years up to the present, now marking sixteen years, the journey can only be defined as miraculous. As I look back, there aren't words to express all that I've lived, that I've learned along the way, and what those words from that small voice implied in my life, but these last sixteen years have turned me into the man that I am. In the words of Paul found in Philippians 3:12 and 14, "Not that I have already obtained it or have already become perfect, but I press on so that I may lay hold of that for which I was laid hold of by Christ Jesus." In the same spirit, I have far to go, but have already begun.

For my thirtieth birthday, I was reminded of those soft words that I felt in my heart almost twelve years earlier, and I began to remember the previous third of my life. God had not only done an amazing work, but He had blessed me with many men and women along the journey who have marked my life. Some will never be known beyond the words in these pages, and others are famous in the eyes of many, but both have taught me what it means to truly live.

I thank my father and mother who have been very faithful and supportive of my journeys, although almost always far away; my sister, who has always been more like a best friend; and my wife, the greatest gift that the Lord has entrusted to me, who has given me two amazing sons and one beautiful daughter. There are hundreds or even thousands of names that will not be in these pages, but as you will see, those that have reflected the mark of the Maker as a part of their legacy have greatly influenced me along the way.

The title of this book comes from two verses: first, the famous words of Jesus found in John 14:12–14: "You will do even greater things than I have done"; and the second from Acts 17:6: "These who have turned the world upside down have come here too." It still puzzles me to hear the debate over these words in the church today, but I have seen that the greatness in the kingdom of God is all too often not the great teaching, most gifted, most famous, charismatic, or prophetic individuals. Rather, it belongs to those who have made the choice to live the ordinary, the most rudimentary part of our design within humanity. Those that embrace the theomorphic to be transformed, to live the image and likeness of God, to be *extraordinary* when nobody's watching, when there are no lights on, and when it's just them before the face of God, living a selfless love with unity of those that surround them.

The process of writing this book began just before my thirtieth birthday and has continued for five years as the ideas developed. This is just a portion of what has brought me to this point in my life as I am so blessed to see that my story began many generations ago. Having two grandparents in the military service, one as a colonel in the Air Force during World War II, and another in the Korean War, I have been blessed to see how the choices of one can influence the many. My parents laid an incredible foundation for my life, for my future, and for my present reality. My choices might not have begun like theirs did, but I'm excited to see the inheritance and impact in the generations to come because of what I have, now, chosen to do. I have a rich legacy of leadership and influence from many generations before me, through my great grandparents, my grandparents, my parents, and my desire is to see that incarnated in my life and multiplied to many generations after me.

My desire in writing this book has three key parts: The first is that, for years, I have enjoyed traveling one or two weeks a month to teach and share in many different cities, countries, churches, and different ministries. Through these journeys, many different teachings have been developed and many hours of processing the depths of apostolic leadership. In a season of life with a growing ministry and three small children, I have had to make a very conscious choice to turn down most teaching invitations, which has been hard for me. I felt a conviction that it was time to begin to write and to leave a legacy on paper that transcends a classroom in any single location. For my kids, for future generations, for our ministry, but also because of a great conviction that I want to be a faithful steward with whatever God places within my hands.

The second is because I have had a conviction to write for many years. Having had a lot of inspiration by John Maxwell, Max Lucado, Reverend John Wesley, Loren Cunningham, N. T. Wright, Darrow Miller, Francis Schaeffer, among others, I've seen the power of writing beyond just public speaking and teaching. My goal is to publish each of my books simultaneously in Spanish, Portuguese, and English as we have a trilingual ministry, and this is my main target audience. *Extra-Ordinary* is becoming an umbrella for daily devotionals, extending into online teachings and ideally a full book series for both children and adults. I currently have several other outlines that I am working on, and this book marks the goal of stepping out in faith as an unknown author with a vision that must begin somewhere.

The third is simply because I have great conviction that God wants me to. It's taken me over five years to finish this book due to fear of man and personal insecurities. What if no one reads it? What if it's rejected? What if it's a complete failure? And to these fears, my only response is—God is worthy of my obedience, even if it's a failure in the eyes of the world. It's for His glory, and He is worthy.

Format

My design within this book gives a dynamic adventure from both my own life and key people that I have crossed paths with through the years. I've highlighted what I consider to be fifteen of the most important principles in leadership and discipleship for anyone at any point in their faith journey. The format allows each chapter to almost be its own story. It's my past-to-present journey with the discovery and application of each principle and how a key person that entered my life was able to most reflect this reality. I hope that this story can be as influential and heart-transforming as it was for me. I've asked each of these men and women to write their own prelude to the chapter so that they can, in their own words, share what this means to them. The stories are all real, based on real people, and events, and to the best of my knowledge, the most honest and sincere expression of my personal perception of my own life to this point. At the end of each chapter, there are application questions and special meditations to consider how these principles can be applied in your own life, family, church, ministry, and with the people around you.

CHAPTER 1

Calling

Inspired by missionary Henry Davis from Venezuela

Calling—a response to the nudge of God, resulting in a change of course, direction, identity and purpose, leading to a new vocation; a response to the voice of the All-Powerful and All-Personal God.

Special Introduction

It's still fresh on my mind, the day when Daniel and I met in Mexico. His team had such eagerness and excitement in their hearts to serve, so it was an honor to be one of the drivers to take him to the location where, together, we built homes for those in need. As I looked at all of you with amazement, I felt that the Lord wanted me to share about His calling through sharing stories about the Lord's plans and desire for our lives. The more I shared, the more excited everyone was. I saw faith rise up in their hearts. This reminded me of when Jesus called His disciples to become "fishers of men," and He was doing this in the hearts of Daniel and his team. In the book of Ezekiel, God said to Israel, "I will first send fishermen." What was amazing about Jesus's disciples was though they were very young and most of them had failed their religious studies and were now working in their trades, they were called by Jesus. Jesus does something that no other teacher does: He went to find these young tradesmen and called them and taught them how they could be like Him. With faith and trust, they were willing to surrender everything, follow Him, and the rest of the story is *His-Story*. These young men changed the world forever. Today, as each of us are called by God, we need to continue to build hope, faith, and love in calling this generation and the generations that follow to be like Jesus to His calling.

Henry Davis
Missionary in Asia from Venezuela

* * * * *

Growing up in a healthy Christian home, I remember having my "good Christian week" each year as we would go and serve somewhere in the world on a mission trip. Even before those trips, some of my earliest memories were somehow connected to youth events at church or our annual church vacation trips to Lake McConaughy in Nebraska. My grandparents on both sides were Christian, as well as my great-grandparents before them: Lutheran on one side and Baptist on the other. I was raised nondenominational. Church and the Bible were just a part of life, as was youth group, Mothers of Preschoolers (MOPS), and many other activities we did. We always had family prayer before dinner, and I remember learning the Johnny Appleseed "prayer song" from the time I was very little. My mom or dad would come in my room every night and pray with my sister and me. My mom would pray for my future wife, and my dad would share how he loved us just as much as the Father loved His Son, Jesus, and share stories with us.

I have a beautiful Bible from my grandfather, and to this day, I am so grateful for the incredible inheritance I have received from the generations before me. The incredible memories of being the "star" in the Christmas story or simply receiving a reality where God was somehow at the center of it.

As I grew older, however, I had to make a choice to step out from my parents' covering and choose to either draw close to God for myself or to walk away. What seemed like very black-and-white truth soon became more like a gray saying from the generations before me.

There were definitely some moments along that journey of adolescence that really marked my life, but a moment came where God was no longer my focus, and soon almost everything I did stemmed from selfish ambition. Even during those awesome mission trips, I was unable to see beyond myself. In general, these weren't trips for me to give and focus on others but rather to experience something for myself and forget it as soon as the trip was over. The issue was my heart. I would go to get, to take, or to fill a void that only God can fill, and I was looking at life with the wrong heart. The craziest part: I was going in the name of God, but He was no longer given space within my life to fill those voids of identity, pain, fear, shame, guilt, or pride. These years became a season to just create what I wanted out of life.

More than one of those trips was connected with a new relationship with a girl that would continue for some time after. I was very superficial, and each decision was solely focused on myself. It came to a point that I would spend time with a group of girls only if they were beautiful, or I could get something out of them. I used them to give myself an identity, and they used me to fulfill their own identity. In some of the godliest environments, sin was there knocking at the door of my heart. It was winning the battle of my mind, and even on a missions trip, all I could do was see myself. Perhaps there were a few moments when I was really challenged that God must be real, but nothing had ever marked me in the way that a trip in July of 2004 did.

I want to pause here and give a special thanks to the McCombs and their ministry of campaigners (a youth ministry for high school students); my mom, and all her efforts to take me on these trips, to keep me in a healthy environment; and the Nollers, for pushing so hard to have God's heart become alive in me; for my dad, leading youth group; and the Brumelles' push to have the Sunday youth services. I may not have made a lot of right choices during my fifteen to nineteen years of life, but I know that these key people that fought so hard to at least provide a healthy environment kept that seed of life within me.

In July of 2004, I had just graduated high school with plans to continue my studies in college. Just like each previous year, an opportunity arose to go and serve for a week on a missions trip. This year, we were going to Chapala, Mexico. A month prior, in May, after my high school graduation, I had a *very* long night at my senior party marking the peak of some of my stupidity and regret. Soon after, I realized that my life and what I was living for was just like everyone else around me who were five to ten years older: party, have fun, pay lots of money to finish college, obtain a good degree, get a good job to pay off college debt, continue partying to meet many more girls that others wanted and couldn't have—but I didn't really want either—to hopefully find *the* girl, buy a house, have the picket fence, have two children, and one day work hard enough to retire and do what I really want to do. I have nothing against the American dream, and for those who truly dream to do something in their life, to be responsible and bless others is amazing, but I just had an awakening moment that I desired something different out of life. Die today or in eighty years, I didn't want to leave any space for what-ifs or should-haves. I wanted to plan for eternity but live as if I only had today.

My first choice to go on that trip to Mexico was a selfish feeling, and it really had nothing to do with God or anyone else. There was no good merit in my desire to change or any deep divine guidance, but as the door opened for me to go, the Lord was preparing the foundation of my heart in a way that I never imagined. I had tasted the normal, and I wanted more. I wanted today to mark the difference in eternity, and I definitely didn't want my perspective of life and the world to be limited to my small town of two thousand individuals in the mountains representing a very small fraction of global reality.

As I arrived in Mexico, something was different on this trip. My heart was open, and I was listening in a way that I had never done before. My eyes seemed to be opened in a way to see things that I had never seen before. Many people say that short-term mission trips have no lasting impact, can leave no long-term development, and are a waste of money and energy, but I disagree. Those short trips growing up didn't transform me, but they kept a little seed alive; and time and time again, I have seen how a simple trip to another culture or country, putting new people in my path, could influence one small choice, which will eventually alter the course of an entire life. This is what happened to me!

This trip is where I met one of the men who forever marked my life. He was a Venezuelan man named Henry. He was working with our church team, and for some reason, I spent hours and hours listening to his stories, and about the man that he was. There was something different about him. When he was speaking with our leaders, the pastor, the kids, the youth, or the women, we would hang on every word and begin to be transformed. I had never met someone that had something so genuine that applied to and challenged everyone around him. He kept talking to me about how God doesn't have grandchildren but only sons and daughters. What he meant was that I couldn't have a relationship with the Creator of the universe through my church, parents, a religion, or anyone else, and it had to be personal and intimate. As he talked with me, he continually referred to the people of the Bible that were called like Abraham, Isaac, Jacob, Joseph, Moses, Joshua, Caleb, Ruth, and Esther, among many others. They were each called to leave their home and culture, their family and comfort zone, and go into the desert and meet God face-to-face. Sometimes they would be sent home again. Sometimes they would never return, but wherever they went, they went because they were in the presence of God. Henry told me that this was the focus of a program they called a Discipleship Training School (DTS) that I could come to beginning in September through the ministry we were serving with, Youth with a Mission (YWAM). Little did I know that the DTS was all over the world, and YWAM was the largest missions movement in the world connected to the University of the Nations, and soon my life would be shifted and altered into directions that I would have never imagined.

I kept thinking, *God doesn't have grandchildren. He only has sons and daughters. Am I a son, or am I grandchild? Is God my Father? Or is He just another story that I have heard from my family?* As I began to process these thoughts, I didn't like where they left me. I had grown up in the church, I had experienced God, I had studied the Bible, and I had even taught the Bible all through high school; but the same question remained: Is God really my Father?

By the end of those ten days, we built three homes for poor families, but the federal police had come to stop us because the local

Catholic Priest didn't want us helping the people. They didn't want the people to have the Bible, to see and experience the outside world, to think independently. I had never experienced something like this—the church trying to keep the people away from the Bible and change—and it made me examine everything I had ever believed.

As this trip ended, I felt like I had an important decision to make. Would I be willing to go into the desert alone with God without knowing what the outcome would be? Did I really want to know God in an intimate way for myself and not because of my church, pastor, or family? Did I live in such a way that *my* story would captivate anyone who would listen like Henry's did? Was I any different than the world around me? The answer: *no*. I didn't have *His* story, but rather my own; and right then, I realized I wanted more.

As I mentioned earlier, I was raised in the church. I had read through the whole Bible. I had amazing parents and some amazing men and women of God who had influenced me. I had been involved in youth groups and missions trips and many wonderful things. I led a Bible study and would often teach from the Bible, pray, and even hang out with Christian friends. When I was three years old, I walked over to my mom and told her that I wanted Jesus to live in my life, and He filled my heart. My first preaching was at the age of twelve, and several people from the congregation said, "You will be a teacher!" I was baptized when I was fourteen because I wanted the world to know that I loved Jesus. I know that the Lord had been working in me, on me, around me, and through me for many years, but that good foundation was just an influence, and now I was a young adult, and I had to decide for myself.

Here I was, now nineteen years old. I had been selling drugs, drinking, partying, and fighting. My vocabulary could offend almost anyone as I excelled in my four-letter words, and I definitely didn't see the image of God in the women around me but rather an object for my affection, and I had lost any idea of who I really was outside of what others wanted. The mothers at church wanted me to marry their daughters, but my friends would never leave me alone with their sisters. My story was definitely not reflecting *His* story that I had heard so much about, that I had studied or even taught, proclaimed that I desired or lived, and definitely nothing like the story of the Venezuelan man, Henry, who turned my world upside down in just ten days. My best friend was a strong Christian girl, and she was always mad at me because she knew my life was wrong. But I knew the Bible better than she did, and I knew it well enough to defend my sin and to stay far from God in the name of truth and the church.

Needless to say, as I returned home and shared with my parents my desire to put college on hold for a semester and take a time in the desert with the Lord and they were very excited. I don't think they knew exactly where I was in my life, but they had seen the signs. On one occasion when I was eighteen, my mom told me that if I didn't clean out my closet, she would. Well, I didn't clean it out, and one day after basketball practice, I came home and saw that my whole room was clean, and so was my closet. This was *really bad*! And sure enough, right in the middle of my bed was a twenty-four-pack of beer, some pornography, and things that I definitely didn't want my parents to see. They might not have seen everything, but they knew that if I was willing to go and spend six months in a foreign country with a bunch of godly people: and possibly straighten out my life a bit, they would be happy. I sent in my application to this DTS program with little to no idea of what awaited me in my desert, but I knew I was being called to go, and that was enough. This one little choice would forever change my future.

It was as if I had been walking on two sides of the fence the last five years of my life: one foot in my life of selfishness, living my plans, doing it my way, in my timing, for the glory of myself while establishing my kingdom and the other with some type of skeptical hunch that God wanted something more and that He must be real, and I needed to change. I was curious enough to keep stepping out into it without ever giving myself over to it. I was doing everything right in the eyes of the world: getting good grades, doing well in sports (for a 2A school), working hard to prepare for college, going to church, and becoming ready for the next step in life. Beneath the surface, though, I knew that it was all just a front. I had the normal high school story of one mask covering another, and I knew it didn't reflect *His* story, and I had come to the conclusion that I wanted more and that He wanted more. So with little to no understanding of YWAM, DTS, or any Spanish, I blindly jumped on a plane to Mexico. This one choice had me begin by walking in my calling as I entered my desert.

As I look back, it's hard to say what would have happened had I never left for Mexico or jumped on that plane. Some say that God will simply have His way with you, and none of it depends on us in some strange fatalism, thinking that nothing I choose can change the fate set before me. In the Muslim culture, it is referred to as "Allah's will" or a concept that God controls all things independent of us as individuals. A lot of my Christian friends would see the God of the Bible the same way, and their excuse for their sin is that if God really wanted them to change, He would change them because He was in control.

The more I reflect upon my life, however, the more I have seen and grown to understand that there is a great weight in the decisions I make. The consequences are very real, and the burden will not fall on God or others to walk forward in what I choose to do. The calling does not depend on us as individuals, as God has called all people, but their response is what transforms eternity. Like David and Saul, Saul had rejected the Lord, so the Lord had to rise up a New king, a humble man, named David because of the hardness of Saul's heart and rebellion. Our choices matter! God didn't change in character. He called three different generations, but Saul had no heart for God. David had a full heart, and Solomon only had half a heart and turned away. Their choices really did matter, and God responded accordingly.

Years later, now being a leader of a YWAM ministry in Morelia, the decision to first come to Mexico seems crazy. I spoke absolutely no Spanish, found no joy outside of my own culture, and I believed that I had a very set pathway for my life. In no way did I imagine I would one day be fluent in Spanish, married to the woman of my dreams with three incredible children, and in a place where the most common language would be one other than my own: Spanish. I never imagined the friends I would have around the world, the journeys that God would take me on, or the lessons that I would learn having traveled to different countries, communities with all sorts of languages, and experiencing many cultures. I would have never imagined what my life would be like today, where I would be, or what I would be doing, but I know that the day I arose to respond to the calling in my life is the day that *everything* else was pushed aside. I'm about to renew my passport, and it has over sixty stamps in it, and I would have never imagined that one step into Mexico would have opened the door to the nations.

Moses began his ministry by responding to a simple call from the Lord: "Take off your sandals, for where you are standing is holy ground." Through the years, God continues to bring me back to this unique verse in the Bible, and I imagine what Moses's life would have been like should he have chosen not to remove his sandals, not to walk over to the burning bush, and not respond to the Call to simply humble himself. Many of the greatest things in life began with someone or something extremely ordinary, whether it is to take off his sandals like Moses did, to get on a plane and fly to Mexico, or simply leave everything behind like Abraham did without knowing where he would go. The greatest journeys seem to begin with the smallest choice to walk into the ordinary in obedience to God and outside of ourselves. A phrase that God has often brought to my mind through the years is, *You will never become someone tomorrow that you don't fight to become today.* I do not know where this call will lead me, but I know that I can never go back. In response to the calling, I have found that there is nothing on earth that can compare to the *extraordinary* and begin to live *His* story for my life.

Through the years, I have heard many people teach or share about calling as if it referred to a place, a physical location, a time in history, a country, or a people group. "I am called to Asia!" or "I am called to serve the Muslims." But I have come to the conclusion that a calling is not a onetime experience for a single place. It is rather an understanding of what it means to find your vocation, to follow the voice of the Creator of the universe, and to fully live God's image and likeness in your own life. It's not about when I get somewhere or what I will do, but more of who I am in Christ and committing to it for the rest of my life.

To give a better understanding of what I mean, I want to share a short story. I know that God has opened doors for me to grow in my teaching gift and that God has given me the supernatural ability to speak and understand Spanish for a reason that in some way connects with Latin America, which I will share more about in the next few chapters. Mexico is where I chose to respond to my calling, and Mexico is primarily where I have served God through this calling. However, I have been in many other nations, worked with many other languages, and have had students from all over the world.

There was a season in my life before I was married that I began to really struggle with the understanding of my calling. I had been in the "desert" for several years, had no money, and being a missionary as my vocation didn't promise a lot to offer for a wife. I loved teaching, and others saw me as gifted in working with large groups of people. I had been in Mexico for just over four years and made a new seven-year commitment to continue serving in Mexico toward the vision that God had given me. In this same season, I was coming closer and closer to getting married, and I hoped that God would miraculously do something different in my life.

This took place in 2008. I was in San Jose, Costa Rica, helping lead a community development school, and I had the opportunity to be a part of an international conference. I was one of the youngest at the conference in my early twenties, and there were pastors and leaders from Central America, Mexico, and the United States. Through casual conversation, I began to speak with a group of leaders from the United States. I was sharing some of my passions, convictions, and communicating a little bit of the heart that the Lord had given me during the past four years. We had some good chemistry, and it turned out that three from this particular group of leaders were a part of a leadership team for a decent-sized church in Florida. Their head pastor had just moved on from the church, and they were looking for a vibrant young teaching pastor to come and take the church into a new direction. We spoke for several hours, and to my surprise, they offered me the teaching pastor position. Not only would I be a pastor at such a young age without seminary and only having finished a few different schools through the University of the Nations, but also I would be able to teach full-time, which I loved, get paid for it, have health benefits, and I would get to move back to my home country and speak English! I was very excited, and this was an amazing opportunity for me to finally use all of my gifts *and* be at a place where future in-laws would have fewer questions and more excitement about giving their daughter to me. I told them that I would pray about it and give them an answer the next day.

As I began to walk away, the presence of the Lord heavily came over me, and I knew that I didn't need to pray about this decision as the Holy Spirit brought conviction. I was excited about my kingdom, my dreams, and what I wanted, but I had forgotten about *His* story in that moment. It quickly changed from serving God for the glory that He could get out of me, to using God to get my own glory, my own influence, my way and establish my own kingdom. I had just made a seven-year commitment because God had shown me that He had a purpose for me in this particular season in Mexico. My calling wasn't to be in the desert or to seek out a new promised land but, rather, to be with God where He wanted me—in Mexico. I turned around and walked back to those leaders and was honest with them. I shared that I was very honored but that I knew God had already spoken to me for something different in this season. It was a great opportunity, but my place was where God already had me. It wasn't about money, opportunity, numbers, or my desires, but it was about walking in *His* story, in His timing, wherever, whenever, and with whomever He wanted.

Similar situations arose throughout the years, and the temptation in my mind was always the same: *Serve God in a small place with between five and twenty-five people that I could influence, or go with the opportunity where I could become well-known and touch many people along the way?* It looked godly, but it was the extreme of humanism and using God to get what I wanted. There is a famous preaching by Paris Reidhead called "Ten Shekels and a Shirt." It reminds me of the dangers of this "Christian humanism" and brings me back to my knees in repentance before God.

D.N.H III

One of the verses in the Bible that I have most meditated upon through the years and continually been challenged by is Joshua 5:13– 15. Joshua had just taken command of Israel and the second generation, and they were on the way to Jericho. The captain of the Host of the Lord appeared to him, and Joshua asked, "Are you for our adversaries or for us?" This question reflects what I think most of us as Christians ask in our lives. "God, are You going to be a part of my plans, what I am doing, and where I am going? Or are You against me and my plans?" The captain of the Host of the Lord answered in a way that has always impacted me, "No." We can't try to take God with us and live what we want. The question should never be, "God, are You with me?" but the question as we walk forward in life must always be, "Lord, am I with You? What do You want from me? Where do You want me to go? What do You want me to do?" We don't get to just take God with us and do whatever we want, but when we have responded to the call of the Lord, we do whatever He asks, even if it is something as simple as, "Remove the sandals from your feet, for the place where you are standing is holy ground."

So through the past sixteen years, I have continually seen that my place, and my calling is to simply say yes because He has said yes, to go because He has asked me to go, or to stay because He wants me to stay. This is the greatest journey on earth. Many times it isn't doing the spectacular, and more often than not, it is actually doing the extremely ordinary, repetition of a day-to-day life because the voice of the Creator of the universe has called me to follow Him. In the wonderful words of Jesus, "I only do what I see the Father doing, and I only say what I hear the Father saying." May my vocation, my life, and my calling be a reflection of *His* story and one day be an example of the *extraordinary* as people remember and think of His story!

Reflection

1. As you think of the verse, "Many are called, but few are chosen," what comes to your mind? Have you responded to the call?

18

2. Thinking of this verse, "God does not desire that any should perish but that all come to eternal life," what does this imply?
3. What was your desert experience? Are you a grandchild or a son or daughter of God?
4. When you share your story, is it *His* story? Or is it your story?
5. When you think of the verse in Isaiah 54:2–3 "to enlarge the place of your tent without any limits," who is responsible to make this happen, you or God?
6. What is your vocational calling? Are you responding to your own passions or the word of the Lord?

Meditation

Jacob had been called from the "loins" of Abraham. Abraham struggled through his calling for almost forty years as he was called at the age of sixty, and Isaac didn't come until he was one hundred. And continually he failed until he was finally able to trust the God of the promise more than the promise itself. At this moment, he was proclaimed as a man of faith and righteousness. Isaac had to have his own encounter with God and choose to follow the promise independent of what his father had already lived. Isaac was the promise to Abraham and therefore had a calling before his birth, but he still had to choose to respond to the calling and have the God of Abraham become the God and Father of Isaac.

Jacob also was chosen from birth, but even to the point where he was going to meet his brother, Esau, in the desert, he first sent his family and livestock in fear that Esau would come and kill him. One night, he had an encounter with the Lord and wrestled Him all night to the point that he was permanently marked in his hip from the struggle. This encounter with the Lord was much more than an experience but the first time that Jacob did not follow the God of Abraham and Isaac. But now he began to follow His God, His own Father. After this encounter with God, Jacob fully responded to the call of God and took on His calling to be the head of his family. As he responded to the calling, his name was then changed to Israel, and he marked what became known as the people of God.

It has become very evident, when we just step aside and give God His rightful place on the throne of our hearts, everything changes, and our story really can become a glimpse of *His* story!

The Bible and Calling

- Abram was called from Ur to have a son by faith and bless all nations.
- Moses was called back to Egypt to deal with his step-brother and free a nation.
- Noah was called to unite his family, build a ship, and preach repentance for all nations.
- David was called to forgive and honor his enemy and become a prince of God's people for the nations.
- Esther was called to become a queen, to combat social injustice, and bless the nations.
- Boaz was called to redeem Ruth, a widow and foreigner.
- Samuel was called to be a moral voice for a nation that rejected him.
- Daniel was called to counsel foreign kings in a foreign nation that oppressed his own family and people.
- Joshua was called to cross the Jordan and conquer the land while carrying the baton of the previous leader.
- Rachel was called to have a family and serve with Isaac in a faraway land.
- Jacob was called to confront his brother and lead his family into a new country.
- Jesus was called to give up everything and incarnate Himself to redeem His people.
- Paul was called to love his enemies and turn into what he most hated and persecuted.

Therefore I, the prisoner of the Lord, implore you to walk in a manner worthy of the calling with which you been called.

—Ephesians 4:1

CHAPTER 2

Truth

Inspired by Pastor Braulio Serratos from Mexico

Truth—the correct description of reality from an infinite perspective, absolute, unchanging, that applies to all people, at any given moment in history, present or future.

Special Introduction

For an introduction to this chapter on truth, and as I think of the value of truth, the following is what comes to mind. Truth is not about any specific religion or philosophy. Truth is simply what it is. The truth is determinate in the life of any individual or society. I grew up in a family in which we didn't know the truth. We believed in religion, we believed in fables, fairy tales, and even lies, which made our lives full of darkness and uncertainty. We lived in constant fear of the present, the future, and even more of eternity. When we know the truth through the Bible, we are totally transformed, and we are set free. For this reason, since thirty-four years ago, I have dedicated my life to sharing the truth of God. The Lord Jesus said in John 8:32: "You will know the Truth and the Truth will set you free." Through the years, I have seen the same pattern repeated many times: individuals and families set free, saved, and totally transformed. May the principles of this chapter do the same and even more in your own life.

Braulio Serratos
Senior Pastor of Jamay Church
Church Planter, Evangelist, and Modern-Day Apostle

* * * * *

I remember the day I got off the airplane as I returned to spend the next six months of my life in Mexico and begin this discipleship program. As I was driving from the airport to the missionary training campus, I had one clear thought: *I must be crazy.* I had just jumped on an airplane to a foreign country, without speaking the language, without anyone I knew, simply because I thought that God was calling me. As my driver said nothing, I sat in silence, whiffed unfamiliar and unpleasant smells; and in my mind, I began to wander. I wasn't even a good Christian or convinced that God existed! As I held back tears, I realized for the first time in a long time, maybe ever, that my walls of protection around my life had come falling down. The masks of my identity were torn off, and I was vulnerable. No one knew my story, the identity I had created and fought so long to possess, or the image that I had portrayed to others. Nothing of what I was existed anymore. I now had no defined past. My story was now what I chose to share, and I could define it however I desired. It seemed just hours earlier I was in control of everything; now all I could do was walk forward and wait for the unexpected. As I was struggling to answer two questions in my mind, I was hit with a new reality: "Who am I?" and "What will these people think about me?"

Having struggled with male relationships—well, not struggled, but having spent much of my time with girls—it was very hard for me when I discovered that I was a part of a school with nearly all guys. Aside from one married Mexican couple, there was only one other woman enrolled in the program. I spoke no Spanish, and I would be rooming with four other Mexicans, none of whom spoke English. I remember the first evening as we all came together. It was one of the first times in my life that I had no words to say, and I had no idea what awaited me. All I knew was this: I didn't want to be here, at this moment, in this place, with these people—but here I was. My first morning, I awoke, half asleep, and tried to put on my hat. One of the Mexican guys began to yell at me, "Peligro!" over and over again while hitting me. I didn't understand what was happening. He made me very angry, but it turns out, he was trying to protect me. As my eyes began to open, I saw a big scorpion sitting in the middle of my hat. I then came to realize he was hitting me and telling me, "Danger!" and not just being obnoxious. This is a pretty good image of what the next three months of my life entailed: me confused and frustrated and usually completely wrong in my assumptions.

It only seems right that after a chapter on calling, I would follow it with a chapter on truth. My whole life, I heard what I should and shouldn't do, what I should or shouldn't believe, what was right or wrong when talking about the Bible; but at the same time, I learned very little about truth. What I most remember about truth from high school and my time before coming to Mexico was that Absolute Truth didn't exist. It was whatever people wanted it to be. If it did exist, one thing was certain: Christians didn't have it. The latter never made sense to me, and I think this is one of the reasons I had the intuition that God must be real somewhere. Some of the most intelligent men I have ever met—scientists from the Middle East, men from NASA, teachers, lawyers, doctors, among others—were all Christians. Some of the scientists even claimed to be able to prove God's existence. I sat through some of their classes growing up, not understanding much, but I knew there was definitely space for reason and God together. I just never really took the time myself to wrestle through the issue.

Day in and day out, I was challenged with the same phrase over and over—"the truth." People spoke of it in an absolute way, with no fear of what others might feel or think, including themselves. The people I came into contact with would teach and share about their lives. They were living their lives for something greater than themselves, outside of themselves, and measured by a standard not of their own. Dean Harvy was one of the teachers that most challenged, inspired, and even angered me because of this concept of truth. He tore through my theology about the nature of God and man, sin and truth, and presuppositional truths. I spent hours arguing with him, trying to prove my point from a posture of independent selfishness, and he would respond with an incredible depth of conviction. He made several statements that forever changed my life. He didn't try to defend or argue theology with me yet kept going back to "Truth," the "Word of God," and the person of "Jesus."

The first statement was, "If you can show me anything I am teaching that goes against the Word of God, the Bible, and not just your opinion or what you believe, I will change what I teach. I trust in the Bible so much as Absolute Truth that if it said 'Jonah ate the whale,' I would believe it." The second thing he said to me was, "With how much you argue against the existence of God and any absolute moral standard or give account for what is and isn't permissible in life, I wonder if you aren't arguing so fiercely because you're worried you might be wrong. If you are wrong, that makes you responsible for your life and no longer a victim. That means you would have to change, and I don't think you want to change."

Could it be possible that some of what I had heard or believed my whole life wasn't completely right? Is it possible that I cared more about being right and defending my sin than finding truth? That week, I made a commitment to God: "If You are real and the Bible is Absolute Truth, then I want to know You for myself, not for what people tell me about You, not for any theology or doctrine, but because I want to discover Truth." I think that was one of the most powerful commitments I had ever made in my life, and it began a process of the Bible and me, Jesus in me, hearing the Holy Spirit. Through the next six months, I read through the Bible, cover to cover, twice! I was tired of people telling me about God, about Truth, and about what the Bible said. I wanted to know it for myself. I don't remember much more of the teachers from that season of my life, but I do remember that if God was real and Truth existed, and that Truth was a person named Jesus revealed through the Bible, I wanted to discover Him for myself.

Every excuse I made in the name of the Bible to live a life of selfishness sounded good. "It's about grace, not works," "Jesus came to get rid of the law," "The Old Testament doesn't matter anymore," "Jesus came to make me free." I was soon to find these were all semi-truths. The real message was about a covenantal relationship in love, a love that transforms everything. In love, there is no space for selfishness. Love makes no excuses but gives everything and expects nothing. Love is an action, not an emotion. The opposite of love wasn't hate but, rather, selfishness. As I began to see Truth, I could see my great selfishness in every argument I ever had. Whether the argument was theological or over a different topic, it didn't matter. At the end of the day, if I had really found love and true grace, which I didn't deserve, I would spend the rest of eternity enjoying the freedom to be responsible for my life. I would be a new creation, reflect Jesus, and enjoy the undeserved gift of a completely clean conscience!

Dean also made a comment that I have carried with me for a long time: "If you read through the Bible every year cover to cover, within ten years, you will have read the Bible more than 90 percent of pastors and ministers in the world today." Whether that comment was right or wrong, it reminded me of what Henry Davies told me once: "God only has sons and daughters, not grandkids." I didn't want to just trust what someone else told me, and I was convinced I had to discover it for myself. I knew that if you could read the Bible in one year by reading three and a half chapters a day, then I could do it in six months reading seven. Yet during those six months, I read about fourteen chapters a day, which has been a habit of mine ever since. I found out it only takes about seventy-two hours to read the Bible, and really, it shouldn't be separated by chapters and verses but, as much as possible, read as whole books—all sixty-six of them.

Sixteen years later, I don't claim I know the Bible better than 90 percent of pastors, but I have discovered that most people I encounter have never read the Bible even once. The Bible is the most reproduced book in the world. It is a book that is quoted, carried, purchased, sold, guarded, and even worshipped, but all too often it isn't read, much less actually applied with conviction and understanding. For sixteen years now, I have read the Bible between two and seven times a year, a different translation every time, and it continues to amaze me how possible it really is to understand the single intended meaning of scripture.

One important principle of studying the Bible has stuck with me—*context, context, context*. And as I always tell our students now, "The Bible can never mean something today that it didn't mean when it was originally written." It was written by real people at a real time in history in a real language, with a real message, and I don't get to change it. My job is to make sure that as I read and study today, I keep the purity of that message. To this day, I still save some "love letters" from my wife that she wrote me as a teenager. Anyone could just read parts of those letters and assume many things. But when you understand our story, what was happening in each of our lives, and just a little bit of context, those words fly off the pages and touch even the driest heart. The Bible has even greater power than one love letter in a single relationship. It can shape nations, transform governments, reeducate a complete generation, and turn darkness into light for obedience to the faith for all nations.

In November 2004, about halfway through my first six months in Mexico, I was sent with a small team of three to go and serve in a local church for the week. We were blessed to meet many people and hear some amazing stories. There was a man we met who has, to this day, marked my life. We were sent to stay at a pastor's house, and Pastor Braulio received us in his home with open arms.

Braulio is a large man, very dark skin, large glasses, broad shoulders, and for a Mexican man, very big and quite intimidating at first encounter. I remember he had a very sweet, soft-spoken wife, one son, and two daughters. I grew up with a healthy respect for my own father as he was a big man with large tattoos, and despite never seeing anything I had heard from his past, I had no doubt that I didn't want to push him too far. I loved him and had a healthy reverence for him. A very similar feeling came over me as we entered Braulio's house. I was nineteen years old, afraid of nothing, but felt like a fourteen-year-old boy again, almost fearful to talk. Not that it mattered since I was the only one in the house that spoke English, and I still spoke almost no Spanish.

I have never been the best listener in life, but living in an environment where no one understood me and I didn't understand them, I began to learn the art of watching, listening, and picking out the smallest details to not be lost in what was happening around me. A smile, a glare, a tear, mumble, or the slightest change of expression on a face would catch my attention. As we sat in the house that first night, I remember studying this man as he looked through his glasses and began to speak to his wife, make a phone call, or get the attention of his children with a simple look. He carried a presence that I had never experienced before. My experience with pastors was expansive. I met men of mercy, counselors, and men I could relate to easily. I also met men who enjoyed talking a lot or teaching, evangelists, or famous public speakers. However, I had never met anyone like this man. He was a man of few words but a great presence in every moment, every word, and with every look. He stepped into the room, and things were different. The question began to build in my mind, what is different about this man?

As we awoke early the next morning, we drove for a long time. The pastor was driving a small minivan with several other men, the two guys in my team, and me. After a while, passing village after village, we arrived in a small town. As soon as the pastor stepped out, all the men came out of their houses, almost like soldiers before a general. We quickly switched vehicles and now, riding in the back of a pickup truck, traveled for hours to a community in the distant mountains.

As the pastor got out of the truck, again people stood at attention. He spoke a few words, but it was evident this man carried something very unique. Day after day, we spent long hours working with the people. We gave out Bibles, shared about Jesus, prayed, and saw miracles. The hunger and need for Jesus was evident.

I don't think I was able to understand the depths of what I was experiencing in these communities until years later. This area of Mexico, the eight Central States, is known as the *Circle of Silence*. It is the least evangelized area in all of the Americas with a percentage of Evangelical Christianity of about 1.5–2.5 percent. To this day, they run out Christians with machetes, and I have heard tremendous stories. You can go to town after town and not find a single Christian church. On most windows, you see little stickers that say, "We don't accept Protestants here." To my amazement, it was town after town of communities that didn't have the Bible either, and many hadn't ever seen one. They really are silent when it comes to the Bible, and many have given their lives to try and change this in the middle of a region controlled by a sect of the Catholic Church that has done everything in its ability to keep the people from receiving the Bible or education.

When I understood this reality, I was able to truly understand who this man, Braulio, was. He had dedicated his life to the Bible, Scripture, the proclamation, application, and dedication of the Word of God. He was born into a reality where truth wasn't taught, proclaimed, or heard. He is one of the best speakers I've ever heard, and I have heard Bible teachers from all over the world. A few years back, in 2017, I ran into him and was blessed to hear him in a church where I was preaching. It was like old times, and I was just as challenged as ever. Braulio is different than most pastors or leaders. He has no money, no fame, no glory, no great name, no great inheritance, and he's downright crazy by the standard of most men in this world. His children are now grown up with his son in college and girls graduating high school. Thanks to him, though, community after community now have vibrant, biblically solid churches. Some are as small as just one couple, with others over one hundred people, but there is a light blazing of radical men, women, and children who have risen up and broken the chains of history. Machismo and the matriarch society, drunkenness and cartels, corruption and violence have now become healthy marriages and families of love and peace. Children are going to school and being educated with very hardworking parents. These have become the people of the Living Word. Almost no one will ever know about them, but I will forever be marked by these amazing people and the man, the modern-day Paul, fully dedicated not to teach, not to sell or to make gains, but to be a man who has given up his life for Christ. He is someone who believes that Truth is absolute and is defined in the person of Jesus Christ by the power of His Holy Spirit through understanding the Holy Bible.

I don't know what this life holds for me, but one thing is certain: Truth is absolute. It is not to be invented or determined by experience. It is to be discovered and is open to anyone who has a willing heart. Pastor Braulio will not likely be known outside of the pages of this book or his small region of the world, but he has forever marked my life. In a way, he has been like a general, showing the men of this world that you can stand strong, you can walk with your shoulders high, no matter what people say. He has exemplified the phrase of Paul: "To live is Christ, and to die is gain" (Philippians 1:21). The Truth allows us to live the message, to multiply it and embrace it in our lives. It transforms everything. Jesus Christ is the Living Truth. He who was, and who is, and who will forever be. I have seen that I can follow Him and become a man like Him. This is my desire—to be a man that reflects the heart of God, to have a marriage that reflects the relationship of Jesus and the church, that I might die daily, and that my children and wife would grow and thrive in the love that we share. In the words of the Moravians, "May the Lamb that was slain receive the reward of His suffering."

For years as I traveled and taught, I would think back on incredible men like Dean and Braulio. They knew the Bible so well they could just teach without notes, flip through the pages, and share with conviction. This was always a dream of mine to know the Bible so well it would become the word of my heart. I have tried multiple times to memorize Psalms 119, and I've never gotten beyond the halfway point, but I will one day. I have an oral Bible overview I can share in just fifteen minutes, and I've memorized books like James or parts of the Gospels, and my wife has the whole book of Mark memorized. At one point, I even had Genesis memorized through the first ten chapters. I remember taking full weekends studying the Bible and seeking God. Something began to shift in me during this time with Braulio, and like Jesus did with the disciples in the end of Luke, my eyes were opened to the Scriptures. I still teach and preach a lot, but almost never with notes anymore. Just my Bible, what's in my heart, and what has become real in my life on whatever God is showing me at that time.

Each year I desire more, and the Bible can never be read enough, pondered enough, explored enough, or applied enough. Just this past year, a Bible translation organization offered to cover my costs to return to school to become a Bible consultant for Latin America because they think I fit well into what they need. These types of invitations seem almost illogical, knowing my own story. What began as a seemingly impossible challenge sixteen years ago by a young man that doubted the existence of God has exceeded my expectations, and I've discovered that I can find truth, I can understand the Bible, and I can become a living letter, putting on the mind of Christ, knowing and understanding God!

I could have never imagined how this process of discovery and Truth would open doors for me. Just a couple of years ago, my buddy, Dale, and I were at a conference where there was a focus on Bible translation, oral Bible translation, and the need in Mexico. We prayed that night and made a commitment to try to do something about the Bible-translation needs in Mexico. Neither of us have any background in Bible translation, but we both have a passion for the indigenous of Mexico and years of experience working with them. We adopted some of these unreached people groups of Mexico and began to pray. That prayer turned into a short mission trip that Dale led in faith with a few other people to try and have a first encounter with the Otomi people of Veracruz in Mexico. All we had were longitude and latitude coordinates.

After much prayer, they hopped on a bus, then took another bus, and another bus, followed by a two-hour taxi to finally arrive in the middle of the mountains. Dale went to the top of the mountain and prayed. They made first entry in the community and eventually found a Catholic church. Upon meeting the priest, the team was honest with their reason for being there, and the priest told Dale that he had never seen anyone in history come into their community to help save their language and translate the Bible for them. He let Dale into the cathedral, and while praying and filming a video, Dale felt God speak to his heart. He felt there was an Evangelical Christian family within the community, and Dale committed to finding them. Within six hours, they found the family with a tiny little church! They were bilingual, a Mexican married to an Otomi woman with kids.

A few hours later, a missionary pastor arrived, who was also working in this community. He had been heading on a trip out of the community when he came to a river, and God told him, *Return. I have sent you people.* He returned to find Dale and our team who were able to minister to him and greatly encourage him! Within two years of that first trip, we have done six different trips with them. We have had some of their leaders travel to Morelia to be trained with us, and we now have a first draft of the Jesus film script and a first draft of the book of Luke. What an incredible story!

In January of 2019, I had another incredible opportunity and was invited to go to the Mexican Congress as the new government took their place. Together, with part of our team from the Council of Michoacán, we united with key Evangelical leaders throughout the country and were able to give a Bible to every new Congress member. We were also able to share about the role of government, the family, and the church within the nation. I was one of the only non-Mexicans invited, and I was the only participant under fifty years old that I could see. How did this happen? How could a man without any degree, without any formal training, and just a young American missionary in Mexico be in a place like this? Simple: the Truth transforms nations. When we become the Living Word, God opens doors to multiply His Truth for His glory. What began many years ago gets deeper, more mature, and stronger each year. God is worthy, and it is His Truth and His story!

In September, of 2019, I was on a trip to teach in Madison, Wisconsin. In the airport, I received a message from a leader in Central America. He had been given the task of pushing forward the Bible-translation Process of Latin America. He knew me, and because Brazil and Mexico have the biggest needs of all of Latin America, he asked me to take on Mexico. It's an intensive eight-month project of beginning the oral Bible translations of forty unreached people groups in Mexico as we enter the global year of the Bible: 2020. To accept would mean stepping out in frontier missions like never before and sending at least one team a week to meet the deadline. I prayed, said yes in the airport, and sent the list to Dale. In just two months, thanks to Dale and his wife, Jesus, Roberto, Gustavo, and a few others, we have already done the first four Bible stories in seven of these unreached people groups. We've experienced miracles, have been the first to enter certain people groups, formed an alliance with government organizations, Bible-translation organizations, and key indigenous leaders, and once again we are doing things that I would have never even dreamt of sixteen years ago.

The influence of Truth isn't what we can teach others from our mind or teaching notes. Truth is imparted more than it is taught. It is contagious. It has an impact and power when it is visible within the life of the messenger. If Truth is absolute, then the power is seen in the fruit of the application. As a living letter, truth must be seen to be effective. May my life align with the lives of many incredible men and women all over the world that have made a choice to become a living letter of His Truth. May each of our stories create a message of His story. As we always say in one of our Bible schools, "The character of the messenger must be consistent with the message that he or she carries."

Reflection

1. What does it mean for you to be free?
2. If the opposite of love is selfishness, and selfishness is to do whatever you want, then what is love?
3. If Truth is absolute, then what is the absolute standard for what you live?
4. If Jesus is God, and Jesus is the Word, and the Word was in the beginning with God, can you fully know God without understanding the Bible?
5. Do you have a clean conscience with pure thoughts?
6. What does it mean to "be renewed by the transforming of your mind"?
7. Where could God's Truth take you in the next sixteen years?
8. How often do you read through the whole Bible?
9. Who is God, what is the Bible, and how have they transformed your life?

Meditation

Deuteronomy 10:12–13 says, "Now, Israel, what does the Lord your God require from you, but to fear the Lord your God, to walk in all His ways and love Him, and to serve the Lord your God with all your heart and with all your soul, and to keep the Lord's commandments and His statutes which I am commanding you today for your good?" Braulio taught me what it meant to understand the fear of the Lord, to begin my life in Genesis 1:1, and remember, "In the beginning, God…" and that all things are sustained in Him, but this is also what's best for me.

Thomas Jefferson wrote a letter one time called "a conversation between my head and my heart," and I think this can be seen in the church of today. We feel or we think, but reason in itself is not enough, and an experience in itself doesn't change anything. It's not about the what, where, or when but more the why and who.

Truth is absolute, and it is not to be created but rather to be discovered. If God created me, He knows what is best for me. If He asks something of me, it is for my good, according to the above verse. God's dreams, desires, and plans for me are continually good, but I need to get out of the way. To discover Truth is the only thing that can fully set me free. Not in my head with knowledge, or in my heart with experience, but a choice to believe with great conviction that I would get up and walk with Him, that it would transform me, and I would become like the God that I worship in thought and character. I have come to a place where I don't just believe the Bible; I understand what it means to love and trust the God revealed through the Bible. He has created me, and my reality is defined by Him. My desire is that I will live my life in such a way that I'll reflect the great commandment, "Love God with all your heart, with all your soul, with all your strength, and with all your mind."

I believe that most people desire to "feel" God. They desire to have their will follow Him, and most people put great effort into doing so. At the same time, I don't believe we have really understood what it means to love God with our mind. Truth is simply the correct description of reality, and I am not the source of Truth, but rather

I have the ability to discover Truth, to apply Truth, and to abide in Truth. "You shall know the Truth, and the Truth shall set you free." I have given up everything, but I have gained everything. I have died to every dream in my life, but I have discovered the real desires of my heart. It took me getting out of the way and discovering Truth to discover who I really am.

The calling was not enough, but to be set free, to become a reflection of the image and likeness of God and learn to really be His image bearer. Only in Him can this take place. Only in Him can I fully live a life of love, of freedom, and a completely pure conscience with no regrets and no shame. As I discover Truth and apply it, I have been set free and will be free indeed. So many years ago, my ideas had no room to turn me into the man I am now. I was a reflection of what I worshipped: myself and my own way of thinking. My desire is that as I discover more and more of the Truth of God, that I will reflect Him more and more. My dream is to be a life learner, willing to trust, even when I don't understand, because I love God!

The Bible and Truth

- Jesus proclaimed that He was the way, the Truth, and the life.
- Pilate looked at Jesus and asked, "What is Truth?"
- When choosing the judges and leaders, Moses chose the men who fear God and were full of truth.
- As the Lord passed before Moses, He proclaimed, "The Lord, the Lord God, compassionate and gracious, slow to anger, and abounding in lovingkindness and truth."
- The people told Joshua that they would "fear the Lord and serve Him in sincerity and truth."
- When Samuel spoke to the people before anointing Saul, the first king of Israel, he spoke to the people and said, "Only fear the Lord and serve Him in truth with all your heart."
- When David was made king, he looked at the people and said, "Now may the Lord show loving-kindness and truth to you; and I also will show this goodness to you."

- "Lead me in Your truth and teach me, For you are the God of my salvation; For I wait all the day" (Psalm 25:5).
- "All the paths of the Lord are lovingkindness and truth, to those who keep His covenant and His testimonies" (Psalm 25:10).
- "Into Your hand I commit my Spirit; You have ransomed me, O Lord, God of Truth" (Psalm 31:5).
- "You, O Lord will not withhold Your compassion from me; Your lovingkindness and Your truth will continually preserve me" (Psalm 40:11).
- "Do not let kindness and truth leave you; Bind them around your neck, Write them on the tablet of your heart" (Proverbs 3:3).
- "He who speaks truth tells what is right, But a false witness, deceit" (Proverbs 12:17).
- "A false witness will perish, but the man who listens to the truth will speak forever" (Proverbs 21:28).
- "Buy truth, and do not sell it, get wisdom and instruction and understanding" (Proverbs 23:23).
- "For the law was given to Moses; grace and truth were realized through Jesus Christ" (John 1:17).
- "But he who practices the truth comes to the Light, so that his deeds may be manifested as having been wrought in God" (John 3:21).
- "But an hour is coming, and now is when the true worshipers will worship the Father in spirit and truth; for such people the Father seeks to be His worshipers. God is spirit, and those who worship Him must worship in spirit and truth" (John 4:23–24).
- "So Jesus was saying to the Jews who had believed Him, "if you continue in My word, then you are truly disciples of Mine; and you will know the truth, and the truth will make you free" (John 8:31–32).
- "But Paul said, 'I am not out of my mind, most excellent Festus, but I utter words of sober truth'" (Acts 26:25).

CHAPTER 3

Intimacy with God

Inspired by missionary Loren Cunningham from the United States

> *Intimacy*—to know the character of another to such a degree that life becomes a depth of love and trust, openness and honesty, humility and transparency so that two can become one without any shame. Learning to love what he loves, to hate what he hates, and to abstain from anything that might negatively affect the others emotions. IN TO ME YOU SEE ALL THINGS.

Special Introduction

Hearing God is not all that difficult. If we know the Lord, we have already heard His voice—after all, it was the inner leading that brought us to Him in the first place. But we can hear His voice and still miss His best if we don't keep on listening. After the what of guidance comes the when and how.

If we want to be known in heaven and feared in hell, we must be willing to lose our reputation here on earth. May this chapter challenge you to dare to live on earth in the same way that Daniel has been trying to do this in his own way.

"For from the days of old they have not heard or perceived by ear, nor has the eye seen a God beside You, Who acts on behalf of the one who waits for Him" (Isaiah 64:4).

Loren Cunningham
Author, Missionary, Founder, and Leader
Youth With a Mission International* and University of the Nations†

* * * * *

I remember a late night on Halloween in 2004 where a friend and I were sitting at a bonfire that overlooked the city playing the guitar during my missionary training program in Mexico. We spent hours talking, singing, and watching the stars. I remember hearing sirens and knowing what was happening all around me, but at the same time, it seemed so peaceful. After my buddy went to bed, I stayed up for a while longer and began to share my heart with God. As I looked around me from the mountain where I was sitting, over-looking the city, I had this strong feeling of how selfish man had really become. Even within the domain of the church, self-centered-ness had become a theme of the Bible preaching: the creation for man, God for man, angels for man, miracles for man, salvation for man, heaven for man, earth for man, life for man, death for man, and everything that could possible "feel good" for man." My prayers quickly shifted from simply pouring out my heart to actually break-ing within my spirit and identifying with this spirit of selfishness. I had given up everything to follow God: my family, my culture, my language, my job, and so much more. Then it hit me. I felt like God owed me something. I was living a life of transactions with God. I gave, so now He *had to* do what I wanted. I was on the mountain, in a new culture, language, and country, and I realized I only wanted God for what He would do for me. I was hiding under the mask

---

* A global missions movement
† A global university for knowing God and making God known in every country on earth

of ministry or Christianity, but my heart motive was the same. I remember humbling myself before God while shedding a few tears, and as I arose again, the story of Noah and the ark came to my mind. It wasn't an audible voice, but the details of this Bible story that surfaced did not come from me. It was God talking to me, and three questions popped into my mind:

- How long was Noah building the ark before the flood?
- How many people listened to God?
- How many times did God speak to Noah during this time?

As my mind began examining the details of the story, I saw a man working hard with his wife and kids for one hundred years on a boat, no one heeding his message. While building the boat and preaching repentance to the people, I didn't see long conversations with God. Noah didn't serve God for what he could get out of Him, but he simply served Him because he trusted Him and therefore was willing to be obedient no matter what the cost, or the results, which were zero converts in over one hundred years of evangelism. Again I humbled myself before the Lord and began to repent of the many times I felt like God had to do something for me; that I had to feel Him; that for me to obey Him, I must first get something. I was nothing like Noah. I had been a man serving God not because I trusted Him but because I had fear of His power and, at the same time, expected His power to bless me before I had to do anything. There was no foundation of a love-and-trust relationship that brought forth radical obedience, just transactional choices while I waited for the reward. That night marked my life. All alone on Halloween, I made a covenant to God. If He never spoke to me again, never used me again, and never allowed me to experience Him again, I would still serve and obey Him for the rest of my life because He was worthy, and I trusted Him.

Many times through the years, God has brought me back to that covenant with a simple question, "Do you trust Me?" I haven't always made the right choice, and to my regret, I have fallen into the humanistic Christianity that believes God is for me like a magical genie. However, with great patience and love, the Holy Spirit has brought me back to that one experience that I will never forget on top of that mountain. After a few tears from conviction and repentance, the decision becomes easy: God is good, I trust Him, and He is worthy, no matter what the cost.

This experience was preparing the soil of my heart for an experience that would forever shape the way that I saw God and how I interacted with Him. After a couple of months in Mexico, everything in my foundation was being rocked. The areas that were weak were being broken, and I found, to my great surprise, that God Himself had begun to build a new foundation within me. After that Halloween night, I went very extreme and began to live as if it was wrong to experience the presence of God. I shied away from prophecy, the miraculous, and the gifts of the Spirit. As I saw the great destruction that a few movements focused on "God experiences" had done, I had become cold in my personal relationship with God. To fully pursue God, however, I had to first put my heart in the right place. As I humbled myself, He then took the job of bringing me into the balance of living a daily covenant full of loving intimacy with Him.

Six weeks after being in Mexico, I was soon to experience something that would challenge everything I had ever believed. I was at a pastoral and missions conference with about three thousand people attending. On the second day, the founder of Youth with a Mission (YWAM,) Loren Cunningham, was the guest speaker, and he began to share about how every country on earth is an open nation. He said, "I can get you into any country on earth if God calls you, but you may never come out. God says, *Go*. He doesn't necessarily say, *Return*." Loren didn't say it with fear or force but rather with love and excitement. He really trusted God, not just because He was worthy but because Loren knew Him. He had experienced Him, and he had a very unique relationship with the Creator of the universe with hundreds of stories to prove it. His testimony spoke to me more than his words, and I saw how Loren didn't teach a message but rather lived a message full of power and experience. He said yes, even at the cost of his own reputation. When he did say no, he was quick to repent and return to the place of saying yes in the fear of the Lord, knowing that God was there to do the impossible. He exemplified sincere love to me, living the kingdom of God here on earth, here and now.

After the conference, there was a time to minister to the different ages, and I went forward and began to call out for God. This was a decisive moment for me as I had been convinced that God was real, that He was good, but that I wasn't right with Him. Since I was the only English speaker, I began to pray out loud in a way that I'd never done before, knowing that no one understood me, and I began to fight with God. I remember saying, "I know You are real, I know You are good, and I know You have more! I can't continue living a divided life anymore. Either tonight You take everything, or tomorrow I am going home and never looking for You again. Either take it all or let me go!" While I was praying, something very unique happened, especially since I didn't believe in the gifts of the Spirit and I had never experienced any of them. I fell down, and as I climbed to my knees, I began to pray in a language that I couldn't understand. I tried to stop, but I couldn't shut my mouth or control it. All the people around me understood what I was saying as I began to pray for them. I was praying in perfect Spanish. This continued for about two hours in a way that to this day I can't fully explain, but I definitely can't doubt that it took place.

After the conference ended and I was back where I was staying, I began to read the Bible to try and figure out what was happening to me. I began looking into speaking in tongues and started to read 1 Corinthians 12–14. I felt like the Holy Spirit spoke as clear as can be to my mind. *You are right. I am real, and I am good, but I am a gentleman, and I won't take anything from you. I am knocking and waiting—you must choose. I knock and wait. I don't break down the door and force you.* I laid down my Bible, looked into the heavens, and I spoke to the Creator of the universe about how I wanted more than to just trust and obey Him—that I wanted intimacy with Him. I wanted to know Him and understand Him in a personal way. With a deep conviction, I knew that no one else could do this for me; I had to do it myself. Loren had left me very challenged. I wanted what I had just heard Loren speak about, but I knew that I couldn't have his relationship. I would have to develop my own intimacy with God. Just like Loren, I wanted something genuine and real, something very personal and intimate. I wanted my own personal love and trust relationship with God, and I was tired of seeking it in all the wrong places.

About three months later, a similar experience happened in El Salvador on the island of Monte Cristo when I began to pray for a woman, and I felt God's heart for her. I didn't know what to say, but the words began to flow out in her language. She understood me in her own language, and God used me to speak to her. What a privilege! I saw that God was all-powerful, all-personal, and all-relational. I realized that a large part of what my relationship with God looked like depended on me. If I was willing, He was always ready and eager to teach, but His willingness wasn't enough; I had to choose daily as well. This has happened in different places, in a few different languages, and I'm always amazed at how obeying the all-powerful and all-personal God here on earth changes everything.

A few years later in 2006, I had the privilege of flying to South Korea for an international workshop. It was my first experience in Asia, and everything marked me: the people, the culture, the bathrooms, and the beauty. My grandfather had fought in the Korean War, so I had heard many stories about Korea, but nothing that I had heard was visible. It was a beautifully developed country. One night during a worship session, I began to ponder and communicate with the Father, Son, and Holy Spirit as I was learning how to relate individually to each person of the Godhead. Very quickly, the Holy Spirit took me on a trip down memory lane of dancing with my mom, dad, and sister while growing up. My mom and dad were incredible dancers, and we used to go out dancing as a family once a week. To watch them move when they danced was like watching one person, not two. As I was caught up in that memory. I felt like the Holy Spirit spoke to me and said, *May I have this dance?*

"Here in front of thousands of people?" I responded. But then I realized that the Creator of the universe had just asked me by name to dance alone with Him, so I did. I shut my eyes and began to dance with the Holy Spirit. I don't know what the people around me thought, and frankly it didn't matter, but the principle that I had discovered came springing up in my life again: God is a gentleman, and He knocks and waits on me. He is faithful and personal, but I must choose to answer. He initiates and pursues, but I have to respond. That dance was one of the most spiritual moments I have ever experienced in this life with God. In the middle of a multitude on the other side of the world but alone with the Father, Son, and Holy Spirit. He called me by name, took my hand, and touched His heart while His Spirit overflowed within mine with a profound love and trust. He is the perfect leader. He is the right guide, and He knows each step to take. As I stopped dancing, I felt that the Holy Spirit spoke to my heart and said, *I want your life with the Father to be like this dance. That each step would be guided by Him, just like Jesus did. Jesus did this by listening to Me and following Me. Let Me teach you how to glorify the Son by obeying the Father.*

One of my biggest frustrations in ministry has been the continual debate and comparison of Spirit or Truth as if they are somehow separate or opposites. I have met many passionate young men and women along the way that call themselves prophetic with a desire to live by the Spirit, *but* they have never once read the Bible. They proof text Scripture, trying to get Scripture to affirm what they feel and desire, despite what it actually says. They struggle more often than not with moral/habitual sin and believe that freedom comes from an experience but feel unable to continually live with a clean conscience, so they never reach freedom and instead seek the next experience. They believe a magical touch by God will heal everything and that somehow a special experience is more important than a genuine covenantal relationship. They seek power, signs, and wonders, with little to no concept of covenant and character. The other side has jumped into an extreme just like I did, loving the Bible but ignoring the message of an intimate God, who is very active and personal. Being so afraid of the negative experiential Christianity, they have jumped into a concept of covenant without relationship. They are good soldiers, fighting the good fight but lacking the sign of the fruit of the Spirit and expectations of the power of God, almost falling into humanism where man has the final word and God's power is only seen in the future resurrection and their concept of a future heaven out of this world.

As I have dealt with and continue to encounter these two very unhealthy extremes, I am thankful for God's mercies that have brought me to my knees, for men like Loren that have challenged me with something more, and for continual experiences that prove that He is here with me. In 2019, after being married with three kids, I believe that God has given me a beautiful picture of a loving covenant with my wife and what He desires with me. He expects experience and intimacy, but the majority of my daily life comes from a love and trust relationship seen by my commitment, many times in spite of my emotions. He desires for me to enjoy His presence, yet He also expects me to live by principles and truth even when my limited perspective doubt and question within my emotions. I obey because I trust and love Him and have no expectations of experience, but just like with marriage, without intimate experience, there would be no healthy covenant either. God overshadows me with His presence and conquers my heart, but I am called to live for Him without any expectations—I live a covenant.

It is not a debate over Spirit or Truth like so many churches have argued throughout the ages, but we must open our minds to understand that it is the Spirit of Truth. We are to cover our minds with Christ. Truth is Jesus, the Spirit guides us in all Truth, but the Word was in the beginning. Jesus is the Word, and the Spirit renews our mind by the Word. Truth sets us free, and it is all by the Spirit of Truth. An experience might mark us, but the Truth is what sets us free. The Spirit of Truth fills, cleanses, and transforms, using the Scripture that we have filled our minds with. I thank God that He showed me my roots of humanism and selfishness, but then conquered my heart as I humbled myself. The balance of intimacy, both covenant and experience, is a hard balance to find. Without the correct balance, it is impossible to live a life of intimacy though. It is time for the head and heart to align with Scripture and fight for the quality time of intimacy to make loving obedience the fruit of this transformation.

From my first trip to Mexico to until now, I have understood that God is enough. If I have no tomorrow, what I have with God today is enough, and I expect even more tomorrow because I love Him and trust Him today. I might never make it to eighty years old to look back on my life like Loren Cunningham has and leave this type of legacy, but my dream of today is to never look back in regret. I walk forward with great joy because I love and trust the Creator of everything, and I need Him today—in a multitude or all alone! In the light of what others see or in the loneliness of no worldly glory, my intimacy doesn't change, and He is enough!

It's amazing how so many years later, Loren continues to challenge and influence my life and relationship with God. When Loren was a little boy, he wanted to write John 3:16 on the moon so that everyone in the world would know about the love of God and learn about Jesus. He didn't know about everyone speaking different languages. Loren was the first man, according to the Guinness Book of World Records, to travel to every country on earth. He has dedicated his whole life to one goal: get the truth of God into every home on earth in the mother tongue of every individual. At the age of thirteen, he committed his life to missions at an altar call and has been faithful in his calling.

This gave birth to the largest missions movement ever in history with one goal: to *listen to God and obey Him*. Bible translators thought Loren was unrealistic, and most denominations thought he was trying to do the unachievable, but how could he have the Word of God in his hands, have understanding and intimacy with the God of creation, and someone else on earth not have that same opportunity? God has used Loren's vision to get our ministry of YWAM Morelia, Mexico, involved with the indigenous of Mexico, with oral Bible translation and the Jesus Film, Wordy by Heart, and putting a Bible in every home within our city and state, and saying yes when so many people are saying "it's not possible," and to just keep believing for more.

In 2 Peter, it talks about us adding to our faith, virtue. Faith and character come before knowledge. Faith is contagious! When we encounter men or women of faith with genuine and deep intimacy, it takes away our excuses that God isn't real. The power of testimony is stronger than we could ever imagine. The power of impartation within teaching over simple knowledge is more transformational than any one truth. To have a man of faith like Loren in my life has removed my excuses to say no. If he can do it, why can't I?

Once or twice a year, I still get to hear Loren teach somewhere in the world, and I've even had the privilege to translate for both him and his wife. One day, my wife and I even brought him to the airport and shared some of our dreams and visions. So many people would say we were crazy, but he said, "You can easily do that," "You can do much more!" and "You could translate every one of the last languages in Mexico with just a small team in a year or two if you wanted." Some people told us our future vision wasn't possible within a whole lifetime, but here was Loren telling us to dream bigger! Then he looked at me and my wife and said, "If you don't establish it within two years, it will never happen." What a shock! He was right, so within two years, we worked to every extent of our capacity and energy to give all that we could, and we are beginning to see those solid foundations now.

Obviously in just two years, it wasn't visible to everyone else, but the foundations that were placed will never be moved. Even though my wife and I had three kids and were foreigners in Mexico, Loren didn't give us excuses that would allow us to bow out of our dream, and he pushed us to go further and deeper in our dreams with God. Loren is a man of great vision, birthed from great faith in God because of an incredible depth of intimacy with God, and this never ceases to encourage me to go deeper and further.

One day, my wife and I were coordinating a conference for all of Mexico and Central America, and I was responsible for hosting Loren. A friend of mine, Giacomo, who knew Loren well, said, "Don't feel bad if he just wants to go to his room and not talk at all. He might not come out all day, but just leave him alone. He needs to watch the news and to have alone time with God." Loren's wife, Darlene, told me one time, "Loren was on a trip and had disappeared in his room for a few days, and no one had seen him, so they called me because they were worried. I told them that he travels all over the world, and sometimes he needs to just be with God. Make sure he has some nuts and snacks, water, and the news in his room and leave him alone. When he's ready, he will come out." He has strong convictions, and he cares more about obeying God and hearing Him clearly than getting lost in all the little details around him or all the other people. This was so impacting to me because it made me feel like I'm not crazy, that it's okay to just be me and run to God for what I need first.

During that conference, after the first day, Loren met me and said, "You must have command as your number one strength in strengths finder. Surround yourself with really strong leaders and just keep pushing forward." He had no idea who I was, but he could see through me, and he just encouraged me to keep going to God and to make sure I was surrounded by other strong leaders. I really don't know if Loren and Darlene remember me any more than just being another face in the nations, another driver, another translator, or another young leader, but my encounters with them have always had the same result. Go deep with God, listen and obey, and never give up!

In different seasons, this intimacy with God has looked different. Through singleness, marriage, family, serving in ministry, or leading a ministry—all brought different seasons and different needs. I've had years of reading through the Bible every month, weekends of prayer and just a lot of extra time for intimacy with God. There have been seasons where I needed to wake up at midnight because the day was too busy to have that time. There have been seasons where the reality of my season of life didn't give me any free time, other moments with audible Bible and worship in the car while I would drive to work, go to the bathroom, or just a quick prayer on my pillow in the morning while my daughter was jumping on me to wake me up. I've been on trips teaching where I literally just wander off and get a hotel for a couple nights because I need to be renewed alone with God. I've learned that it's not about the activity, the what, or even how. It always comes down to the why and the position of my heart first; then the details of the how, when, and with whom are very important clarity. In every season, He alone is enough.

Currently, I'm in a season with three kids, all aged six or under, and a growing ministry, so I don't have much free time from the moment I'm awake to the moment I fall asleep. A couple of years ago, we opened a prayer and Bible-reading room in our ministry. I've found that if I can go just once a week or even just once a month at 4:30 a.m. to get an hour or two to just sit and pray, listen and read, worship and renew my mind in His presence, it is all I need. To be a good husband, father, or leader, I must find the place to be first a good son, to be renewed by the transformation of my mind in His presence. It seems to me that there is a crazy cycle in which the more I learn about loving my wife and my children, the more I learn about God loving me; the more I learn about loving God, the more I learn about what my wife and kids need from me.

My highlight of my week has become my day of fasting, where I begin with an hour or two with God in the prayer room, some special time to write or express my heart with God's during the day; and then I break my fast with a special date with my wife. The success of my love with my wife and kids is always a fruit of my depth of intimacy with God. If I could change anything about my life, it would be for me to have greater self-control and consistency on my quality-time days with God and my wife, which overflow into everything else that I do. This has become the only way that I can ensure to function out of debit, what I have stored up, and never out of credit, to give out of my emptiness.

Reflection

1. What is eternal life?
2. Do you seek only spiritual experiences? Do you just hide in the Word and your mind? Or do you live in a covenantal relationship with Jesus with the Spirit of Truth?
3. Where is your secret place?
4. What is the standard of your Absolute Truth?
5. How do you relate to the Father?
6. How do you relate to Jesus, the Son?
7. How do you relate to the Holy Spirit?

8. Has God ever spoken to you?
9. In what areas can you grow in to begin to function in ministry out of debit and never credit as you serve and give to others?

Meditation

In 2007, a few years after my first training program in Youth with a Mission (YWAM), I continued to serve as a missionary. One day, I was in a big hurry to get back for lunch at our YWAM campus. As I was driving back, I passed an older man who was almost naked and walking on the side of the road. The Spirit told me to stop, but I was in a hurry and didn't. As I was reaching our YWAM campus, the conviction was too much, so I drove all the way back to town and picked up the man. He was an older American man who had retired in Mexico to drink. Here he was, sitting in my car basically naked, completely drunk, and telling me how his Mexican girlfriend had just stolen all of his money and taken off. I drove him home, went inside, and prayed with him. The smell was unpleasant; he was very sweaty, and the alcohol was strong. Nothing special happened, but when God asked me what I saw and I was honest, He responded to me with what He saw which was completely different. I saw a drunk old man that smelled bad. He saw a young child who was lost and alone, and God's greatest desire was to simply hold this man in His arms. So I did. I leaned over and held this man and shared that the Father wanted to hold him and hug him. As tears poured down his eyes, I knew I had only seen what I smelled, but God knew his name.

As a Bible teacher, I believe strongly that transformation comes through a foundation of Truth, but I have also seen that without love and relationship with the Spirit of Truth, there is only death. One day, I had just finished teaching a week in a discipleship training school with lots of content. I was praying for some of the guys when all of a sudden, the strongest, most macho, dry, tough, and closed guy came to my mind, and I heard the Spirit say to my thoughts, *Tell him I know he is a man, and he doesn't have to do anything to be a man. Simply being My son makes him a man.* This made no sense to me as it didn't really fit with my teaching, but as I remembered Genesis 1:1—"In the beginning Not Daniel," I trusted the Spirit and shared. Immediately, this tough Mexican man broke into tears, and he began to share and weep like a child. There was a story I didn't know, but the Spirit of Truth did. His older brother was living a homosexual lifestyle, so his whole life of fighting, drugs, violence, and rebellion was built on a lie that he wasn't macho enough. I knew some truth, but the Spirit knew this young man's story. When the two united, there was freedom!

As I continue to learn what it means to be intimate with God, a few things have become clear. He desires what is best for me, but I don't know the desires of my own heart, and I need to release everything daily to be filled because God can't fill hands that are already full. He has also shown me that as I work with others, the Spirit of Truth will do way more than I ever could. He desires to bring freedom; He desires to get very intimate and close and has no fear of getting His hands "dirty." These moments of experience that are fully connected to the Truth are what will sustain a life of freedom. Experience without covenant is adultery, but covenant without intimacy is death and suffering. God touches us to touch the multitudes, to transform the nations, to really be a missionary in all that we do. Intimacy with God is not a means to an end but rather the foundation that we can graduate from, and every day it just goes deeper and gets stronger, creating the foundation for everything to come in our obedience to what He will speak next of where, when, with whom, and how?

The Bible and Intimacy

-   "Then God said, "Let Us make man in Our image, according to Our likeness; and let them rule over the fish of the sea and over the birds of the sky and over the cattle and over all the earth, and over every creeping thing that creeps on the earth" (Genesis 1:26).
-   "God blessed them; and God said to them, 'Be fruitful and multiply, and fill the earth and subdue it; and rule over the

fish of the sea and over the birds of the sky and over every living thing that moves on earth'" (Genesis 1:28).

- "For this reason a man shall leave his father and his mother, and be joined to his wife; and they shall become one flesh. And the man and his wife were both naked and were not ashamed" (Genesis 2:24–25)

- "To Seth, to him also a son was born; and he called his name Enosh. Then men began to call upon the name of the Lord" (Genesis 4:26).

- "Then Enoch walked with God three hundred years after he became the father of Methuselah, and he had other sons and daughters. So all the days of Enoch were three hundred and sixty-five years. Enoch walked with God; and he was not, for God took him" (Genesis 5:22–24).

- "By faith Enoch was taken up so that he would not see death; and he was not found because God took him up; for he obtained the witness that before his being taken up he was pleasing to God" (Hebrews 11:5).

- "And God blessed Noah and his sons and said to them, "Be fruitful and multiply, and fill the earth" (Genesis 9:1).

- "Now when Abram was ninety-nine years old, the Lord appeared to Abram and said to him, "I am God Almighty; walk before Me and be blameless. I will establish my covenant between Me and you, and I will multiply you exceedingly" (Genesis 17:1–2).

- "Yes, he wrestled with the angel and prevailed; He wept and sought His favor. He found Him at Bethel and there He spoke with us" (Hosea 12:4).

- "As they were going along talking, behold, there appeared a chariot of fire and horses of fire which separated the two of them. And Elijah went up by a whirlwind to heaven" (2 Kings 2:11–12).

- "Speak to all the congregation of the sons of Israel and say to them, You shall be holy, for I the Lord your God am holy" (Leviticus 19:2).

- "And you shall be to Me A kingdom of priests and a holy nation" (Exodus 19:6).
- "For you are a holy People to the Lord your God, the Lord your God has chosen you to be a people for His own possession out of the all the peoples who are on the face of the earth" (Deuteronomy 7:6; 14:2).
- "For You do not delight in sacrifice, otherwise I would give it; you are not pleased with burnt offering. The sacrifice of God is a broken spirit; a broken and contrite heart, O God, You will not despise" (Psalm 51:16–17).
- "For when Solomon was old, his wives turned his heart away after other gods; and his heart was not wholly devoted to the Lord his God, as the heart of David his father had been" (1 Kings 11:4).
- "After he had removed him, he raised up David to be their king, concerning who He also testified and said, "I have found David the son of Jesse, a man after My heart, who will do all My will" (Acts 13:22).
- "But you, Israel, My servant, Jacob who I have chosen, Descendant of Abraham my friend" (Isaiah 41:8).
- "And the Scripture was fulfilled which says, 'and Abraham believed God, and it was reckoned to Him as righteousness,' and he was called the friend of God" (James 2:23).

CHAPTER 4

Fear of the Lord

Inspired by missionary Jose Curiel from Mexico

Fear of the Lord—to understand God in such depths of His greatness, beauty, and supreme capacity in power and love that He alone becomes the first focus in life: in every decision, in every relationship. He is of greatest value, and the natural honor and respect that He deserves is given fully to Him as the ultimate answer in all direction, discipline, and wisdom in life. He is the One of highest value and therefore worthy of all worship. The only correct response is to fully obey in a relationship, birthed out of love and trust, resulting in a clean conscience because of the revelation of how a Being of such is still personal and intimate with every member of humanity.

Special Introduction

In this moment in history, the nations have lost all sense of reality, and it becomes necessary to have a reference point that gives meaning to this journey that we have embarked upon. Even though we hear about the importance of living a life based on certain values, our social values have been distorted into self-fabricated ideas that have brought us into great despair. Within this list of principles, Daniel unpacks the fear of the Lord as an essential element for success. The fear of the Lord is important because it not only brings us to the beginning of wisdom, but it also keeps us far from evil. May this chapter inspire you to return to the beginning and to flee from all evil in your own journey!

"Oh, that they had such a heart in them, that they would fear Me and keep all My commandments always, that it may be well with them and with their sons forever!" Deuteronomy 5:29

Jose Curiel
Founder and Leader, Youth with a Mission, Guadalajara, Mexico
National Leader for the Discipleship Nations Alliance for Mexico
Missionary

* * * * *

It was 1995, and we had been laughing and having lots of fun. It was after 9:00 p.m., and everyone else in the house was sleeping. We were supposed to be asleep as well, but instead, we just watched a movie about making swords and knives. Since both my friend and I loved the mountains, hunting, fishing, and had spent our child-hoods together in the outdoors, we decided to make little swords. We were ten years old and had decided that we could take his mom's nice stainless silverware set, and by burning the knives with fire, we could bang them and turn them into sharp knives. This seemed like a great idea for two young boys, but we quickly realized that the knives began to turn completely black. They were scratched and damaged, and the kitchen began to smell of smoke and fire. We quickly tried to scrub the silverware, hide the knives, and spray some cleaning stuff to take away the smell, but with no success. At that exact moment, his dad came into the kitchen angry, asking about what was on fire. We looked at each other and quickly lied as we were both afraid and said that we were just looking for a snack. His dad saw the lighter, looked in the drawers, and saw the black knives. We were terrified. He spoke sternly to us, clearly being angry, so we quickly went to bed.

The next morning, my friend's dad acted normal, but my friend and I were still afraid. He was afraid of his mom and what she was going to say, and I was afraid because within a few minutes, my dad would be picking me up, and I knew that I would get in trouble for what we had done. When my dad arrived, with a very uncomfortable and awkward smile, I watched him talk to my friend's dad. He smiled and grabbed my hand and began to take me out the door. My friend's dad called me, and I ran back, and he whispered into my ear, "See how I didn't tell your dad? I know you didn't try to do something bad, and I don't want you to get in trouble, but never do it again." I remember riding home in the car asking myself two things: Why was I afraid of my dad? Why was I afraid of my friend's dad and didn't tell him the truth?

Throughout my life, I have done many stupid things, and I have many memories of my childhood that go back to these same moments of fear. After each incident, though, I always remember asking myself, "Why was I afraid, and why didn't I just tell the truth?" There was something about the mystery of the unknown response of my dad or someone else: the lack of intimate knowledge and doubt that just maybe there might be a bad reaction that I needed to hide from—yet I was always wrong. My dad told me my whole life, "If you do something really bad, just call me and tell me. It will always be better for you and easier for you if you just tell me the truth from the beginning. I will pick you up wherever you are, and I'll come and get you out of whatever has happened. Just don't lie to me and tell me the truth—trust me!" It took me years to understand this, but I remember as I was a bit older that I made a few mistakes, and the fear took on a new meaning. As a child, my fear was almost like being scared of the worst possible response, knowing that my dad had great strength and power and could hurt me if he wanted. As I grew up though, it changed because I knew my dad and who he was in his character. He may have had great strength and power, but I had no fear of him using it simply because he could. It was no longer a fear of what he would do but rather a fear of how he might feel and how it could affect my relationship with him. That love of a good father is what began to prepare the way for me to understand a life-transforming truth about God and fear of the Lord.

As my plane landed in Mexico in 2004, I was nineteen years old, and it was my first time to travel internationally on my own. I had listened to my MP3 player the whole flight, remembering the last few years of my life, who I was, and what I had done. I had no fears or worries, but the reality hit me while driving that suddenly I was alone. Doubts began to enter my mind that I had made some mistakes, but at least I had the expectation that upon arrival at my discipleship training school, I would be with some other people like me, or so I thought.

I was very wrong, and not just the culture or language, but there was no one like me. I was completely and utterly alone, and the only things I had were my thoughts. They seemed to jump around without purpose or reason, quick to judge others and make assumptions, and even quicker to convince me of the mistake that I had made. Our opening night was one of the longest nights of my life. I remember thinking that for the next six months, I wouldn't have a single friend, and I didn't want to get to know any of these people. The students in my class weren't "my type of people," the leaders were all Latin, and the only family with kids was the leader of the ministry, who seemed very quiet and a bit distant from the rest of us. Everyone was laughing and playing, but he was off to the side in his dress pants, leather shoes, button-up dress shirt, black leather jacket, hair combed back, and glasses. He seemed to have joy watching us but, at the same time, seemed to prefer to watch from the sideline.

I remember going down to my dorm room and lying on my bed, and the son of the leader soon after walked down to our room where I was lying. He must have been about ten years old at that time, and Jose Daniel—or JD, like many called him—walked right up to me and asked, "Would you like to hear a story? I can tell it to you in Ingles o in Spanish." Being polite, I said yes, and he began to tell me the story of Jacob and Esau. He told me the color of their eyes, their hair, the clothes that they wore, the way they walked, and just about every detail imaginable. His story proceeded for almost two hours without even the slightest pause. The thing that most impacted me, however, was the detail that this young boy knew of the Bible. Later I found out that he and his sister would memorize chapters of the Bible at least every other week. I had memorized a few verses in my life, *but* this young boy, a mere ten years old, knew almost every Bible story better than I did! After those two hours, I kindly paused him and told him that I needed to go to dinner. Without hesitation, he agreed and walked up the hill to the eating area with me and said, "Let me know when I can finish the story."

The next day, this young boy found me while I was out in the grass and asked if he could finish his story. Not seeing any way out, I agreed and listened to a couple more hours of this story in Genesis. I was both intrigued and frustrated at the same time. I was amazed at his ability, but I had never spent time with kids before, yet much to my surprise, this young boy was soon to become one of my own little brothers. There was something very different about him: the way he talked, his sense of humor, and his entire reality. This young man lived as if God was the only thing that mattered, and it made me wonder why he lived like this.

It wasn't just JD. His sister, Nicole, was also very quick to open her heart and welcome me into this new environment. She would tell me the stories of the things they had done as a family, what it was like to grow up bilingual with a Nicaraguan mom and Mexican father who both had US citizenship. She would share about all the fights with her brother, and very quickly I felt as if I had inherited two younger siblings. She would share about how hard it was to see people come and go all the time and not have any friends her age, but also how much she loved meeting new people. She would share about the challenges of being Latin but also having a heart language of English. She was fluent in Spanish but dreamed in English and emotionally expressed herself in English, but she lived in Mexico. Looking back, it is very interesting that I couldn't relate to anyone and felt like I wasn't a part of anything, but these two kids were able to so quickly find a way into my heart and life. To this day, there isn't a day that passes that I don't think about them, pray for them, or remember them and wonder what they must be living today.

Besides those two kids, I was only able to connect to one other person. The day that we were sharing our testimonies, there was a very unique-looking Mexican guy with dark curly hair, dark skin, and a little mole that looked almost like a teardrop. As he shared his story, I felt like I was looking into the mirror of a darker version of me, and we quickly became friends. We spent every free moment together, and even when in groups, we really only focused on us. He was the brother I never had, except he spoke no English at all, and I spoke absolutely no Spanish. My school leader would get frustrated with us because we had a similar sense of humor with practical jokes, and with everything from taking the wooden slats out of our room-mates' bunk-beds so they would fall on top of each other when trying to go to bed, to locking people in the bathroom, buying plastic bugs or fake poop to leave on the teacher's doorstep—we enjoyed laughing hysterically at everyone else. Our school leader would become so frustrated with us and couldn't understand how it was possible for us to be so close without being able to understand a single word from the other person. We would go on long walks and catch tarantulas, do exercise together, worship together, and pray together, without understanding a single word. I think everyone around us had to laugh because we were the strangest friends that could have come together, and I thank God very much because I needed it during that season of my life. We had a lot of fun together, but often I would think about JD and Nicole and compare them to Usba and myself; they had something that we didn't have. Usba and I didn't care what anyone thought about us, but Nicole and JD seemed to base everything they did on what they believed God would think about them, and I would continue to wonder why they lived that way.

As the weeks passed, I began to develop relationships with others in our class, and once I was able to speak in Spanish, I slowly drew closer to the whole team. I still remember, however, always wondering how I felt so close to my friend Usba, two young kids, Nicole and JD, and yet couldn't connect with anyone else and had little to no communication with the leaders of the ministry, the parents of these kids. They were very friendly, but they were very busy, and I just didn't see them very much. My first real experience with the leader,

Jose, was when he taught a week in our school. I don't remember many classes, but the week that he taught on the fear of the Lord literally changed my entire being. Through the years, I have heard Jose teach on many things, I have traveled with him to many places and translated for him more times than I can remember, but to this day what most impacted me was that first week I heard him teach. It was the most sincere I had ever seen him. He was honest, humble, and it was a major principle that I saw in everything I can remember about him as a man, father, husband, and leader.

This was a man who grew up in a tiny village in Mexico, where there doesn't exist a single Christian church. He received no education other than elementary school and left illegally for the United States, where he became a Christian. After entering YWAM, he quickly returned to Mexico to do things right. He began to full-heartedly serve the Lord. He became self-educated and finished high school, and eventually he graduated with an executive master's degree from the University of the Nations. He was a part of pioneering a ministry in Guatemala, where he married a young Nicaraguan woman; and then with two very young kids, he returned to his home area in Mexico to follow what he felt God was speaking to him. He has been a part of working with key pastors throughout the country and has a conviction and passion to teach the local church and to work with other pastors. He's an incredible student of history and one of the best in Spanish grammar that I have ever met. But who would have imagined this possible, knowing where he came from?

As he taught that week, what most impacted me was, I don't ever remember meeting a man that full-heartedly lived his personal convictions before God: with his family, with his wife, and with his kids. He was very honest, and he wholeheartedly lived what he believed to be biblical truth because he was convinced of whom he was doing it for and that God needed to be the center of his life. I remember while he was sharing about being transformed by Jesus and that everyone around you should be transformed and experience the fruit, and I was clearly able to connect his choices to his conviction. As he shared stories about writing letters to make things right again from his past, about returning to Mexico because of his conviction to not be in the

United States illegally, about his process of courtship with his now wife, about the clothes he wore, paying taxes, his spiritual disciplines, his conviction to live before God with a clean conscience, and so many other things, I began to feel deep conviction.

That weekend, after his class, I had a cleansing in my heart like I had never had before, and I desired what this man shared about having a clean conscience. I took out a piece of paper and began to write down many names—of girls I had hurt in these past years of selfishness, of guys I know that I had done wrong to, and even a business that I had stolen from when I was little. I quickly got on my MySpace account and began to look up everyone from my past that I knew I needed to make restitution with. I wrote many letters to people from my past, and *yes*, I even wrote a note with $10 to the business from which I had stolen. What surprised me the most wasn't just the clean conscience that I now had but the response I had and how my radical obedience could also mark their lives and give them freedom. I began to understand that as I saw God first and His authority over my own, my steps of obedience in obtaining a clean conscience while walking in humility could impact others. Not everyone responded, but many people did, and there was one that *especially* really marked me.

There was a girl whom I was friends with, and we had a summer church trip together. Knowing that she liked me, I took advantage of all her emotions and then completely ignored her. In comparison to everything I had done, this seemed like an extremely small thing, but it felt so heavy on my heart, heavier than many of the other horrible things I had done. I wrote her a long letter, and within a day, she responded. She forgave me and shared about how amazed she was, knowing me, that I would dare to humble myself to contact her, and she asked what had happened in my life. She had been hurt by many guys, and I had opened a wound in her life, in her identity, and even in her thoughts about Christian men. I quickly shared about what I was doing in Mexico and how Jesus had gotten a hold of my heart and how I had finally understood the weight of all the choices I had made. I also shared their consequences and how my sin didn't just affect me but greatly affected others. I went further to share that God wasn't like that, and He had never desired for her to be hurt by me or any other guy, but it was the fruit of me not knowing Him and not reflecting Him. I shared how my one desire now was to live life with a clean conscience in the fear of the Lord and guard anyone and everyone from my own weaknesses and about how I had to think twice about the consequences of my actions, words, and thoughts. This impacted her in such a way that for many years afterward, we continued to communicate.

Jose had been right in what he taught. When I was transformed through my humility and obedience with God as the center of everything, then those around me would be touched by the power of God and experience some of that ripple effect. To this day, I try my best to never forget this principle. Out of everything that I have learned in life, it all means nothing if I don't have a clean conscience, living right before God today in the fear of the Lord!

Outside of that class, I had very little interaction with Jose during those few months. I remember clearly a week that I was in Puebla hearing Loren Cunningham speak, and to my surprise, Jose pulled me aside and confronted me. I had been playing with his kids, and his daughter loved to try to wrestle with us because she said she never had an older brother and wished she could have had one to play with her and wrestle with her, and he walked up to me and pulled me aside while we were wrestling. He shared about how his daughter is a young woman and that a young woman needs to be treated like a young woman, and that no man should touch her or wrestle with her like that, especially a Christian man. I was shocked because in my culture, this was very normal. I don't even know if I agreed or disagreed, but I remember thinking that one day when I have kids, I want to worry about them in the same way that this man worried about his kids. He was very different from my own father in the way he expressed his love, and yet there was something very genuine and unique about him, and I could see that his love was just as deep and sincere as my own father's. I had never in my life met someone that I could honestly say, his heart motive was to always please God and have a clean conscience. He loved his family with his whole heart, and one of my greatest joys is knowing that I was able to walk alongside him for almost ten years and learn the meaning of fear of the Lord.

A year after Jose had confronted me, I had returned to Mexico, and I began to know Jose beyond just being a leader. It was very different being a full-time missionary in Mexico than just a student. Through this change, however, I began to work closer with Jose. I began to travel with him, and I began to feel his support in a very special way. I was blessed to have an incredible mother, father, and sister, but this Mexican family took me in and treated me like their own. Throughout our trips together in Korea, the United States, throughout Mexico and Central America, I learned much from this man. I learned incredible things about the Mexican culture and the villages of Mexico. I had the opportunity to travel and live with his family and watch them pray and seek God together every morning. They didn't live one way during ministry and some other way on vacation, but they simply were who they were, in spite of what any-one else thought or even expected. With tears in their eyes, I saw his kids get up and walk away from a card game because they had said something they shouldn't have, not because anyone said anything but because they didn't have a clean conscience in that moment, and they needed some time alone with Jesus to make things right.

One day our car broke down on a trip, and Jose called his wife, and her response was, "Ask God what to say to the driver. It's possible He has you there for a reason—don't miss it!" Throughout all those years, however, the one thing that always came back to me when I was with Jose was the fear of the Lord. This will forever mark my life, and I hope the life of my family and ministry in the future.

Noah was called to build an ark and have a family, and he was faithful, and that was his ministry. Abraham really only had a wife and two boys, and in much of it, he was faithful. Even in all his mistakes, God looked down on him and called him a man of faith. David was an adulterer and murderer, but God called him His friend. As I have studied the Bible for many years, and I see the lives of some great leaders, and some not-so-great leaders, some that had huge minis-tries, and some that had the ministry of their family, like Noah, or even lost their family like Hosea—I can see they all made mistakes, they all failed, but they all had to make daily choices and live with the consequences. When everything was over and done, each one had to give account to God and do so with a clean conscience.

I've seen Jose do some of the most incredible things and literally walk out faith that is miraculous. I've also seen him in tears of humility and repentance, asking for forgiveness and acknowledging his weaknesses. Just like every character in the Bible that people have many different opinions about, I've seen how leaders like Jose suffer what others think about every choice. Beyond the successes or failures in the eyes of others, I have no doubt that God will look at Jose and respond, "Well done, my good and faithful servant." This principle of God first, in the fear of the Lord, Jose taught me many years ago. Now I have my family and my kids, and I have the responsibility of making tough decisions as we are now leading a ministry birthed from God's heart for the nations. We've already had our own successes and failures, and many seem to have an opinion, but I'll never forget that I must first go to God and give account to Him and that today I can live with a clean conscience, even when it means that I need to humble myself before God and others. It's worth it, if that means I can live today in peace and freedom.

I think it was in 2009 that I had sold my car and was trying to bring my new car into Mexico, but I was having some issues at the border. I called Jose for some advice, and his answer will always be with me. He said, "I don't want to sound religious, but you need to pray and ask God and then obey Him." He gave me his opinion, but he said that I needed to do what God showed me, that God was wiser, He could see what we couldn't, and that only in first seeking Him and obeying Him could I really have the conviction of what to do in this difficult moment that wasn't cut and dry in others' opinions. He could have easily told me I needed to do one thing or the other, but he didn't; he pointed me back to obey and trust God. This is a principle that I have now tried to implement with my family, my team, and my staff. When I feel myself wanting to tell someone what they have to do because I think it's best, I remember the fear of the Lord and that they also must first give account to God with a clean conscience and that my job is to point them to God and not to me. God is God; I am not! By trying to assume a role in the life of another that doesn't correspond to me would mean that I've completely rejected the beginning of all wisdom: the fear of the Lord. Again God has sons and daughters; He doesn't have grandchildren. I must give account directly to God, not to what my leader thought.

Out of all my stories through the years, this is the area in which I have been most influenced and what has most impacted my life. Every trip back to the United States, I have to fight to not fall into a cultural norm where God doesn't need to be consulted. For some reason, it seems so comfortable in my own strength returning to where I grew up that I can almost convince myself that I don't "need" God in the same way that I need Him while serving in other nations.

A few years ago in 2017, my wife and I were at dinner with a young couple with whom we are good friends and who are also supporters of what we do in Mexico. In the restaurant parking lot, there was a man sitting in the car in front of us and had been waiting there for a long time. I think he made many people feel uncomfortable, but I had the heaviest conviction that I needed to talk to him and felt God had given me a word for him. Since we were in a dinner meeting, I shrugged it off and tried to ignore what God was saying to me. The man left, and my heart melted as I felt conviction. If I was back in Mexico, I wouldn't have hesitated, but here at home where I was comfortable in my own strength, I hid from God. For an entire year, that weight was on my heart, and I remember telling God the following year that I never want to let my comfort come before what He is saying to me. I want my story to always be His story, no matter where I am or what I am doing.

A few days after that dinner experience, I was talking to an old friend and mentor of mine, Chris Noller, in Evergreen, Colorado. She was sharing about how easy it can be when we are comfortable to just stop seeking God. When we have everything we need, all the finances, the blessings, the provision, and relationships within our family and around us, we can quickly forget to depend on Him. It's so true, and more and more I've realized that the message of the Bible is not one of comfort and self-glory or blessing but a context of perseverance and dependence upon God. There is no time to take a vacation from His guidance, in the good or bad, the mountains or valleys, rich or poor—He must come first, and His perspective must be what guides us. A guidance where, in many cases, the why isn't revealed until we first obey the what.

A year later, in 2018, I had another opportunity to be in Colorado. A similar situation arose, and I was given the opportunity to respond to God in an uncomfortable moment. A friend of my sister came over to the house to see our kids, and we were all talking and laughing. She was going through a very difficult situation, and again in the middle of a room with people that weren't Christians, I felt God say that we needed to pray for her. I felt very uncomfortable, but I grabbed my son, and I asked if we could pray for her before she left. I told her that I believed in a God of miracles who is close and present to us and that if she permitted, we wanted to pray for her healing and for her relationship with Jesus. She said yes, and my son surprised me and stood up, put out his hands on her, and shut his eyes. We prayed together, and then my son gave her a big hug, and there were tears in her eyes. There were tears in my sister's eyes, and something had shifted within that room. Nothing magical happened, but I could feel the joy of the Lord showing His closeness to her, to myself, and my son, and incredible peace filled me as I knew that I had a clean conscience in my small step of obedience to Jesus.

Little by little, I continue to grow in my understanding of the fear of the Lord. It begins in knowing who is God. From there, it grows in my intimate relationship with Him, learning to love and trust Him in all that He speaks, even when it doesn't make sense. I continue to discover that having a clean conscience seems to have two different aspects. The first is what I learned for ten years living with Jose: to have God as the center of everything and live with a clean conscience in my personal relationship with Him. The second has been what I've been learning throughout the more recent years. A clean conscience and living the fear of the Lord is for my relationships with everyone else around me. By being sensitive to His Spirit and obeying His guidance in how to relate to others, I have seen incredible miracles, healings, and just wonderful conversations as God's power seems to be most used in learning to love and reflect Him to others.

Just like many leaders from the Bible and other leaders before me, I know that I will make mistakes and offend or hurt people, make wrong choices, etc., not because I desire to or because I'm malicious, but because I am so finite in my understanding and knowledge of those around me. All too often, what I see is myself, not seeing others or hearing what God is saying, and my lack of empathy or context doesn't allow me to see the big picture. My desire is that in my success and even in my failure, people would know, and most importantly, God will know, that I have no fear of humbling myself and turning to Him and being radically obedient. My dream is that anyone who lives around me and who comes into contact with me or who only shares a few words with me would be touched because of the greatness of my God; that as I am transformed, they can be touched and transformed as well; that it would be seen first in how I relate to God. But I earnestly hope that it would be greatly seen in how I lead, speak, interact, and relate to others in the fear of the Lord.

Too often in ministry, I have seen our young leaders superexcited to bring in a new, very gifted, and charismatic teacher. We are in a season of life where gifts and charisma are glorified over character and integrity. There was a season in ministry our staff kept wanting to invite a couple to teach, and my wife and I had an opportunity to listen to them over lunch. They clearly carried some strong gifting and charisma, but as I was listening to their story, I felt like the part of their marriage, their dreams, their convictions, and the daily reality when not in spotlight was missing, and we had some reservation. Through the next year, they had been invited back a couple of times, and we couldn't quite figure out what was happening, but we just felt that something wasn't right. A year later, they were divorced, and some major moral sin had come into the light. My heart broke for them, and I continue to pray for them both; but more and more, I see the dangers of seeking after leaders and people for the experience or show over the fruits of character and moral purity within the fear of the Lord. I love the moving of the Spirit and to see the gifts working within the body of Christ, but "the beginning of knowledge is the fear of the Lord."

In a similar way, many youths of today addicted to pornography and masturbation have a lie in their mind that after marriage, their temptations will just go away. Time and time again, I find myself meeting with a young married man in tears sharing about how the addiction is even worse after marriage, that his wife can't meet his lies and fake ideas of intimacy, and that he always feels dirty. When I tell him that he needs to talk to his wife and confess, he begins to cry, saying he can't because he knows how much he will hurt her. For some reason, as much as he speaks of his fear of hurting her and shame of her discovering the truth, it wasn't enough to stop him from doing what was wrong. His love for God and his wife isn't enough; he needs radical choices, and it won't begin without the fear of the Lord.

When I teach on the topic "the fear of the Lord" in different places, people give away their phones and computers. They get rid of their clothes sometimes and show up in class the next day in a plastic bag. I've seen guys and girls shave their heads or girls give away their makeup. I've never said they should, but I always ask, "What keeps you from drawing close to God and having a clean conscience? Get rid of it! Anything that you aren't mature enough to administer well, get rid of it until you are!" Who we are in the depths of our heart and conscience is much more important than what others might think or see!

Some of the most incredible men and women of God that I have had the pleasure of meeting and be inspired by are not charismatic. They are not the typical apostolic visionary leaders, an A-personality type, but they are radical in their consistency of life with God. They might be overlooked by everyone around them, but they are the faithful servants. As it states in Matthew 7:13–23, "Many will say to Me in that day Lord, Lord, didn't we do miracles and cast out demons in Your name, and I will say to them, depart from me doers of iniquity, I never knew you." Gifts and talents continue with or without God, but a clean conscience and intimacy is all too often not what people first see or remember.

Some of my most shameful moments in ministry are those in which other people were inspired by my gifts, a teaching, my knowledge of something, or my charisma because I knew that I wasn't walking in the fear of the Lord. In my sin, I didn't magically forget what I know, lose my gifts and talents, or develop a new personality. Maybe I was in a fight with my wife, and my pride was too big to ask for forgiveness; or I had hurt someone as their leader, and I didn't want to humble myself and admit that I was wrong; or even something as small as knowing that I had promised something to my kids and then didn't fulfill it for whatever reason. I can remember through the whole class how I didn't have a clean conscience because I hadn't obeyed God, and I was walking in hypocrisy, and no one knew it but me. I was still anointed because I was teaching His truth that is real for everyone, and God didn't take away my gifts, but I wasn't walking in fear of the Lord.

One of my desires as I walk forward in ministry is that the secrets of my heart—my weaknesses and failures—wouldn't define me, yet at the same time, they would never be hidden either. That I would never walk alone but have good accountability within my team and that God first would never fade away. I desire that my kids would grow up with understanding why we do what we do more than just what we do and how we do it. I desire that our disciples and coministers would understand the value of radically living the message we teach every day, more than wanting to teach the message or be in the public light. May my story become His story, and may the ordinary aspects of daily life become the *extraordinary*!

Reflection

1. Do you feel like you know God well enough to trust Him and what He desires for you to do or not to do?
2. Based on what you have seen in this chapter, have you experienced living in a clean conscience?
3. If you ask God about your past relationships (family, friends, etc.) and choices that you have made, do you still have a clean conscience?

4. What can you do in obedience to God to bring resto-ration in those relationships or choices to now have a clean conscience?

5. Are the practices of your life, in both private and public, reflecting the God that you profess to follow? If not, what steps can you do to align your life?

6. Have you asked the Holy Spirit to give you the power to obey what God is showing you? How can you be more obe-dient to what the Holy Spirit is showing you about yourself and relationships with others?

7. What defines you the most? What others think, what you feel, your gifts and calling, your experiences and knowl-edge, or what God has to say about you?

8. Is your past fully in the light of confessing to God and knowable by others? Is it a testimony of God's power, or are you still hiding the shame? God wants you to be free!

Meditation

For a few years, one of my main focuses has been leading and supporting a Bible school. We dive deep into the Word of God and begin to process some of the bigger and more difficult ideas about God, man, creation, sin, and much more. During the school, I always see so much freedom as students see the reality that, just like me, they have no excuse for their disobedience. God is good. God is personal. He is all powerful, and He is always willing. We learn to draw close to His heart, trusting Him and desiring a greater intimacy.

It never fails, however, that about six months or a year after the Bible school that some student will call me and want a very theolog-ical answer to some crisis in their life and want to use the Bible to "prove" whatever they want to believe or do. I have learned in these moments that the issue isn't theological. Everyone wants theological answers to defend their sin or choices when they aren't seeking God, and I won't give them one. I ask them three questions: Do you have a clean conscience? How is your intimacy with Jesus—have you spent time with Him today? Are you walking in the fear of the Lord?

Almost always I get the same answer: no and no and *no*. Deeper knowledge should always have a fruit of loving God more and trusting Him in what He desires in our life and relationships with others. It should never be to defend my sin or to affirm hurting someone else. Before knowledge, before experience, before the fruit of the deepest of studies, we need the fear of the Lord. "The beginning...is the fear of the Lord."

One of my prayers is that I would never deceive myself, creating a God in my own image and using my knowledge for what I want to do. When I find myself shifting into any type of theological excuse that would encourage me that I don't need or can't have a clean conscience, I know that I am in trouble. Studying God is to open the doors of love and trust with God; and if what I discover or want to believe would tell me that I don't need to love, that I'm okay in my shame fleeing from my God, then I know that something is wrong. Before knowledge comes love and trust. Love and trust come from intimacy, and intimacy is birthed out of a willing heart and obedience. This can only happen in the fear of the Lord.

The Bible and the Fear of the Lord

- "How blessed is everyone who fears the Lord, who walks in His ways. When you shall eat of the fruit of your hands, you will be happy and it will be well with you. Your wife shall be like a fruitful vine within your house, your children like olive plants around your table. Behold, for thus shall the man be blessed who fears the Lord. The Lord bless you from Zion and may you see the prosperity of Jerusalem all the days of your life. Indeed, may you see your children's children. Peace be upon Israel!" (Psalm 128).
- "The Fear of the Lord is the beginning of knowledge; Fools despise wisdom and instruction" (Proverbs 1:7).
- "Then you will discern the fear of the Lord and discover the knowledge of God. For the Lord gives wisdom; from His mouth comes knowledge and understanding" (Proverbs 2:5–6).

- "Do not let your heart envy sinners, but live in the fear of the Lord always" (Proverbs 23:17).
- "The Spirit of the Lord will rest on Him, the spirit of wisdom and understanding, the spirit of counsel and strength, the spirit of knowledge and the fear of the Lord. And He will delight in the fear of the Lord, and He will not judge by what His eyes see, nor make a decision by what His ears hear" (Isaiah 11:2–3).
- "Then those who feared the Lord spoke to one another, and the Lord gave attention and heard it, and a book of remembrance was written before Him for those who fear the Lord and who esteem His name. 'They will be Mine,' says the Lord of hosts, 'on the day that I prepare My own possession, and I will spare them as a man spares his own son who serves him.' So you will again distinguish between the righteous and the wicked, between one who serves God and one who does not serve Him" (Malachi 3:16–18).
- "So the church throughout all Judea and Galilee and Samaria enjoyed peace, being built up; and going on in the fear of the Lord and in the comfort of the Holy Spirit, it continued to increase" (Acts 9:31).
- "Therefore, knowing the fear of the Lord, we persuade men, but we are made manifest to God; and I hope that we are made manifest also in your consciences" (2 Corinthians 5:11).
- "Who will not fear, O Lord, and glorify Your name? For You alone are holy; for all the nations will come and worship before You, for Your righteous acts have been revealed" (Revelation 15:4).

CHAPTER 5

Redemption

*Inspired by founder and leader of Foundation,
Emmanuel Hilario Morales*

Redemption—the action of saving or being set free from sin, bondage, ownership, error, or evil. To be touched by God in such a way that the result is genuine repentance. To stop living for oneself in selfishness, and to begin living for God supremely with love for Him and others, literally changing from the kingdom of darkness to the kingdom of light here on earth, now, in the present.

A Poem of Redemption

The Road to Redemption

The Road to redemption
Is a daunting path
It's an uphill battle
That is slippery and steep
It goes against the current
In the frigid rough rapids
With rays of blistering sun
A jagged wall of obsidian
And a sea of sand

There are no shortcuts
Only cuts, scrapes and bruises
What you did in the past will never be forgotten
But what you are remembered for will have changed.

—Brandon Amberger

* * * * *

I remember clearly, at age fourteen, when I was baptized. Two of my dear mentors from church baptized me at a lake with our entire church in attendance. It was a very special memory, and for years the picture of my baptism hung inside my room. I remember sharing about my heart to be with Jesus, my desire to have Him fully alive in my life, and that I wanted to spend eternity with Him. These were all true, and I believe that they came from the depth of my heart. Jesus understood them. The Father was with me, and I was being filled with the Holy Spirit. However, I do not remember in any part of these memories having any type of understanding of supreme motives, lordship, being set free from anything in particular, or the heart of sin. I remember identifying the external bad actions and good actions, but not really the depths of being set free from selfishness to love. This is probably a part of the reason for why, not even a year later, I began living an extremely pagan life. I was a "born again and baptized believer in Jesus" who was living supremely for myself. I had missed something big in the heart of real redemption and supreme motives.

One of the sayings that I most remember hearing about the church growing up and I continue to hear to this day is, "The church is a giant hospital. We are all sick, and we come in to connect ourselves to the Holy Spirit, and we must simply wait for the return of Jesus." There might be some partial truth in that declaration, but I remember that one of the things that most impacted me within my first six months in Mexico was to see the journey of redemption here on earth now. It wasn't a picture of a bunch of sick people that weren't able to do anything, but time and time again, I would encounter people with every excuse in life to reject God, to reject their family, and to live as victims, but they didn't. I encountered men and women that not only knew of His story but also believed with all their hearts that there was a genuine before and after. When you meet Jesus, things really do change without a desire to ever go back to a past life.

I was nineteen years old and had grown up in the church. I was blessed to grow up in a Christian family and environment. I had said the sinner's prayer, and I was even baptized, but I was just like the world. There was no before and after in my life of meeting Jesus. I was like many others, just connected to the IV and not wanting to do anything. The before was me living for myself and the after was me not wanting to die but me wanting to be happy and have life for me. What had I missed? Here I was in a new culture, a new language, and I'm sure with just as many lies as my own culture, but there was evident redemption within the people I was encountering. Everywhere I looked, I heard real testimonies of what their life was like before and after. People were baptized because they believed with all their hearts that the old life was dead and gone. By going under the water, they showed the world that they were dead to sin and now alive in Christ, a new creation, an evident before and after now living in obedience to the faith in Jesus Christ and Lord.

I believe that this is one of the reasons that I struggled so much in my first few months in Mexico. I would argue with every teacher not because I was in complete disagreement but because I didn't have a memorable before and after change in my life. I felt like God owed me something, as if I deserved to be saved, and my understanding of the cross was that I had a legal right to be saved. I believed I could be completely out of relationship with Jesus, having no clean conscience, living no truth at all, and having no fruit of love in my life, but that God still had to save me. Being saved was completely transactional within my mind and not at all relational. I soon realized that it wasn't just me, but most of the people my age felt the same way. We were second-generation Christians that wanted the rights of being a son or daughter of Jesus without ever having tasted the real death of our choices or real life of God's goodness. We had the vaccination, just a shot of truth to not want anymore but think that we had all we needed, even when our lives didn't reflect a healthy new creation.

One of the men that I met in this journey was an older missionary who had begun the missions movement for the Tarahumara people group in Chihuahua, Mexico. His name is Alfredo Guerrero. This man had been kidnapped by his father, who then lied and told him that his mother was dead. His father beat both him and his brother until they ran away to live on the streets. This man raised his younger brother by finding success in the dark world of the streets from the time he was eight years old with rage and anger toward his father. Years later, his mother showed up, old and sick, and she had spent the latter part of her life traveling through every school in the entire state to try and find her boys. When she finally did, she had used up most of her life.

When this man discovered the truth of his past, his hate for his father only grew stronger, getting deeper into the streets with knives, robbery, alcohol, and much more. Years later, he was married; and out of nowhere, he met this American missionary who eventually shared the Gospel, the kingdom of God, and Alfredo's entire life changed. Within just a few years, he was walking down the street with his wife and kids, and he ran into his father. He was drunk and asking for money. For many years, his promise to his brother and himself, to his mother, and to every person his father had hurt was to kill his father the day he found him. Now being face-to-face with his father once again, all his past anger began to burn up from deep within. Yet something was different. He was a new creation. His father was still an alcoholic living on the streets, but he was no longer a reflection of his father. He was different: Christ lived in him. Rather than killing his father, he invited him out for breakfast and began to take care of him until the day he died. More than being a man that is now in encyclopedias for what he has done in missions, this man challenged me to fully understand the meaning of being redeemed.

As I heard this man's story, all I could do was ask myself the same questions: Who am I? Where do I come from? Where am I going? What is my before and after?" This man had every excuse possible, but he wasn't a victim. I hadn't lived a life like his—I had no excuses—yet somehow I was a victim. What had I missed? What was this story of redemption that seemed so alive around me but so dead within me? Was it possible that the church was more than a hospital, that salvation was more than just a gift that only carried power of transformation after death? That justification was not a legal right for me not to go to hell but rather the grace to be transformed? What was I missing in His story?

These men and women that I met made me want to run away and hide. I know that I had no excuse, but at the same time, I had believed every excuse possible to continue to live as a victim of my circumstances, of myself, and of God. I knew all about Him, but nothing brought me to Him. I wanted to understand that He was guiding me, that I could have certainty in the direction that He was taking me, and that my life reflected a reality where He was sitting on the throne of my heart, directing every decision of today!

There was another man that I met within my first year in Mexico, a man who, to this day, just like Alfredo, I continue to come across and hear about year after year. A man who has a story that has touched many individuals who have come in contact with him and continues to transform lives just as powerfully and real as it did to me fifteen years ago. I would like to introduce you to Hilario.

I remember that before actually having a personal encounter with Hilario, I would always hear about him and about his ministries. Teams and different people that came to serve with him, wouldn't stop talking about Hilario. I met him several times from a distance and heard his testimony through many people, but it wasn't until I drove with him to the border to legalize a vehicle that I was able to see with my own eyes who this man was.

Hilario appears to be a very hard-looking man with very stern facial features. He is very big and reminded me of a Native American. He is the type of person that you meet on the street, and you choose to cross to the other side because you fear what he might do. He looked at you, and you could imagine a very long and difficult story behind those scars. That was exactly what his story used to be. He was put in jail for being just that type of man. Even in a high-security prison, he was considered a man to be feared, but one day all this changed.

A missionary would come every week and share about the redemption of Jesus, what it meant to have a before and after, and what it meant to be a new creation, never looking back. He shared about the goodness of God and how the suffering of man isn't because God is bad but, rather, because God is so good that He created man with the power to make choices. Those choices are so powerful that they will have a ripple effect to others around us every time we make one. When we use those choices for love (seeking the highest well-being of God first and then others without thinking about oneself), the consequence is incredible, and that blessing is heavenly. When we use those choices for selfishness, the opposite of love, then we have what we see around us: brokenness and suffering, pain and abuse. Through one of these days, Jesus clearly got ahold of Hilario's heart, and there was a before and after—he was a new creation.

The prison guards didn't believe it was real. They didn't believe that a man like this could be redeemed. They actually warned one another, assuming that it was either a show to try to get his very long sentence reduced or to seek an opportunity to hurt someone else. Day after day, Hilario's transformation didn't change, though, and it happened in such a way that against the wishes of the guards, Hilario had his sentence reduced and was miraculously set free. To the surprise of everyone in jail, especially the guards, Hilario showed up the next day to preach in the prison. He might have been set free, but they couldn't keep him out of jail sharing the message of redemption. The goodness of God transforms *everything*. Yes, *everything*. Soon this feared man was multiplying his heart in multiple jails, through Christian rehabilitation centers, through orphanages, and through any means possible. This man that appeared to have no life within, eyes sealed shut, was awakened and set free from himself because he understood what it meant "to live is Christ, and to die is gain."

Somewhere around 2009, I went with Hilario to the border to legalize a vehicle for his ministry. As I spoke with Hilario on this trip to the border of Mexico and the United States, I began to see and understand why I had heard so many stories throughout the years about this man. He was real, and there was nothing hidden. He had testimony after testimony of what God had done within him, through him, and around him. Throughout the years, I keep hearing the same incredible stories about this man's redemption. Almost anywhere I go in Mexico, if we talk about jails or rehabilitation centers and God, they know Hilario. The redemption that God had in his life not only transformed everything about him, but it has transformed everyone that has come in contact with him.

After that road trip, I remember getting home after having time with this man and asking myself if there was anything different about me now. Was there a before and after in my life? Was it real? I had given up my car, my family, my culture, my language, my girlfriend, and the little bit of money I did have, but was I any different? Were people different because they met me? God began to show me my life as if it was a movie, and yes, I didn't even believe it at first, but my story had finally become *His* story.

I was no longer a young boy seeking God for what I could get, but I finally knew God. I had known His goodness and had experienced it. It was no longer about what I had to do but what I get to do. My life and works were not a task but a privilege. I was no longer a servant to the master but a prince of the King. In the words of Paul, "Look at me, do as I do, because I do what I see Jesus doing." Or in the words of Jesus, "I only say what I hear the Father saying, and I only do what I see the Father doing." These weren't lives of men that made a momentary choice in their past, a onetime decision of salvation, and that was the end of it. Rather, these men that knew Jesus and His Spirit of redemption were alive, vibrant, real, and powerful today.

By walking in this daily journey of knowing God, I learn to know who I am. I'm not proud of where I come from looking at the selfish choices of my past, mostly because I have absolutely no excuses. I had a great family, education, and experiences in life, and I simply hid away from all the open doors. I chose me over God. But now I know that I have no excuse to hide away from an *extraordinary* life of redemption. I'm not just sitting in a hospital waiting for the return of Jesus, but rather, I am made in the image and likeness of

God; and by His Spirit, I can do even greater things than Jesus has done as a part of the body of Christ in order to see my life transformed and bring positive influence to those around me and to see the kingdom of God here on earth. I believe it with all my heart! Not for some experience of today or for a season in my life or because it's some means to a better end of salvation and heaven. No, I am in the promised land today! I am in Jesus today! I am where He wants me to be today! It's not about what I have or haven't done or even who I am but rather who He is. By His strength, by His love, by His power, I have been redeemed; and whether it is just one more day or another sixty years, I can have His story, and there is no turning back. I have seen men and women of faith who have every excuse imaginable to give up on God and life, on humanity and redemption, but they have simply said yes and been renewed, have been redeemed, and I choose to be one of those people.

Throughout the years, within each new season, one of the challenges with redemption is that the victories of the past don't count for the present and future. There is no merit for a well-lived past if the freedom of redemption isn't lived and seen today. After getting married in 2011, there was a whole new life that opened that was incredible and amazing but also had some major challenges. The good was always twice as good, but the bad was always twice as hard. I was told that I needed to imagine living 24-7 with a mirror (my spouse) that can and will talk. My wife is incredible, but it's true. In all the areas that I had thought I was transformed, I realized that there was no merit if my wife didn't see it in our marriage, and I had to learn to live redemption again. With my first child, my second, and my third, it happened over and over again: learning to live redemption here and now and not just one time in my past. Within each new season, there must be a new level of redemption and letting God write the story.

Within our ministry, there are people walking in all stages of life from being new believers to seasoned intimate lovers of God and from singles to families with multiple kids. Personally, I have three kids, two dogs, two cats, a snake, and a full garden. My life begins with my daughter waking us up early, our son waking up throughout the night while he nurses, trying to get both kids ready and changed, go to the bathroom, brush their teeth, eat breakfast, and ready for school. We need to feed and water the dogs and take them for a walk or let them into the yard while finding time to water the grass and garden. We do the dishes and try to clean up a bit while grabbing a quick coffee and sometimes breakfast so the kids aren't late for school.

From the moment I arrive to where I serve in ministry, people are waiting to ask questions, to process problems, to deal with complaints, to make decisions, among other tasks. Right after lunch, one of us runs to pick up the kids from school. We do our afternoon activities, have dinner, and begin the process of preparing for bed. This includes baths for the two eldest and sometimes the baby, doing the dishes and cleaning up the kitchen, letting the dogs out and getting them water, brushing the kids' teeth, having them go to the bathroom and sometimes doing their homework. From there, we continue by telling one a story, followed by a song and then a prayer; and then telling the other a story, followed by a song and then a prayer. And on a good night between eight or nine, we can try to sweep and mop downstairs and rest for a bit before trying to get a bit of sleep. This is 24-7, sickness or health, good or bad. This is a part of being married and having kids in ministry. In this season, being redeemed and living God's story is radically different than any season before. We need His grace just as much as ever before, but it can be even harder now. We don't get to live on the merits of our past redemption, but each day we must allow God to write His story rather than us writing our own.

It's easy to get up and preach for an hour from a pulpit, to teach for twenty to forty hours during a week, and then fly home, or to write content or a book in free time. To live the everyday reality, the stuff that we just can't change, the repetition of daily life and love in marriage, or respond as a father in the middle of high tension, tiredness, and just the weight of the world—it takes an incredible grace of God and commitment. It takes an incredible power of redemption to say yes when everything in you wants to say no, or to be patient and not react when you desire something different. The story of redemption, to have a before and after that never turns away, is a story where the daily author must be Jesus. It must be full of His Spirit, and it must be renewed by the grace that is found in the presence of the Father. Ten years ago, I would have said that it would be impossible for me to live what I live today. In God's grace, He didn't show me my own capacity as a single man. One day at a time, living today, trusting that what He says is enough and His grace is sufficient.

Over and over again, I'm amazed that what most impacts the people around me isn't my teaching or classes, my leadership, or what we do. But day after day, person after person, I hear the same thing: "To see what you do as a husband and father, still being a good son of God, and somehow still finding a way to love us and lead this ministry—it just amazes me. I hope to be a father and husband like you one day." This almost always brings me to tears and reminds me once again that the *extraordinary* isn't all the big stuff that others see but the day-to-day, ordinary, normal, real life redeemed by Him!

Reflection

1. At what moment do you see the before and after in your life? Do others see that same change?
2. If we are redeemed by the goodness of God, do you know the character of God?
3. Who is guiding your life, the smallest choices of your relationships, your words, and what you do or say today?
4. For you, what does it mean to be a Christian?
5. As you read through Jeremiah 9:23–24, what does this mean?
6. When other people see your life, what do they see, and what will they say?
7. When the lights are on you, what does your redemption story look like? What does that story look like when there are no lights on you?

Meditation

Today the word *Christian* or *Christianity* is just another religion. There was a time in history, however, when the word *Christian* actually meant something. It wasn't a word used by the people of God but rather by those who hated the people of God. In the early church, many Jews thought that the Christians were simply Jews who had taken the Nazarite vow in numbers and many times were referred to those of the "Way," the path of Jesus. It wasn't until the Roman persecution of the Jewish Christians that we see the birth of the term *Christian* in a new light. Those that were so angry about this group of people that lived so radically different weren't like anyone else in the Roman kingdom, who were nothing like the other Jews or Gentiles but lived radical lives. They wouldn't give into corruption; they couldn't be bought or be bribed. Their families were different. The way they talked and lived was different, and it was always the same reason: they were living like Jesus!

To be like Christ, "Christian" would end in being eaten by lions or killed in the Roman Empire. It meant that you believed so much in Absolute Truth and the conviction that Jesus was the only way and the essence of love, that you would profess it and live it to the point of death. You were a new creation, and there was no going back. You had died to sin and are now alive in Christ, who is resurrected and sitting on the throne. You were a citizen of the kingdom of heaven without any cultural passport or nationality but simply a reflection of Jesus, living love, because you had been redeemed, living the kingdom of God here on earth as it is in heaven.

Today, all too often we see redemption as a past-tense act on the cross that has little to no implications of what we live and do today. We even say, "You don't have to do anything now. It's just grace"—as if you could experience grace outside of relationship and intimacy with Jesus and His Holy Spirit. We must continually go before the throne of the living God and ask ourselves if we know Him, if we have a relationship with Him, if we are like Him, and if we have been redeemed to draw close to the Father. To be Christlike is not a title we can give ourselves, but it falls into the eyes of the world that looks at us. When they see us, do they see Jesus? If not, what does it mean to be a Christian? Either we have been redeemed, or we haven't! Either we live the ordinary of the world, or the *extraordinary* of the kingdom of God.

The Bible and Redemption

- "In your lovingkindness you have led the people whom You have redeemed; in Your strength You have guided them to Your holy habitation" (Exodus 15:13).
- "And Moses gave their redemption money to Aaron and his sons, according to the word of the Lord, as the Lord commanded Moses" (Numbers 3:46–51).
- "But as for me, I will walk in my integrity; Redeem me and be merciful to me" (Psalms 26:11).
- "Awake! Why do You sleep, o Lord? Arise! Do not cast us off forever. Why do You hide Your face, and forget our affliction and our oppression? For our soul is bowed down to the dust; our body clings to the ground. Arise for our help, and redeem us for Your mercies' sake" (Psalms 44:23–26).
- "The works of His hands are verity and justice; all His precepts are sure. They stand fast forever and ever, and are done in truth and uprightness. He has sent redemption to His people; He has commanded His covenant forever; Holy and awesome is His name" (Psalms 111:7–9).

CHAPTER 6

Forgiveness

Inspired by my dear friend, great father, and wonderful husband, Martin Garcia from Mexico

Forgiveness—a conscience, deliberate decision to release feelings of resentment, vengeance, hurt or anger, toward a person or group who has harmed you or failed to meet your expectations whether they actually deserve your forgiveness or not. This release turns the individual or group of people over to God to continue to do a liberating work in their lives without you expecting any type of restitution; you are getting out of the way. You become freed from your own emotional slavery by forgiving others as well.

Special Introduction

Forgiveness is a choice. It is a process of brokenness and restoration, of pain and healing through which your pride is forced to die. In this process, God brings the wounds of the past back to our mind, not to hurt us but rather to heal our heart, which allows us to walk in freedom. Freedom that helps you to trust, to relate to God in a new way and to see Him as a Father. This will affect you in such a way that your relationship with Him will affect everyone else around you. May you find this same level of forgiveness as you encounter the love of the Father God. May this chapter inspire you to forgive without any reservation and to release anyone and everyone that you have held onto bitterness toward. Be free by setting others free!

Martin Garcia
Teacher by Vocation
Discipler of Many
Father, Husband, and Dear Friend

* * * * *

My sister is three years older than me, and we have been blessed to become close friends. My mom loves to tell me the story about how at the hospital after I was born, my sister held me and smiled, and then handed me back to my mom and said, "You can send him back now!" My mother always laughs and said she had her hands full trying to get my sister to want to share her life with me. Now my oldest son is two years older than my second child, Abigael, and he still likes to tell us that he is the special child—he was the first and is extraspecial.

As I grew up, I loved my sister greatly and did everything in my power to get her to love me and want to be with me. No matter what I did, where I went, or whatever took place, I wanted to do something special for my sister. In kindergarten when there was a party at school, I wouldn't eat my cookies or snacks because I wanted to bring them home as a present for my sister. No matter what happened and how she would respond, I would wake up the next day and love her with full forgiveness and forget what had happened the day before.

Watching my oldest son, Caleb, interact with Abigael in the same way never ceases to amaze me. No matter what Caleb does to her, she wakes up with great joy to see her brother and love him again. I'll never forget the day that I was in the bathroom and heard Abigael screaming. Caleb had her on the ground and was standing on her head so she couldn't get up. Aside from him getting a quick consequence, we had a long talk about loving his sister. Within ten minutes, they were downstairs playing together and loving each other.

Abigael had fully forgotten what had just happened ten minutes earlier. No matter what one or the other does, the sun will not set on their anger or sadness, and they awake best friends again. This sincere love and forgiveness teaches me every day the power and freedom found within forgiveness.

I have to confess that it took several years for the power of forgiveness to really sink into my life as I was growing up. The sincere and unfailing love found in quick forgiveness seemed so difficult to bring into my adolescence and early adulthood. Having lived an incredible six months in Mexico with God challenged me in so many areas in 2004, but one of the principles that seemed to most transform others found little room in my life. The concept of forgiveness and brokenness, deep expressions of emotion and regret, anger and tears, or sadness just wasn't something that I completely understood. To give a deeper understanding about how my mind works, after taking different personality and processing tests, I came to realize I am an INTJ on Myers Briggs, which many call the mastermind, but low on empathy and emotion; and my top three on strength finders are *command, context,* and *strategic,* which really helped me understand why getting things done is so important for me, why I really care about understanding history and the context of people or situations, and why my mind is always looking at what is the best way to accomplish goals. All of these are in the area of mind, with lower levels of emotion and relationship. It is very natural for me to disconnect from my emotions and be more like a robot, simply looking at the context, facts, and how to do what is best. It can be very complicated for me to really break into the depths of my heart, emotions, and empathy toward others.

I remember hearing classes on forgiveness and repentance, and it seemed to just be a dry mirror in which I really did need to repent and ask for forgiveness. I sent letters, e-mails, and even made phone calls, as I previously mentioned in an earlier chapter, as the Lord changed my heart over my selfish choices and began to bring redemption. I knew that I needed forgiveness, that I needed to repent, and that I had greatly hurt others. As tough as that reality was, it made much more sense to me to do something to move on without any emotional response. I did not understand what my classmates were going through. During different classes in that first missionary training experience in 2004, I would witness classmates broken and in tears as God convicted them of all the people they needed to forgive or ask forgiveness from. They would burst out of class to go and make a phone call as they received revelation of bitterness, hurt, and lack of forgiveness and would call a friend or family member and ask for forgiveness.

This was such a foreign idea to me, and connecting their actions and emotions was difficult for me. Even the message of the cross, which brought me to my knees, my natural way of processing information left little place for an emotional response. I had always somehow been able to understand and extend empathy as I would reason within my own mind on how an individual must have had a good reason for doing whatever it was they were doing, even if it hurt me in the moment, but not an empathy within my own emotions, only within logic. The common trend seemed to be that after the weeklong teaching on the Father heart of God, or internal healing, big issues would come up in people's lives. As they grew in understanding of how great God was—loving, patient, and faithful—they would quickly identify where all their ideas and lies had come from, which they somehow projected onto God's image and their own personal relationship with Him. Usually, the commonality of hurt was the relationship with a parent, key leaders in their lives, or influential person from their past that had hurt them.

Very different from most of the other students, I was encouraged to look back and see how greatly blessed I was by an incredible family, church body, and even friends in school. I am also quite thankful for the way that God created my mind and how I process information. It can make it a bit tough to relate to others sometimes, but it has been a huge protection as well through difficult seasons. Yet despite my relative stability, there was one story that would come up over and over again through my life that God would one day use to humble me and give me the strength to forgive and release in the most difficult moments of my life.

My friend Martin, an elementary teacher and man that spoke absolutely no English, had a season in his life that forever marked me. In the first two years of knowing and working with him, we had little to no relationship at all outside of just seeing each other at work. He was a little bit older than me. We couldn't communicate easily, and he was nothing like me. One day during class in 2004, he burst out during a break to make a phone call; and when he came back, this is the story he shared.

He grew up with only one last name. In a Latin American culture, this is a huge shame because every child has two last names as they take both their mom and dad's last name. If you only have one last name, it means that your father refused to recognize paternity. He was bullied from the time he was a child about not having his father's name, and he eventually created a fantasy story in his own mind that his father had lost him by accident and was desperately out looking for him and would do anything to get Martin back in his life. In his mind, this little boy only had to find his father and everything would be better. So that is exactly what Martin began to do: he began to seek out who his father was and where he lived, believing that his father must be searching for him and wanting him to come home again. This childhood dream and fantasy soon took a turn for the worst.

It took a few years, but Martin was able to find who his father was from a relative; and to his surprise, his father didn't live that far from where Martin went to school. One day for Father's Day, Martin made his father a very special gift and was superexcited to go and have his first encounter with his father. He had heard that his father drove by a certain street every afternoon, coming home from work, so Martin went there, so sure of the excitement his father would have upon his arrival, encountering his son that he had been looking for. As a car drove up, Martin saw his father, who looked out the window. His father shut the window of the car and just drove by. Martin took his gift and broke it that day, turning his tears of childhood pain into hate and bitterness. He stood on that corner for a long time before he accepted that his father didn't want him and that he no longer wanted or needed his father.

For years, there was no contact, but eventually Martin showed up at his father's house. A worker received Martin and told him that his father didn't have any other children and to never come back again to that house unless he wanted to get into some big problems. With a broken heart and anger, he left without seeing his father.

A couple of years later, Martin returned to the house again. This time, he was allowed in, and his father knew exactly who he was and didn't care. He had a wife and multiple kids, and he didn't want anyone to know about Martin, so he began trying to pay him off so that he wouldn't come back again. Martin had wanted a relationship, not money, but his dad only offered money to get him to go away. For years, their only relationship was that Martin would show up to have his father give him money and then leave again. No relationship, no love, and he was still a little boy, lost and wishing that he would have never discovered the truth.

Now this twenty-eight-year-old man was sitting in a class, realizing that all the lies he believed about God were his projections of what he had never had with his earthly father. When God revealed His great love, He also showed Martin that he needed to forgive his father and even ask forgiveness from his father for holding on to so much bitterness, hurt, and anger. When he called his father in tears, a child now trapped in the body of a man, he broke down and began a new relationship with his father.

This phone call opened the doors for another future conversation where he could finally say, "Daddy, I forgive you, and I need you to forgive me for everything that I have thought, felt, and even said or done against you. Thank you for giving me life! I need nothing from you, and I am thankful for you!"

Like I said, it was hard for me to grasp the reality of what took place in the classroom that day. How could pain and forgiveness be so deeply emotional and so liberating? I had little experience in this type of emotional pain, but I couldn't imagine living what this man had lived. My dad was my hero and best friend, my mom the best mom I could have ever asked for, and my sister was like my best friend. Even with that, I was a selfish man who felt I had an excuse to be a victim, and yet here was Martin, willing to humble himself as he had found real forgiveness before God, releasing and forgiving his father. Martin's personal redemption with God brought him to a place to forgive the unforgivable, extending redemption outward to those around himself.

Martin eventually became one of my good friends. For sixteen years now, we have walked, cried, laughed, and lived this journey of life together. I was there when his brothers rejected him, but I was also there when his father fully accepted him and finally loved him as a real son. When his father was dying, not one of his kids loved him and wanted to be close to him, but Martin went and took care of him. He changed him, nursed him, loved him until the point of death; and then his own brothers gave him nothing, saying that he wasn't a legitimate part of the family. They didn't give him any of the inheritance and shamed Martin to the very end of his dad's life and after. All that Martin did in response was simply give self-sacrificial love. Martin has lived through more than I could imagine with his family, but with the incredible strength of his mother and the forgiveness he found in God, he was able to forgive and restore things with his father, finding freedom from bitterness and anger.

In 2006, two years after witnessing this intimate moment of forgiveness with Martin in the classroom, the biggest storm of my life hit me. I found out that my dad had left the house, and my parents were getting a divorce. I knew my parents had struggles like any other marriage, but I would have never imagined what was taking place. It seemed like everything that I had dreamt of, identified with, and loved within one day became everything that I never wanted to become. I don't blame either of my parents, and I love them both. Fourteen years later, now that I've been married for eight years with three kids, I have understood the reality of how hard marriage can be. As I was just a twenty-one-year-old young man, however, this hit me in a way that I would have never imagined. There are many details that I won't share as I love my mom and dad both very deeply, but the impact was very real, and a limitless amount of questions arose. Who am I? Who is my family? Who are my parents? Is anything from my past nineteen years real, or was it all fake? I had a crisis that I had to walk out of, and I was all alone with no one else to turn to.

Not only was I walking in the midst of this battle, but my girl-friend at the time and I weren't talking, my sister and I had a falling out, and in this same week I was getting deported from Jamaica. That's right. I had flown to Jamaica to attend a missionary school to further equip myself called the Community Development School through the University of the Nations because I wanted to pioneer it in Mexico. But in the process of getting my student visa, the government had lost my passport in the mail. I might have been crazy, but I felt like God said, *Just go.* When I boarded my flight in Denver, Colorado, without a passport, the airline staff said I could fly to Orlando, Florida, but that I wouldn't be able to continue, so I went. In Orlando, they let me fly to Miami, saying the same thing. In Miami, they said that because the plane was empty, they would let me fly to Jamaica, but most likely I wouldn't be allowed off the plane. When I arrived in Jamaica, the man in immigration didn't ask for my passport and just let me in. That's right—miraculously I flew and got into the country without a passport because when God says yes, no one can say no. What I thought was miraculous soon became the loneliest place on earth.

This really was a miracle because in order for me to have pio-neered this school into Mexico, I needed to be present the first two weeks to understand the administrative details of how the school functioned. In the midst of all that was happening in this one week, I had no money, and immigration showed up on Thursday saying that I had until Saturday to leave the country, and my entire body began to break out in blisters and react in sickness. This was the toughest moment of my life up until then and that Friday night I was unable to sleep, but in the middle of the night, the Lord began to speak to me. I sat out on the hill overlooking the ocean, under the stars and moon, all alone, and I opened up a journal from two years prior. I had made a long list of things that I believed the Lord wanted me to do and had written them all down a couple of years earlier. To my amazement, I had done all of them except for selling my car, which I would do soon after. As I looked at this list, I realized that even if everything was as perfect as I thought it was just a short time ago, or as bad as it felt in this moment, I wouldn't change anything I was doing because I knew who I was. I was finally in the right place for the right reason, and nothing could change that. It was a crazy moment, the most alone and broken I had ever been, but also the first time I was at perfect peace, as if I was sitting directly before the face of God Himself.

To make a long story short, miraculously I was able to get an extremely cheap ticket to Miami, fly out, get my student visa in two days, and return to Jamaica by the end of the week. To this day, it seems that the toughest moments of my life have been the moments that I have most seen God and have been able to cast all my burdens on Him. The biggest miracles seem to have come through the biggest tears, but God has always been faithful when I've felt most alone. I was most alone in Jamaica, without anyone to reach out to, to cast my burdens on, but God held my hand and carried my heart. I believed that He was enough, but just a couple of years later, all these hurts came rising up again.

For years, I lived with others, sometimes larger groups in a dorm room and sometimes just one other guy. In 2008, just two years after my parents' difficult divorce and my time in Jamaica, I was living in Mexico. My roommate had decided to move back to the States, and the leaders decided to let me live alone. I eventually acquired a couple of snakes, a tarantula, a large scorpion, a gecko, and my parrot, Bell. My room became a small zoo with myself and my beloved animals. Bell was a very special gift for me from my girlfriend, who is now my wife. I had Bell for several years. She would come down to my bed and give me a kiss every morning, and she used to ride on my shoulder while I walked around campus. I had become the training director for all of our missionary internship programs, and while I worked there, she would sit in my office in a little tree I had, periodically flying to me while I worked throughout the day. One morning, a perspective discipleship training school student came into my office for an interview and tried to pet Bell. My window was open, and the parrot got scared and flew right out the window. A large hawk saw her and began to chase her as she flew away into the horizon screaming, never to be seen again.

It's crazy to remember and think about, but my parents had been divorced, my best friend and I had lost contact in Mexico, my sister and I weren't close in this season, and various other difficult things had transpired, including me breaking up with my girlfriend. But I had never shed a single tear through those storms. The night that Bell left, however, was different. I had placed all my emotion, strength, and hurt on this silly little parrot; and when she flew away, I broke. I sobbed like a child. It wasn't even necessarily the parrot, but Bell brought out all the emotion that was deep within me. It was several years later, but everything that I hadn't understood with Martin began to make sense to me, and I kept remembering that phone call he made to his father forgiving him and asking for forgiveness. Through a long night of great brokenness, reopening many wounds, and feeling completely alone again, I remembered the power of forgiveness.

It took me a few months, but that is exactly what I did. I had to call and talk to my mom and share that I loved her and forgave her and asked her for forgiveness while we both cried. I ended by telling her that no matter what she chose, I still loved my father as well and that I never wanted to hear her talk badly about him. With my father, it was even harder because, as close as we were, neither of us were big talkers. We would spend weeks together hunting or fishing yet never talking. I actually lost complete communication for almost half a year with my dad until we were able to talk, and I told him basically the same thing that I had told my mother. Then almost a year later while in Costa Rica, in the same month, I had to deal with a phone call from both my mom and my dad asking the same thing: their blessing to begin a relationship with someone else, someone new, someone who wasn't my mother or father. I gave it, remembering the incredible story of my friend Martin. Who was I to not allow my redemption with Jesus, His forgiveness to me, to not be multiplied to others? So I fully gave it, remembering how brave Martin had been.

I have been hurt, even in my very introversive way of processing information. I have been broken and abandoned by friends alone and had expectations fail over and over again throughout the years of my life. There are two things that I have kept ever present in my mind: the first is that it has always been during the most difficult moments of my life that I have been closest to God, and I know that He never fails me; and second is that there is nothing that I can't forgive. I am not a victim, and through Jesus, all things are possible. If Martin could love and live with joy and right relationships with brothers who have hurt him over and over again, with what he lived his whole life, and still be an incredible, loving, patient, and forgiving man, then so can I. Jesus is worthy of my life, and in all things, I desire to honor him; and if He could forgive me, then there is nothing that I can't forgive.

Today Martin is an incredible husband, and I had the privilege to be in his wedding. He is an incredible father whose children will never experience the pain and brokenness that he lived most of this life. In just one generation, what could have turned into great bitterness and brokenness for future generations has turned into an incredible story of divine forgiveness and redemption. When I want to say no, I remember those that have said yes when they had many reasons not to. Today I can forgive and be set free because my children, my wife, my friends, and my future generations deserve a legacy of freedom and complete love!

Every year, with each new ministry or leadership opportunity, every step is connected to new relationships. Relationships seem to never get easier, and the failure of relationships always result in great pain and hurt. As our ministry grows or my influence in different spheres of relationship, there is one guarantee: people will fail me and hurt me. Even worse, I will fail others and fail to meet their expectations. It's not the desire of my heart, and I don't wake up desiring to hurt someone else, and I now understand that no one else has ever woken up with a malicious heart to intentionally hurt me, but it still happens.

As finite beings created in the image and likeness of God, there is one guarantee: I need forgiveness. I need to forgive others, and I need them to forgive me. I need to forgive my wife and kids almost every day. I still have to learn to daily forgive my mom and dad, my sister, and many people that I love greatly, whether they ask for it or not, whether they deserve it or not—I just need to forgive. Our team of nine different nations and five different languages now only makes it harder. If within my own marriage, with the woman that I love above all other people on earth, I unintentionally hurt and need her to forgive me, or she can still hurt me and I need to forgive her, then within our ministry, it's a daily choice. Some days I feel like it's a daily battle, to have to fully forgive to be able to walk forward, over and over again, no matter what the cost because it's the only way to keep moving onward.

Unfortunately, I can't make others have a right relationship with me, but I can take away all of their excuses and do everything possible to be right with them. I can forgive daily, go to sleep with a clean conscience, and wake up without any prejudice or bitterness. Every day is a new day and a new opportunity to forgive again. As Paul says in Romans 12:17–19, "Repay no one evil for evil. Have regard for good things in the sight of all men. If it is possible, as much as depends on you, live peaceably with all men. Beloved, do not avenge yourselves, but rather give place to wrath; for it is written, 'Vengeance is Mine, I will repay,' says the Lord." God is King. He is infinitely wise and therefore the only right Judge. I can't sit in that seat; I just need to forgive.

Reflection

1. Is there anyone you have chosen not to forgive in your life?
2. How has bitterness and lack of forgiveness affected you? How will that affect your future relationships if you don't deal with it?
3. What can you do to fix this area of bitterness, anger, and hurt toward others?
4. Do you need to ask for forgiveness from someone that you have hurt or failed who now has bitterness, anger, or hurt toward you?
5. Do you trust God as the perfect judge, wiser and abler than you to do what is right?
6. What would your life look like to live in freedom and complete forgiveness toward others?

Meditation

There are some dear friends in my life that I assumed would be quick to forgive me and move forward but have responded in a way that I would not have wanted when I asked for forgiveness, and we've never spoken again. There are also those whom I have forgiven but have chosen to never change at all, and we still have no contact to this day. I have lost one of the dearest relationships in my life, a best friend and brother, and there are other relationships that have been broken along the way, but forgiveness is a choice, not a feeling.

We choose to do it not because someone deserves it or not, or whether they will change or not, or even if our relationship is healed or not. We do it because God forgave us. I am no one to judge, but God is the perfect Judge, so I can turn any individual over to God without any expectation, independent of my pain. I trust God to work in their lives. He is perfect and wise, and only He can really change the heart; and at the end of the day, it depends on the individual to allow it. If you want to be free, you need to forgive—no excuses, no victims, no way around it. Freedom is no guarantee to change someone else or to even change what you feel, but it sets you free to walk forward in life and to no longer be trapped and stuck. If Jesus forgave you to the point of death, even when you didn't want Him, you can forgive others, even if they don't ask for or want it. No one deserves forgiveness, but we can still forgive!

The Bible and Forgiveness

- "Show me Your ways, O Lord; teach me Your paths. Lead me in Your truth and teach me, for You are the God of my salvation; on You I will wait all the day" (Psalm 25:4–5).
- "Blessed is he whose transgression is forgiven, whose sin is covered. Blessed is the man to whom the Lord does not impute iniquity, and in whose spirit there is no deceit" (Psalm 23:1–2).
- "If You, Lord, should mark iniquities, O Lord, who could stand? But there is forgiveness with You, that You

may be feared. I wait for the Lord, my soul waits, and in His word I do hope" (Psalm 130:3–5).

- "O Lord, to us belongs shame of face, to our kings, our princes, and our fathers, because we have sinned against You. To the Lord our God belong mercy and forgiveness, though we have rebelled against Him" (Daniel 9:8–9).

- "And whenever you stand praying, if you have anything against anyone, forgive him, that your Father in heaven may also forgive you and your trespass. But if you do not forgive, neither will your Father in heaven forgive your trespasses" (Mark 11:25).

- "Then Peter came to Him and said, 'Lord how often shall my brother sin against me, and I forgive him? Up to seven times?' Jesus said to him, 'I do not say to you, up to seven times, but up to seventy times seven'" (Matthew 18:21–22).

- "Therefore, as the elect of God, holy and beloved, put on tender mercies, kindness, humility, meekness, longsuffering; bearing with one another, and forgiving one another, if anyone has a complaint against another; even as Christ forgave you, so you also must do" (Colossians 3:12–13).

- "The God of our fathers raised up Jesus whom you murdered by hanging on a tree. Him God has exalted to his right hand to be Prince and Savior, to give repentance to Israel and forgiveness of sin. And we are His witnesses to these things, and so also is the Holy Spirit whom God has given to those who obey Him" (Acts 5:30–32).

- "Therefore let it be known to you, brethren, that through this Man is preached to you the forgiveness of sins" (Acts 13:38).

- "I will deliver you from the Jewish people, as well as from the Gentiles, to whom I now send you, to open their eyes, in order to turn them from darkness to light, and from the power of Satan to God, that they may receive forgiveness of sins and an inheritance among those who are sanctified by faith in Me" (Acts 26:17–18).

CHAPTER 7

Dependency

Inspired by Pastor Adrian Casillas Piña from México

Dependency—the quality or state of being influenced or determined by or subject to another. To have deep trust and reliance upon another for all choices, even when great influences rise up to stop you from walking in dependency. A choice to not rely upon yourself.

Special Introduction

> The Lord is my strength and my shield; My heart trusts in Him, and I am helped; Therefore, my heart exults, and with my song I shall thank Him.
> —Psalm 28:7

One of the most difficult things for all mankind is to trust in God and to depend completely upon Him with a full heart. When we try to take control, our flesh is revealed, trying to be happy and achieving a state of complete joy while making sense out of life and then finally being confronted with reality. Mankind living independently from God will never continue forward, be complete, find meaning in life, and find complete joy and peace."

Blessed is the man that understands that it is better and more excellent to do things God's way because, many times, depending upon our own intelligence, strength, charisma, opportunities and wealth only leads us to fall into an emptiness and loss of the truth. We must completely depend on Him. My own life and the life of my family was totally changed by God. He achieved in a short time what my father and mother had desired their entire lives for their family: unity and real love within the family. This understanding came through His wisdom in situations like my brother Jaime's accident and even music, the talent that God had placed within our hands. He called our attention, and He made us see that even in music we would find Him. Above all else, the fervent prayer of my mother that had known and believed that God is real changed us. We stopped doing everything that we had done in our own strength, seeking fame and recognition from man and all the money that this fame could give us. This happened to such a degree that we burned all of our band's bright clothes, all of our music, and all the CDs and tapes of any worldly music that had kept us from living in real freedom.

In this way, we began to learn a new beginning that depended completely on God. I was no longer going to make $1,000 in an hour or to sing to hundreds or thousands of people, but we didn't need this anymore because we now had a Boss who paid us in something much more valuable than all the gold in the world. Our safety and protection was now in Him alone. May all glory, honor, and thanksgiving be given to the One who is sitting on the throne, who lives from generation to generation.

I have known Daniel for sixteen years now. May the words of this chapter challenge you to walk in complete surrender and dependence on God in the same way that my family has learned to do since we first encountered Jesus, and Daniel has been learning to do throughout his journey in ministry.

Adrian Garcia Piña
Senior Pastor in Zapotlán del Rey
Father, Husband, Musician, Evangelist, and Dear Friend

* * * * *

From a very young age, my father was like my strength. It did not matter what happened around me or within me. If I could look into my dad's eyes and see his affirmation, then everything else was okay. My confidence, identity, overcoming of fears, and believing what I thought was impossible, was all possible because of the incredible heart my father showed me. A major part of my identity and essence was fully embraced within the dependency upon my father and who he was for me. I did not need to hear his words, just seeing his eyes, smelling him from a distance, or even knowing that he would be there tomorrow no matter what happened, influenced my identity in a supernatural way. Despite so many cultural lies that I would accept through my life of independence, there was something engraved within me from the time I was born: that if daddy was there, things would be okay. I might have forgotten it throughout part of my journey of life, but by God's grace He was able to bring me back to the roots of understanding that I fully need Him and that if He is for me, then no one can be against me.

I was blessed to be born in a moment in history where my family, culture, and reality gave no space for a legitimate excuse to not fully trust God and others while taking full responsibility for my life. Looking back on my life, all too often an excuse seemed to be the only answer that I had to not fully follow or trust God. I never lived any type of abuse; I did not have any substantial family issues; and I never experienced life where my basic needs of food, shelter, education, relationships, or health were not met. I was offered incredible educational opportunities, had good social and sport communities, and work was never an issue for either myself or my family. Although we were not rich in the standards of many, we had more than the majority of the world. I never experienced living on the streets, any real need not being met, or doubts about what I could do or become one day. I have wonderful family memories, dinners around the table with my mom, dad, and sister, and incredible experiences of vacations, travel, and extended family.

If anything, looking back, I was maybe even a little sheltered from the world. Our community was probably 95 percent white, middle-class American. It was like an island of sameness. Generation after generation of the same families, the same cycles, with similar general stories. One might almost find comical that anyone that comes from this lifestyle could have any complaints or find any excuse to be a victim, but just like every other member of our human race, when choosing whether to stand up and be responsible or look around and blame others as an excuse to be a victim, many times I fell into those same patterns of the world. Lost in my own mind as an adolescent and teenager, I began to believe that I was the only one that had to deal with my thoughts, emotions, dreams, fears, and challenges of understanding singularity and diversity in a world that begs for conformity.

Like most young men, I began to find my comfort and independence in the uniqueness of becoming like what everyone else around me also wanted to become, the exact opposite of unique. My style, my clothes, the music to which I listened, the hobbies I enjoyed, and even what I depended on turned me into just another Colorado, Rocky Mountain boy. A world of myself deceived into thinking that this was any different from anyone around me and completely blinded to any world outside of my own head and heart. Whether it be football or basketball, snowboarding or skateboarding, hunting or fishing, drugs or drinking—we all looked alike. As King Solomon said in Ecclesiastes 1:9, "That which has been is what will be, that which is done is what will be done, and there is nothing new under the sun."

I had the privilege and benefit of traveling to many different states as none of our extended family lived nearby. For example, I visited Minnesota, Kansas, Nebraska, Florida, Texas, cities in California like San Francisco, Los Angeles, and even the Bahamas and Mexico, all before the age of 18. My only real culture shock was in the twin cities of Minnesota where I experienced real racism both toward me for being white and from anyone like me toward all that were not white. All these *experiences* were still superficial in comparison to a global reality and not a full part of the world in which I really lived. My day-to-day values, my normal thoughts, and memories were all incomplete. These were experiences that gave me fun stories or even made me think a bit about people that were different than myself.

I remember clearly the first time I was in Juárez, Mexico, and experienced extreme poverty, or walking in Kansas City and being told that it was not "safe" to walk certain places, or even being in LA and hearing gunshots at night, but that still was not my world.

A friend and mentor of mine, Christine Noller, used to say this: "If everything you need, want, or dream of is at your fingertips and everyone around you lives as if they have already achieved it, it's very difficult to feel like you need God. It's hard to depend on God and seek His heart when it's natural to just depend on yourself." Thanks to her and my family, I did get to experience other things outside of my small little community and world, but at the same time, these experiences never transcended back home.

I remember after going to Juárez with my mom in 2000 and actually "suffering" a bit for Jesus. What marked me most was not the extreme poverty, living with sand fleas every day and having bites all over my body, the limited water and lack of showers, or even the extreme heat—it was seeing how my mom reacted when we went home. She would break down crying as we drove up into the mountains and watched everyone with their nice cars and huge houses filled with only four people. Many around us had more than enough somehow lived without peace and joy. We had just left a place of extreme poverty, and yet the children were happily running around naked, never complaining and with huge smiles. Many families did not even have a house and many times any type of steady job, but they had unity and joy; they had real love. I was touched by this difference, but it radically transformed my mother in a way that I could not fully understand. She would spend weeks of a reentry crisis, unable to take in everything around us and unable to understand how people could not see what was happening in the rest of the world. I, on the other hand, just slid back into my normal life, back into my mind and heart, and all too often back into the ideas that somehow "I was a victim" and deserved something more than what I had.

It wasn't until 2004, when I jumped onto that plane to go and live in another place on earth, did the veil finally fall from my eyes—or, rather, was ripped off my eyes; and the only option left was to allow my sight to adjust to this new reality, to what the world really was, who I really was, and what I had in the midst of it. I felt as if I was wearing extremely dark-tinted glasses for the first nineteen years of my life, not knowing that I was even wearing them, and all of the sudden someone held me down, tore them off, and asked me to stare into the sun for the first time. I had been living my whole life in the middle of a world that I had never truly seen, understood, or acknowledged even existed.

This eye-opening realization took place in different phases. I remember the simple shock of living in a place where I did not understand the language for the first time in my life. "People don't all speak English?" To further demonstrate this point, I never understood why so many places on earth spoke in such a negative way about Westerners or North Americans, particularly those from the United States of America, until my glasses were removed. Myself, like so many others, had grown up with a limited perspective of a global reality, and I was finally being pushed beyond what I had ever known before.

After the language, though, bigger things began to hit my heart specifically in my understanding of what is wealth? The differences between valuing time over people or people over time, money over relationships, or love and relationships over money. A big house and car or investing in a large property to grow something on it with a tiny little room in which to live. One time, I learned that one of my friends in Mexico, who I had previously thought was very poor—his one-room house consisted of only a toilet, shower, outside kitchen, and a huge bed—was actually very wealthy. I asked him why he does not buy a nice car and build a big house, and his answer astonished me: "If you spend all day outside working or out with people, why would you want anything at home other than a nice bed? All you do is sleep there, why would you waste money on things that you don't spend time in?" I then asked him what he did with his money, and he responded that he bought more cows, more property, and I soon discovered that he owned almost half the town. He liked his comfortable boots and didn't spend money on something expensive that he would not wear. He lived everything opposite from where I came from, a world of materialism and consumerism. Even in the area of education, I would be asked, "Why study if I can make more money with my hands doing what I love, working with the people that I love, and being home with my family?"

Another eye-opening realization was the food. I remember the first time I went to a barbeque at the house of someone that was very wealthy. When I opened the pot, to my amazement, there was a full cow head being cooked staring back at me. Right next to it, they were frying intestine and stomach. I have eaten grasshoppers, cow tongue, cow brain, cow eyeballs, cow lips, chicken feet, pig fat, works that look like larva, and much more. To my amazement, one of my favorite foods, sixteen years later, is now cow tongue and grasshoppers, and my wife loves fried intestine and stomach. Some of the foods I had been told my whole life were garbage or waste have become some of the treasures at the table.

I had to unlearn many ideas I had acquired and been taught to reexamine why I had been told certain things and begin to see into the heart of another group of people in the light of a new day. I had to make a purposeful shift from the glasses of ignorance I had been wearing my whole life. Little did I know, however, this same awakening needed to take place with the way I saw and interacted with God. I did not see the world clearly because I had not seen Him clearly.

There are many examples of how God began to show me that I did not see Him in the right way or in the full light of the clarity that He desired. It was not something tangible and real, something that I could measure and really see the before, during, and after. That is, until I came to a little place in the center of Mexico called Zapotlán del Rey.

This small village has little to no outside influence. Even though it sits just off a highly traveled highway, the majority of the residents have never even left this part of Mexico. After my first experience in this community, which I mentioned briefly in a previous chapter, I have had the privilege to continue building relationships with the people, to work with them, to learn with them, and to grow together with them throughout the years. Pastor Adrian continues to join us in different moments and, just a couple years ago, was with us in our ministry with his wife for a two-week Bible seminar I taught for leaders called Bible Education and Leadership Training or BELT. We continue to connect once or twice a year. Sixteen years since I first met him, we have become close friends, and I would consider him and his wife a part of our family. This man is nearly twice my age, but I have learned to love and respect him greatly. God has used him and his family to show me what it meant to remove my glasses and see God in all of His glory, goodness, and clarity, which began to change the way I saw people. He is full of power, but simultaneously very intimate and personal.

Adrian is the seventh sibling and comes from a large family of fourteen siblings. He tells the story of growing up in a family where both his mother and father were very stern, and although they were a poor family, they were very hardworking. He shares how he began to develop a love for music at a young age, and despite how his father was somewhat distant, he came home one day and bought Adrian a keyboard. Little by little, Adrian began to learn music, playing the keyboard, guitar, drums, and even learning to sing. His brothers all quickly followed in his footsteps, and within a short season, they formed a band. I have met most of the brothers and am amazed to see that much talent in one family.

The band began to gain some momentum and traveled and played in some of the biggest parties and even for various drug cartels within the area. They tell stories of how crazy the environment would become and how men would get so drunk that they would pass out, and then their wives would go home with different men or even with one of their own brothers. Some of the brothers got involved in trafficking, growing, and distributing drugs. The environment began to go from bad to worse, and some of the brothers left for the United States, some continued with the band, and others began to live their life in different ways with fast cars, women, alcohol, drugs, and money.

Through this season of their lives, his mom had a little radio and would listen to a Spanish Christian station from the United States every night, and she met Jesus in a very personal way and began to pray for her children and family earnestly. It was during this time that God began to move in their family. As she was praying and opening the door to God in her family in the middle of a community without a single Christian church or any believers, God began to move.

There were many factors that influenced Adrian and his family to encounter Jesus, but one day when one of the brothers was driving, he had a major accident. He was medically pronounced dead, and there was nothing the doctors could do. During this time, the brother shared that he awoke in the presence of Jesus and began to walk down a long pathway with Him, but there were many people on the other side of the path in a place that looked like what he imagined to be hell, and they called and cried out. He was trying to go to them and tell them to leave their way of living and that Jesus was real, and he now saw that life could be different, but he was not able to get to where they were. He continued to share that during this dream, he realized that many of the people he was seeing as dead and in hell were actually real people that he knew, who were still alive in his family, friends, or community. Jesus told him that if he did not share what he saw and if they did not change their lives, they would end up outside of His presence for all of eternity. At this moment, his life returned to his body, and he awoke. The doctors have no way of explaining, but this rebellious and crazy young man awoke as a completely different person, never to be the same again.

Because of the lack of oxygen to his brain for so long, he suffered permanent physical disabilities, but he is able to talk, express his heart, and faithfully loves people on the streets. Everyone that comes in contact with him is impacted by the overflowing love he gives. When he woke up and shared with his brothers and family what had happened, a shift began in their family, and the reality of God was undeniable.

In this same season, a local missionary and pastor, Braulio, from chapter 2, came to their community and began to meet with the mother as well. Just like one would imagine from a book on revival, every one of the brothers, their wives, and all their kids were conquered by the love of Jesus. This community went from zero believers to almost eighty believers because the power of God came over just one family. This did not come without a cost, however. The community stopped selling them food, giving them water, and they were threatened on multiple occasions. As they opened their homes and lives to the power of Jesus and the Holy Spirit, the drunk men turned sober, never drinking again. Those that sold drugs gave up their "good" income and began to work in the fields. Those in adultery fully repented and restored their marriages, their families, and their lives. Even that band that once was the center of dark parties took their gifts and talents and became an incredible worship band. God poured out His Spirit. They began to walk in a lifestyle of repentance, and they were discipled.

Adrian, the seventh brother, is now the pastor of the church, and they continue to grow. The kids are grown and are walking in this truth of Jesus, and other communities are being touched by God through their lives. Externally, most of the family is still relatively poor—they work with cows and goats, bees and honey, and in the fields. *But* they are free, they are passionate, and they are contagious. Poverty is in the mind and not in the lack of or abundance of resources, but liberty lies within the dependency we live in Jesus! Jesus has given them new ideas on working with goats, planting, and starting new projects as they have understood what it means to be cocreators with God.

Growing up, I never really saw a group of people that corporately gave everything over to God, a group of people that gave up everything from their past and started anew. My concept of God was to bring Him into my life but never to give up my life to follow Him. Thanks to this pastor and his family, I have seen the real power of God. I have experienced the depths of His love, and I have no doubt within me of how good and real God is. Adrian has taught me year after year how to be faithful to God and live a life that fully depends on Him. Whether with his wife, his kids, or the ministry that God has given him, God comes first! They can be generous and give from their poverty and in their wealth, for it all belongs to God and can go as easily as it comes. As seen in the Gospels, to one who receives much grace, he will continue giving much grace.

About four years after I first met Adrian and his family, something that happened continued to influence me. I used to go on weekends to work with them in their church and to simply spend time with the family. One of the younger brothers, Saul, became a good friend of mine, and I greatly enjoyed being adopted into a loving Mexican family from which I could learn. I remember one particular night very clearly in a way that only I could have known what was happening within my heart.

Before I did my discipleship training school (DTS) and entered YWAM, like most other young men, I struggled greatly with pornography and masturbation. It was something that I know my parents did not agree with, and they had taught me otherwise, but it seemed so common in the lives of almost every guy I had met. So I chose to just be normal, and it became my excuse to do what I knew was wrong. After understanding real love, I was able to completely walk away from lust. I arrived to the point that I would even close my eyes or turn away if I saw a sensual billboard or scene in a movie, and I was free to not struggle in that area anymore.

This particular day, however, I was having a really hard day, and I returned to an old habit of seeking lust. No one knew about it, but I did, and I did not have a clean conscience. That same evening, Adrian asked me to come to their church to participate in an event that they were doing in the community. After about an hour, Adrian walked off to the side with a few other people. A few minutes later, he came and grabbed me and said that there was a woman that was experiencing demonic problems and that he wanted me to pray with them for her. This was one of the most humbling moments of my life, but I knew that I had no authority to pray for this lady and that my heart had been far from God all day. I had to open up and repent before all these leaders, including Adrian, my friend, and they prayed for me. After that, we prayed for the lady, and she received her freedom that night.

Going home that night in 2007, I was processing so many thoughts. No one from the church had judged me or looked at me any differently, but I felt like I had let God down. I know that He is always willing to forgive and draw close, but I was so ashamed to call myself a missionary and be living in a way that did not depend on Christ on that particular day. I sat out by the stars that night and prayed alone. I had time to worship and love on Jesus, and I made a commitment that I wanted to live a life of dependency on Him. I was willing to give up whatever and do anything to keep myself close to Him.

Looking back now over many years, I have had many types of struggles and had to repent many times with my team, my wife, or leaders for simply being stupid, not thinking, or offending someone, but I can say I have walked in freedom of my conscience, not giving over to lust and not hardening myself to what God would want to do through me. One of my greatest fears is to have God open doors that I shut because of selfishness or self-dependency. My desire is to live in a way just like I had seen and learned from Adrian, that I would be sincere and dependent upon God above all other things without shame.

This dependence can seem irrational to others, and to this day, I know that many friends or even family members that struggle to understand my motives in what we do. The only thing I can explain is that just like my father when I was growing up gave me the confidence to overcome anything in life, in the same way my life is dependent upon the Father of all Creation now. Jesus Christ is my Lord and King, and all I do is just because I love and depend upon the Father. I expect no special reward, and I fear no punishment if I do not obey Him, but I know that I am nothing without Him. He is not a means to some selfish end, but He is my ultimate goal daily. More and more, I have experienced the seasons of plenty and the seasons of nothing, the seasons where we are surrounded by people we love and the seasons that we are literally alone and cannot go to family, friends, or leaders. But God is still present and faithful. Just one look from His face, a small affirmation even if there are no words, a little hug or just the feel of His heart—is all I need to keep going forward.

Even though some of our choices have seemed crazy to others— having all three of our children be born in Mexico, living a life of faith without any set income, traveling and ministering in some very difficult and dangerous locations, giving away our $10,000 car when we have our own needs, blessing others and being generous when we are lacking, and so much more—we have learned that we depend on God first and foremost, above all things.

I have been fortunate to never have been alone in my life, but like everyone, many times I have felt that way. With an incredible wife, three beautiful children, and incredible leaders within our ministry, I can still feel alone. I have learned that this is actually a good thing because there is an emptiness within humanity that can only be filled by God. To be created in the image and likeness of God is to be filled by Him, by His Spirit, to abide within Him, and to follow after Him. Others see the fruit, but He sees the heart. Others judge by their own experiences, but He judges by what He has spoken and asked. God is intimately personal. The God who sees, the God who speaks, the God who knocks, the God who waits, and the God who fills us is enough.

As an adolescent, I assumed that the future would be easier; but I have learned that the only thing that changes is that I have many more responsibilities, more people watching me, more criticism and opportunity to fail or succeed (and consequences seem to be even greater if I fail). Life does not get easier, but the same choice is available every day, as seen in Deuteronomy when God gives His people the choice: "Today I present before you, life or death, blessing or curse, you choose." Today I can choose, once again, to fully depend on God, to fully trust Him, and to fully remember that His goodness is enough for today!

My buddy Usba and I used to look at older pastors and ministers around us, and they would tell us their stories from their youth. They had stories of their past passion and excitement, and so many of them seemed to have lost it. We made a commitment together that we would never let that happen, that we would never lose our first love no matter what the circumstance of life. One of my pastors even told me many years ago after first going to Mexico, "You have a lot of passion, excitement, and charisma today, but it will go away within a few years as you mature and grow up." I hope that he was right in the fact that I have matured and grown up in the last sixteen years, *but* I hope that he was completely wrong in that I am more passionate, more excited, and show even more charisma than in the beginning. I hope my dependency can become greater and that my complete surrender today would give way for Him to be glorified even more than yesterday!

Three years ago, in 2016, we began pioneering a new ministry in Mexico. We do many different things, but one of our foundational values is biblical transformation and WISE: *worship, intercession, spiritual warfare,* and *evangelism.* We do Bible training for pastors and indigenous leaders and have formed a long-term alliance with Wycliffe Bible Translators in Mexico so that they would translate the Bible, and then we could go and train the leaders how to use it. We are putting a Bible in every home in Morelia, Mexico, where we live, which is a project of about 220,000 Bibles. Now we have been pushed into the Bible translation of the last forty unreached people groups in Mexico and much more that seems unfeasible at this time. It's only possible in Him, through Him, and ultimately all for Him.

Through these two values of the Bible and WISE, God began to really challenge me about my own dependence on Him. Do I live for myself, making decisions on my own experiences, or do I really depend on God? One of the questions I felt was, How much time do I spend in the Word and in repentance, fighting for a complete dependency on God in all that I do? I have read the Bible every year for the past sixteen years at least one time and usually more, but there is still more. After fasting for an extended amount of time, I made the goal to try to read through the Bible twelves times in 2017. I cannot go and share about the power of the Bible unless it is a part of all that I live, so I spent a couple hours a day reading, outside of my daily devotionals. I only read through the Bible seven times that year, but it was a great goal that year that connected with new levels of fasting and prayer. He also showed me that my marriage, being a good husband and father, or even a good leader depends on how sensitive I am to Him, not what I know already or have experienced, and that I needed to learn to grow in a lifestyle of repentance with my wife, my kids, and my team.

Interestingly, for so many years, I was trying to achieve this image that I had everything worked out, but I have understood that

I do not need to project this to others, and God does not want me to. What He most desires is that I simply desire and obey Him above all things, that I would not teach theory, that I would not share the stories of others, but that I would learn to grow and live my own stories, my own victories, and have defeated my own giants.

As I was diving deeper into the Bible and spending more alone time with God than before, fasting every Wednesday and taking a full afternoon to just be with Him each week, I began to see more and more how my design is actually to live continually in a posture of dependence upon Him, to thrive in His presence. I need Him in everything I do. I need Him to achieve the dreams that He is giving us as a ministry, which are greater than anything I have ever imagined and thought on my own. I do not need to please man or fulfill his expectations, but I need to simply live on my knees in the presence of God, living before teaching, doing before exhorting, and most importantly, being radically dependent on Jesus and His Holy Spirit every moment of my life to draw close to the Father's heart.

Reflection

1. Do you fully depend on God with all that is in your life?
2. Is there any area in your life that you have not been willing to give to God?
3. Are you living on your knees in repentance every day or building a tower of pride?
4. In the toughest moments, to whom do you look: your past experience and own wisdom or to God and His Truth for today?
5. If you were to lose everything, all physical possessions and earthly relationships, is God enough for you?

Meditation

In the beginning of 2019, I arrived to work in the morning, and one of the young boys of a single mom on our staff ran up to me really excited about our rabbits that just had babies the previous night. I was really frustrated about something, and rather than responding in a positive and loving way, I was very short and said, "Yes, I know. They told me last night," and I walked away. The look in his eyes was devastating as his countenance fell. As the leader of our ministry and being a man, I have much weight in this young boy's life, who does not have a father present with him. The next day, I showed up early, pulled him aside, and hugged him. I apologized and said I was wrong and that God was nothing like me in that moment. I was sorry I did not take time to listen, to be excited with him, and that I would do my best to never respond rashly again. I also humbled myself before our team later that day because I felt so bad and wanted to use it as a teaching moment. Who cares if I can travel, teach, preach, write, or be seen if I cause one of our own young boys to stumble? Dependency upon God is seen in how we react when we are empty, not in what we do when we feel full!

Since the beginning of this year, I've once again had the difficult question knocking on my heart, "Who do I fully depend upon, and where am I being restored and filled?" This year has opened doors to doing more full fasts for weeks on end of just water, early prayer mornings in the prayer room, and a deeper level of self-examination. Does my marriage reflect that I depend first on God? Does my relationship with my kids reflect that I first depend on God? Do my relationships with our team and their kids reflect that I fully depend on Him first? I can't always say yes, but my desire would be that every day my heart's desire would be just a little bit more dependent on Him! If only that was the desire of all humanity—not that we always did it right but that we always had the right heart!

The Bible and Dependency

> When I would have healed Israel, then the iniquity of Ephraim was uncovered, and the wickedness of Samaria. For they have committed fraud; a thief comes in; a band of robbers takes spoil outside. They do not consider in their hearts that I remember all their wickedness; Now their own

deeds have surrounded them; they are before My face. They make a king glad with their wickedness, and princes with their lies. "They are all adulterers. Like an oven heated by a baker—he ceases stirring the fire after kneading the dough, until it is leavened. In the day of our king princes have made him sick, inflamed with wine; he stretched out his hand with scoffers. They prepare their heart like an oven, while they lie in wait; their baker sleeps all night; in the morning it burns like a flaming fire. they are all hot, like an oven, and have devoured their judges; all their kings have fallen. None among them calls upon Me. "Ephraim has mixed himself among the peoples; Ephraim is a cake unturned. Aliens have devoured his strength, but he does not know it; yes, gray hairs are here and there on him, yet he does not know it. And the pride of Israel testifies to his face, but they do not return to the Lord their God, nor seek Him for all this. Futile Reliance on the Nations "Ephraim also is like a silly dove, without sense—They call to Egypt, they go to Assyria. Wherever they go, I will spread My net on them; I will bring them down like birds of the air; I will chastise them according to what their congregation has heard. "Woe to them, for they have fled from Me! Destruction to them, because they have transgressed against Me! Though I redeemed them, yet they have spoken lies against Me. They did not cry out to Me with their heart when they wailed upon their beds. "They assemble together for grain and new wine, they rebel against Me; though I disciplined and strengthened their arms, yet they devise evil against Me; they return, but not to the Most High; they are like a treacherous bow. Their princes shall fall by the sword For the cursing of their tongue. This shall be their derision in the land of Egypt." (Hosea 7)

Now in that day the remnant of Israel, and those of the house of Jacob who have escaped, will never again rely on the one who struck them, but will truly rely on the Lord, the Holy One of Israel. (Isaiah 10:20)

CHAPTER 8

Loneliness

Inspired by two incredible young Chinese men

Loneliness—a complex and usually unpleasant emotional response to isolation. Loneliness typically includes anxious feelings about a lack of connection or communication with other beings, both in the present and extending into the future. As such, loneliness can be felt even when surrounded by other people and one who feels lonely, is lonely. The causes of loneliness are varied and include social, mental, emotional, and physical factors, but to be separated from God, is true loneliness. To be utterly alone with Jesus the Lord and Christ however, removes all loneliness.

Special Words

When foreigners read the Book of Acts, you see inspiring stories. When we Chinese read the Book of Acts, we see it in our lives.
> —Pastor of Underground Church

Of course we're scared, we're in China, but we
have Jesus.

—Pastor Jin Mingri

* * * * *

I have heard individuals tell me their whole life that they couldn't
survive without others, or how they would go crazy if they had to be
alone. Any time I have ever heard someone say anything like that,
all I can do is think back to growing up and how much I loved to
be alone. Growing up in Colorado, outside of a small town in the
mountains where you couldn't see a single house from my house, was
an incredible experience. We had horses and dogs, even a potbellied
pig that used to live in the house. I grew up hunting, fishing, snowboarding, and loving my alone time. If it hadn't been for our "party
line," I wouldn't have known that anyone was around, but it was
always a bummer to try to make a phone call and hear your neighbor
talking on the phone already. There were evenings when I would pick
up the phone and hear the conversation of our neighbors talking, so
it meant that I needed to hang up. I don't know if I have ever seen or
heard of a party line since then, but it was just normal to first check
to see if one of the neighbors was on the phone before trying to make
a phone call, and sometimes while you were talking on the phone,
someone else would pick up and start dialing until they realized that
you were on the phone.

Just having neighbors that I sometimes had to hear talking on
my phone line almost seemed like being around too many people
despite the fact that I couldn't see a single house from where I lived.
I had friends up in the mountains, and we would go and shoot our
BB guns or investigate in the old gold mines or even play down by
the creek and fish in it. But one thing was sure: unless we went to the
main road, we weren't going to see anyone else. This was how I grew
up and the life that I lived. I enjoyed being around people, and as
previously mentioned, I did tons of sports and social activities, but I
loved being alone. From a young age, I would hike up the mountain

and just spend hours alone looking at the trees and the mountains and daydream about what it would have been like to live in these same mountains as a mountain man many years ago. I'd dream of the Indians and wild animals and imagine what it would have been like to be the only white person in all of the mountains. I loved the movie *Jeremiah Johnson* and could imagine myself living like that many years ago.

Despite developing normal social skills, this background of the mountains and being alone left me as a major introvert who just enjoyed being without others. I like people and have the ability to be in groups, but when I need to process or to deal with something I'm feeling or thinking, then I just need to get away and be alone for a while. Many times I wish I could go back to those mountains where the closest person might be an unseen neighbor using our phone line. No people, beautiful smells, animals, and nature. I could spend days like that, all alone, but oh so happy and peaceful.

The quality time with my dad was the same way, being alone while fishing or hunting, playing golf or hiking, and we never invited anyone else. I didn't bring friends, and it would just be us in the mountains or at the lake. My mom never understood it. We could come back from long days of being out, and she would want to know what we had talked about, and we would both just say, "Nothing." One of my favorite trips with him was when my dad took all of his vacation at once when I was in middle school in 1998, and we went to Lake McConaughy, a beautiful lake in Nebraska, for a little over a month. We fished, skied, wakeboarded, swam, walked, and it was incredible because there were no people other than the two of us. To this day, my mom doesn't believe me; but in a month, we had the time of our lives, and we didn't talk about anything. We said simple things like, "You hungry?" or "Want to go fishing?" but nothing more than that, and it was perfect.

Apparently, for many people, this seems really strange or unbelievable, but I loved it. I have always loved being alone, and I have many memories of how being alone never meant loneliness. I had my thoughts to get lost in, my memories to ponder over, and my dreams to imagine. Being alone was really good for me. Actually, up to the point when I was married, almost nine years ago, one of my favorite times each year was driving back and forth from Chapala, Mexico, to Denver, Colorado. I would do it in about three days and be completely alone with my car and the highway. For hours, I would open up the sunroof and roll the windows down and just watch and listen to nature. I would stop on the highway for every sunset and watch every sunrise. Even now, one of the things I most enjoy are my flights when I go to teach or when returning from a trip. I love long layovers when I can just read or be alone and watch the people walking around me. Not long ago, I had an eight-hour layover, which was perfect to read the book of Isaiah and then have time to just be and think while watching and trying to read and analyze the people passing by.

Because of the way I grew up and certain values that were imparted to me, it was a huge challenge moving to Latin America in 2004 to join a "warm-climate culture" where everything is about the group and being together, where everyone has to be invited, and you need to always go to every public activity. Living with multiple roommates, working with people, doing ministry with people, and then having to be with them in my free time was too much. All I wanted to do was to be alone! This caused numerous problems in my first few years in Mexico. Some people thought that I didn't like them, didn't want to be with them; and others were either hurt, offended, and simply did not understand. Little by little, though, I learned that I could be with a lot of people and be okay, at the same time needing to be creative and finding my own alone time and place to renew my energy.

In spite of being "alone" and loving it for so much of my life, it wasn't until I was in South Korea that I understood loneliness. This lesson prepared me for many seasons that would await me in the years to come, and I'll never forget my trip to South Korea in 2006. This was my first trip to Asia, and I was superexcited for what I would learn and experience on the other side of the world. What an incredible opportunity to travel to the Eastern world! I made new friends and learned so much about being in a foreign culture.

I remember the first time I went to use the restroom, and I realized that there were no toilets but just a little hole in the ground. I was so confused that I had to look under the wall of the stall next to me to see that I had to take off my pants completely and squat to make this new process work like a tripod. The next morning when I went into the shower, I was shocked to find a great big open room with lots of shower heads and lots of men helping one another in the shower. This was a little too much culture shock for me, so I would shower early each day before there was a crowd. It was so intriguing to see everything new around me. People would bow to one another, and depending on how far down you bowed, it meant something different in this honor culture. The language was tonal, so every word had multiple meanings depending on whether you started with a high pitch and ended with a low pitch, or low to high, or unchanged.

My third day of the conference, I remember realizing that out of the three thousand people, most of the men all sat together, and the women all sat together. The men would give one another massages and physically be very close, and the women as well, but I didn't see any interaction with the men and women together. The normal was to show same-sex affection if you were heterosexual and to be self-controlled without anything to prove, which was the opposite of my part of the world.

On that same day, we had a special session to pray for China. I had never heard the extent of the persecuted church in China, but it was heartbreaking to hear the stories and what many people were facing but encouraging to know what God was doing. After hearing so many stories and testimonies about China, I headed back to my room, and that third day is when I began to really understand loneliness for the first time.

I roomed with a dear friend of mine from the Bahamas, Dale Bourne, who has walked together with me for many years, and with a couple of Chinese guys. That afternoon, we had a conversation that moved me deeply. They spoke almost no English, and neither of us could speak Mandarin. I remember each night that the two Chinese guys would come in to talk to us in our beds. They were just wearing boxers, and they would get very close to us, and it was very uncomfortable for us at first, being from the West, but it was evident that their hearts were very sincere without any weird motives. One of these guys began by trying to use a dictionary to show me a picture of a girl. He told me how he loved her, but because he was a Christian, she couldn't be with him, and her parents wouldn't let her see him anymore. He shared more and more stories of what it meant to live as a Christian in China, and it impacted me a great deal. With tears running down his face, he spoke about his dreams of getting married and having a family, but that because he was a Christian, it was very difficult to find a wife or ever have kids. Throughout our conversation, he shared many difficulties he faced because he was a Christian; and at the end of the conversation, I realized that he wasn't looking for pity, but he somehow believed that all Christians lived and experienced the same thing and was just looking for brotherhood, for someone to pray with him and stand strong with him. He had no shame, and in his loneliness, he was complete in God alone.

Here I was, traveling to the other side of the world for an experience and adventure, having every opportunity in my life to do whatever I wanted and with whomever I chose. This man did not have that same freedom, yet he had everything at the same time. He was full of Christ and had made a choice that loneliness to be with Jesus was better than any dream on earth without Him. The day these two guys left, they left me a little piece of cardboard with a special note on it. To this day, I have kept this note and daily remember to pray for these two young men. I have no idea what has become of them. Did they go to jail for their faith? Did they ever find a wife or have kids? Did they ever get to experience their dreams, or did they die for what they believed? I may never know, but what I do know is that every day I pray that they did or that they someday will experience their dreams! As I watch what is happening now in China with the burning and tearing down of all the Christian churches, the state religion, and the continual increase of persecution, it makes me think more and more about how these two must be living now because of their Christian faith.

These were the first two men that I had ever met who were truly alone, who were without anyone, simply because they loved

Jesus. I would think about them many nights in the weeks, months, and years to come, but something that stuck with me was the joy that they had in the middle of their loneliness. There was something about that loneliness that had forever marked their lives and, in just a few days, had forever marked my own.

Being alone was always a choice to get away from people, to do what I wanted, and to be free to follow my own heart or dreams. Here were two men, though, who represented millions of Christians throughout Asia, the Middle East, some parts of the Americas, and islands throughout the Pacific who had lived lives where being alone meant not doing any of the dreams they wanted, not fulfilling most of the desires of their hearts, and being alone because others either didn't want them around or didn't want to be around them. This was more like rejection than being alone, but as I watched their tears and listened to their dreams, I was touched, and the question came into my mind, "Would I still faithfully follow God, love Him, and trust Him if it meant that I would be left completely and utterly alone—if it meant that I would have to give up all my dreams and surrender everything that I had? Would I still love Jesus if I had no family, no friends, no wife, and no promise of kids one day?"

I had never thought about these types of questions before, and in spite of complaining about everything that I had given up to follow Jesus into Mexico, Central America, or the Caribbean, the reality was that I didn't really have to give up much. I had the freedom to choose to follow my heart and what I felt that God was saying in a very open way with few to no consequences. I could go back home at any time and be welcomed with open arms. These two men, however, had no open doors or future "dreams" or "calling" and no place to go back to, but they seemed so much closer to Jesus than anyone I had met up to that moment in my life. Something had taken place in their loneliness that had marked them for Jesus in a way that I had yet to experience. The depth of faith, the depth of love and trust, and the incredible daily choice to be faithful even if it came at the ultimate cost was very inspiring.

God has greatly used that experience to prepare me for what loneliness would really look like in life. Through some very complicated moments, the following years would take me on my own journey of loneliness. I have now experienced this type of being alone a couple of times, and in spite of leaving some scars from different relational challenges, what most stuck out was the way in which God picked me up, touched me, held me, embraced me, and sustained me in such a way that can only be done by Him. There are tears that only He can catch and wash away, and moments of brokenness that only He can sustain.

Back in 2007, I had been through multiple difficulties within ministry, within my family, and even with other leaders around me. It was one of the first moments in my life that I felt truly alone and didn't know who to go to or what to do. The story that came to my mind several times was how Jacob on his journey to encounter his brother, Esau, had a very special encounter with the Lord, which marked him forever and changed his character. Up to that moment in Jacob's life, he was in hiding and was willing to let his family be killed by his brother; but after wrestling with the Lord all night, he woke up and finally took his place at the front of the family, unafraid of being alone, no longer worried about what might happen but finally confident in who he was with God.

In spite of losing contact and communication with most of my family during that year for multiple and very painful reasons, losing my best friend in ministry, and then being isolated from many of the people I knew the most, all because I chose to stand on principle as opposed to certain relationships. To this day, most of those individuals still don't speak with me. Despite feeling very alone while also dealing with some very difficult situations within my family and friends, I never remember crying or even expressing how I was feeling about my parents' divorce, losing dear friends, or being hurt by people very close to me. Rather, I kept moving forward in life and ministry. Many nights I was unable to sleep and all too often felt tormented by my ever-racing thoughts, but the tears never shed. I was alone and really had no one other than God Himself to process in this season, but it all seemed to be fine. As mentioned in a previous chapter, all that I had to share in my heart, I shared with my parrot, Bell. She was the one that listened to me and the one that was there to love and comfort me during that perfect storm. During this season, I probably spent hours and hours sharing with her about what I was dealing with, feeling, and struggling with, and it was she who kept me from being alone and giving up completely on family, friends, leadership, and ministry.

The day she flew away broke me. For days I would dream that she would be back on the porch in the morning or fly home at night, but she never did. It was in that moment that I finally broke in my emotions. I had built up all of my emotion, my struggles, my hurt and pain, anger and mistrust, and placed it all within this silly relationship with my parrot. When she was gone, I broke. I remember sitting in my room one night, and I just began to cry like a child, like I have never cried before in my life. It was like a dam had been broken and a river was set free. In complete loneliness and brokenness, the tears were released and began to heal and wash away the wounds of the past. I began to process all the details, all the relationships, some deep wounds as I hit the reality that there was no longer the option of going home to my mom and dad together, that I no longer had contact with my sister, that I no longer had a best friend to walk through life with in ministry, that I no longer had my girlfriend, and that most of the people I knew in Mexico had turned their backs on me as well for staying faithful to our leaders. I was completely and utterly alone in Mexico, and if I tried to go home, I would still be alone!

I no longer had my dreams or even my plan B. All that I had was God. As I wept before Him and began to worship Him, which lasted much more than one night, a few days, or even a few weeks, I realized just a little bit of what those guys had in China. They had made a difficult choice to follow Jesus and had done it with great understanding and with all of their hearts. They knew the cost, but they also knew Jesus, and He was worth it! I finally understood all those things. I was no longer called to Mexico, called to a specific ministry, or serving as a missionary. I was just a young man who had nowhere else to be and no other plan. I had no idea what the future would hold, but God was worthy of everything, and that was enough. God had spoken to me, and I had obeyed, and He was all that I needed to be complete. In spite of being in one of the most difficult moments of my life, this was also one of the best seasons of ministry that I had ever experienced; and from that day on, something shifted within me. Being alone meant to have nothing between my relationship with God. Staying or leaving a given ministry, going somewhere new, or returning to my roots, leaders, friends, or what other people thought or any individual relationship—none of it mattered. All that mattered was that God was first.

True loneliness is being willing to make those same choices we tell people we have made, but with understanding when we are all alone. In the end, I am not really losing something but gaining the world, even if that leaves me alone with God. I've never shed that many tears in worship as I did for several months and almost every night in my room. I had never questioned myself or my choices as I did in that season, doubted people or family to that degree, while at the same time being completely free and honest with myself and God. That desert of loneliness soon passed, but the oasis of life that was birthed was a lesson that I have had to grab on to over and over again when the only place left to look is up. Throughout the years, as a leader, when moments got tough, others were able to leave or turn on me, but I had no place to go because I have always known I was where God wanted me in that moment. Many times I've found myself alone with God, but He is and always will be enough.

Almost nine years later, after having met my Chinese brothers, after getting married and having begun our own family with a small boy, my wife and I found ourselves in a moment of loneliness once again in 2013. We had made the choice to continue serving in Mexico with our newborn son, despite the previous two years having been more difficult than anything we had lived together. We had never imagined we would walk through some of those storms in marriage, and definitely had not expected it to happen within a ministry environment. We had been the only Americans serving where we were serving in Mexico. We were the only young married couple, and now the only young family in that particular ministry. We still loved Jesus with all of our hearts and wanted to serve Him, but all of our direction and passion seemed to be lost and had faded away.

As we struggled on individual levels and together, we made some bad decisions and got into a large debt trying to make things easier by at least creating some physical comfort within a home environment even if we were unable to control the rest around us. We tried our best to create a feeling of being okay, hoping that this would make things easier, but in every attempt, nothing seemed to become easier. As our son was born almost four weeks early, God began to show us that there would be a move on the horizon, and it would be much quicker than we thought. We began to seek wisdom from different leaders, our family, and our friends as another storm seemed to overtake us without an end in sight.

Within a very short season, things became very complicated, and I stepped down from leadership, and a doorway opened for us to move. We had no money, and most of our relationships and leaders from the last few years closed their doors to us. We shared with our family and some friends about what had happened with our debt and some of the things we were really struggling through, and as a result, we entered a very difficult season within some of our family relationships as well. Everyone loved us and cared about us, and everyone had their own dreams, thoughts, or ideas for our lives. We didn't want to do it the way they wanted, and doors began to close very quickly. They all loved us greatly, but we really had to make a choice: to be with God and all alone, or to give up everything that we believed He was saying to us to be closer to them.

One morning, Katie and I were sitting at our table eating breakfast, and God gave both of us the same word: no matter what happens, we weren't supposed to leave Mexico; and no matter what anyone said, God would provide, and He was with us. The peace that came in that moment is something that I am unable to explain, but it was the peace that comes before the storm, and we lived on that peace for close to a year. We were asked to leave where we were living several months before we had planned, and we didn't have the money to do it. Our legal covering for our Mexican visa stopped covering us by not allowing us to renew our visa through them, and we had no place to live if we moved. In this new city, we didn't seem to have a single friend, but we knew where God was calling us.

Miraculously, through very random people and primarily Mexican missionaries, we were able to pay for our travels to this new city in Mazatlán, Mexico. Upon arrival, we found a house, but we didn't even have enough money for the deposit, yet another Mexican missionary paid for the deposit. We didn't have enough money to pay our rent; we had no idea what we were going to do and were strongly discouraged against what we were doing by the closest people in our lives, but we had peace, and God continued to miraculously provide through the nationals and a few very faithful mentors and friends.

Our first night was in the middle of the hot season in Mazatlán, and there we were—lying on the floor in one bed, in the middle of the heat and humidity, with just one little fan! It was *ninety-six* degrees in the middle of the night with high humidity, and as I looked at my wife and son sweating while they slept, my Alaskan Malamute dog looked at me, and I knew that we were thinking the same thing: *What on earth have we gotten ourselves into?* We couldn't afford to get air-conditioning, and we didn't even have a refrigerator to cool off milk or food for our baby. With great reason, most of the people that knew us and loved us thought we were crazy and irresponsible. I remember walking every morning and just asking God how on earth we would make it through today. I would ponder the idea if I had just made one of the biggest mistakes of my life or if we were really obeying God.

As a family we experienced many tough moments those first weeks. As a husband and father, I felt like I was failing. I had no friends to share with or express my heart to in this new city, and most of the people that loved us believed that we were making a very bad choice and did not know how to respond to us, and I didn't know how to communicate with them. Despite our circumstances, this was one of the greatest seasons of our lives, and I had never been closer to God. Through this moment of loneliness, we began to learn new levels of living in complete dependency on Him.

I can't say that I miss the heat of living in Mazatlán or living in the way we did in that difficult season, but I would like to share an experience we had. One morning, just after waking up, I had read Numbers 6, which speaks about the Nazarite vow. So I shaved my head, my beard, and humbled myself before the Lord while entering a fast. I knew He was my only answer, my only provision, and the only One who could really cover my back. He was the only One who could provide for my son or take care of my wife. Only He could heal our pasts and stabilize our present to bring us into the future. Only He could find a way to pay the rent, keep us where He had called us, and open the doors for our Mexican visa. Only He could restore and redeem relationships again with some of the challenges from others and some of our own failures. My reputation didn't matter. It didn't matter what people had said, were saying, or would say about our failures, our mistakes or immaturity in certain decisions, or anything else we had or had not done. A past leader had even written some people defaming us and encouraging others not to trust us in leadership. Learning and living as a young married couple in family and in ministry had been very challenging, yet even in our failures, God had always been faithful. He kept telling us, *Trust Me and obey. I will honor you and protect your reputation.*

Miraculously, within just a few months, He did everything He had spoken to us and much more! We were able to get three different AC units. We purchased a refrigerator and stove, and we found ourselves surrounded by people who loved us, who embraced us, and who began to greatly encourage us. My wife, Katie, bloomed more than I had ever seen her bloom before. Doors opened to begin to pay off our debt, and God blessed us with some incredible friends. And most importantly, we knew that only God could provide for our needs. It didn't matter where we were, where we would go one day, or what we would do. We had been alone with God, and He was enough. He was more than we could have ever asked for or dreamed of, and He was no longer a means for our own goals; but rather, He was our daily goal—in our marriage, in our family, and in our ministry. Our faith was nourished to such a degree that we knew nothing was impossible if we were with God. He eventually used friends, family, and complete strangers to provide for us, to encourage us, and to show us that we weren't alone, but it was in that loneliness, that we first found freedom.

I've learned that God doesn't want us to be alone, but at the same time, loneliness is a necessary part of the journey of really struggling with God and finding victory in life. Sometimes loneliness is the fruit of our mistakes, and we learn from them. At other times, it's the fruit of just obeying God. These are the moments that determine who we are and who we will be one day. These are the moments that build the foundations of our faith and remind us that we are not the center of things. The focus and main point is not our calling, vision, dreams, achievements, or desires. What it is really about is our learning to fully depend on God in all that we are and everything we will ever do!

A few years ago, in June of 2016, we set out to pioneer a new ministry with our son, our baby girl, our pets, and a few young staff. We had been promised many things by some people and dreamed of many other things with others about how this pioneering process would be and many promises from the previous years about how we wouldn't be alone and that they would be with us. The truth, however, is that it was very difficult. I'm sure what most people promised us or had said they would do for us was sincere in their intentions at the time, but it was superlonely when we stepped out and once again experienced that godly loneliness. In these moments, there are two sides of the coin of how to interpret things: either it's about us, and we look to others in what they have or haven't done as if we are victims; or it is about God, and we look to God and His faithfulness. He is faithful. He celebrates and encourages us in our victories, and He holds our hands and protects us in our failures.

These last three and a half years of pioneering have been full of ups and downs. On one side, we have felt completely alone; but on the other side, we have been embraced and affirmed by God like never before. We've had huge failures and incredible victories, but the affirmation comes from Him. Many people that we thought would be close to us on this journey have distanced themselves and many others that we had never thought of before became like family. This love and suffering built a new family, a new community, an incredible team, and there is no longer loneliness. We are one of the closest teams that I have ever worked with. We are thirty adults that represent four different languages and eight different countries! It's one of the sincerest "love and support" communities that I've ever experienced. Now, looking back, I can remember both: there was some deep loneliness, but it's remembered not with tears but with great joy!

Reflection

1. Have you ever really walked through loneliness where God was all that you had to hang on to?
2. If yes, in what way did God mark you and respond to you?
3. If you haven't yet experienced loneliness, what is the foundation of where you go, and what do you when things get really hard? Do you hide in what just seems logical or easy in the moment or deal with what God is really saying to you?
4. If everything was to change tomorrow, and all that was left was you all alone, without family, friends, or leaders, would you still follow God?

Meditation

The other day, one of our guys asked me why I thought that YWAM or Mexico was the best place to serve and be. He is a young Mexican and was expecting a deep response to an important question. Very quickly, I responded to him in a way that he did not expect. It was a quick response: "I don't think there is anything special about YWAM or Mexico, and if God leads us, we will leave either or both without regrets." By the look on his face, I could tell he was super-surprised, so I clarified a bit, "I love to serve in YWAM because it's the only place I have found that gives me 24-7 freedom to disciple an individual, a team, a school, or a group of people for minimum six months or up to many years. I love that freedom and the incredible fruit that we have seen. I love what we do all over the world, and I'm humbled and honored to be a part of YWAM. I love the Mexican people, the culture, and the language as well. The reality, though, is that we are here simply because this is where God has guided us.

If He asks us to go to Asia, Africa, or the United States and leave YWAM or ministry, then we would happily do that as well. There is no special merit in being in Mexico or this particular ministry. What makes it special is the One who called us."

Yes, that would imply leaving everything we love and everyone we know or have invested in and walk once again into loneliness, but we've already done that. Walking in loneliness sometimes is just a part of staying with God's path for your life! Let His story become your story!

Ethiopia has one of the coolest stories of how the Gospel actually came to their country. In the book of Acts chapter 8, there is an incredible story of Philip. He was one of the seven chosen by the apostles to serve the tables. He was the first to go in obedience to God under persecution to expand the Gospel to other places. This brought forth the greatest revival and quickest-growing church ever in history. In that moment, the Spirit of God guided him to leave all that he knew and enter the desert. He did. He left everything and everyone and simply trusted God. In the desert, he encountered the Ethiopian eunuch who is credited with bringing the Gospel back to Ethiopia in church history. Philip's choice to be alone and go into the desert still has fruit today. It can cost everything, but God is worthy, and sometimes saying yes to Him means walking into the desert alone without any idea of the future consequences. May your daily, ordinary choices of today, even when you feel completely alone, become the *extraordinary* reality of tomorrow where God is glorified.

The Bible and Loneliness

- "And the Lord God said, 'It is not good that man should be alone'" (Genesis 2:18).
- "Then Jacob was left alone; and a Man wrestled with him until the breaking of day. Now when He saw that He did not prevail against him, He touched the socket of his hip; and the socket of Jacob's hip was out of joint as He wrestled with Him" (Genesis 32:24–25).

- "But he said, 'My son shall not go down with you, for his brother is dead, and he is left alone. If any calamity should befall him along the way in which you go, then you would bring down my gray hair with sorrow to the grave'" (Genesis 42:38).
- "And Moses alone shall come near the Lord, but they shall not come near; nor shall the people go up with him" (Exodus 24:2).
- "I am not able to bear all these people alone, because the burden is too heavy for me. If You treat me like this, please kill me here and now—if I have found favor in Your sight—and do not let me see my wretchedness!" (Numbers 11:14–15).
- "So He humbled you, allowed you to hunger, and fed you with manna which you did not know nor did your fathers know, that He might make you know that man shall not live by bread alone; but man lives by every word that proceeds from the mouth of the Lord" (Deuteronomy 8:3).
- "And he said, I have been very zealous for the Lord God of hosts; because the children of Israel have forsaken Your covenant, torn down Your altars, and killed Your prophets with the sword. I alone am left; and they seek to take my life" (1 Kings 19:14).
- "I lie awake, and am like a sparrow alone on the housetop" (Psalm 102:7).
- "It is good that one should hope and wait quietly for the salvation of the Lord. It is good for a man to bear the yoke in his youth. Let him sit alone and keep silent, because God has laid it on him" (Lamentations 3:26–28).
- "And I, Daniel, alone saw the vision, for the men who were with me did not see the vision; but a great terror fell upon them, so that they fled to hide themselves. Therefore I was left alone when I saw this great vision, and no strength remained in me; for my vigor was turned to frailty in me, and I retained no strength" (Daniel 10:7–8).

- "And a voice came out of the cloud, saying, 'This is My Beloved Son. Hear Him!' When the voice had ceased Jesus was found alone" (Luke 9:35–36).
- "Then Jesus said to them, 'When you lift up the Son of Man, then you will know that I am He, and that I do nothing of Myself; but as My Father taught Me, I speak these things. And He who sent Me is with Me. The Father has not left Me alone, for I always do those things that please Him'" (John 8:28–29).
- "But let each one examine his own work, and then he will have rejoicing in himself alone, and not in another. For each one shall bear his own load" (Galatians 6:4–5).

CHAPTER 9

Compassion: The Eyes of Christ

Inspired by missionary Giacomo Coghi from Costa Rica

> *Compassion* (the eyes of Christ)—The sympathetic pity and concern for the sufferings of others that moves you to draw closer, seeing what isn't present in the immediate moment, but what their reality could be or should be, according to what God sees. To see beyond the current reality, and taking into consideration the entire life journey that has brought the individual to the immediate moment, and understanding the why and how even more than what is actually happening right now, with a personal commitment to walk forward into the future into a new life with the particular individual resulting in friendship and transformation.

Special Introduction

Our greatest treasure is the people and the relationships the Lord has trusted us with. Jesus Himself was surrounded by twelve disciples who did not meet the cultural requirements or expectations of those who could transform the world.

Jesus diligently lived with them and mentored them to the point that He called each of them His friends. He lost one in the process, but at the end, they were all empowered with the Holy Spirit and went on to do great exploits in the kingdom of God.

Jesus aimed for the God-given potential within each of them. This is not a formula but rather closely listening to God's voice and His heart for each individual, calling to life the mixture of gifts within each of them in order to achieve their life's purposes. His commitment was for them, even when they didn't see what He could see in their own hearts.

May this chapter inspire you to do the same, to find the diamonds in the rough, the people that many leaders just pass by or miss completely. May you find the *eyes of Christ*.

Giacomo Coghi
Missionary, Founder of YWAM, San Jose, Costa Rica
University of the Nations Latin America Representative
Father and Husband, Mentor and Friend

* * * * *

Having been born and raised in a culture that measured someone's success by the amount of studies they've had, the college degrees they had received, and the type of families that they came from, it was a culture shock to see a new reality as I left my home culture of the United States when I moved to Mexico. I began to see leaders that hadn't even finished elementary school, authors that hadn't been formally educated, pastors and leaders whose greatest training came from jail or the streets, and my concept of a "healthy life" or "successful people" was soon very challenged by the new reality staring me in the face.

In the first groups of men that I met, a large part of them had never known their father. They'd lived through and experienced abuse and brokenness like many of the stories already shared within previous chapters. Many of them had eventually turned into something similar in their own lives, having left a wife and kids, or having engaged with many different girls or prostitutes, or fathering kids with different women. Their stories continued to impact me and challenge everything that I had believed. I met men that used to be involved with drug cartels and even had been paid assassins, and now they were good fathers and husbands, loving God, their family, and their neighbors while living as good citizens. They had been dealt a hand of cards in life that seemed like a complete loss and were to change their life into something that everyone had said was impossible. They had every excuse to be a victim and do nothing with their lives, but here they were, living a normal and successful life, and no one would have been able to guess what they had lived through.

Growing up, I remember a few friends who had divorced parents or had experienced some type of abuse, but I had never had a friend who'd been forced to live on the streets and "survive" since they were as young as two years old or been born into a world where rape and prostitution were the daily reality. I had never lived on the streets, taking care of my brothers and sisters fleeing for survival; to live by stealing, stabbing, or even selling my own body. A life where you choose to either be killed or kill, where suffering was so great that great evil would appear to be almost good within the middle of the situation. A life where abuse and brokenness was the normal, and simply surviving would have been a success. A life where a meal was a miracle, and a cardboard box was a blessing to be protected from the cold.

If I had ever met a man or woman, a child or adolescent like this, I'm sure that just the smell or the external sight of them would keep me far enough away and that I would have never asked for their stories. Besides, what type of a story could these people have anyway? From a young age, I had embraced a story of humanity that wasn't complete. I had been given a cultural story where anything that wasn't clean and orderly, educated and cute, just couldn't fit into that story. It was a story where being different or brokenness must be a result of laziness, of race, or just because that's the way that some people were destined to live.

This wasn't a story that my parents had taught me formally or a story I had even heard in school, but it was the story that had been written in my heart from a young age, that my empathy or lack of empathy came from ideas believed as absolutes without having ever heard why. This was a story that TV and most people around me had created and believed, churches and leaders had affirmed, and mostly because no one had lived through a different story to tell another version. It was a story that had been told from the outside in without ever seeing or hearing the heart of anyone different. A middle-upper-class, educated, heterosexual, white, limited reality.

In the next chapter, I will dive much deeper into one of those stories that most impacted my life, but one of the things that most impacted me as my eyes were opened to a new face of reality was that maybe there was something within the center that I was missing. Maybe my reality wasn't really His reality. It's easy to judge the story that someone else tells you, and it's easy to be free if you have never suffered; but with great understanding, Jesus talks about how someone who has received much mercy will then extend and multiply much mercy. It's hard to give what we haven't received, and to my surprise, I had believed a story that basically concluded with the first chapter of someone's life. There was a man, however, that would soon enter my life and radically change the way that I would forever see people.

It was 2005, and I was interpreting at a conference, and there was a man from Costa Rica speaking. This was the same conference that later that year took me on a long journey to Jamaica and finally to Costa Rica. By 2006, I was arriving in Costa Rica to begin working with this same man, Giacomo Coghi. I remember some of our first talks. His questions were much different than any leader I had worked with up to that point and without knowing any of my story. Knowing that I was only twenty-one years old, he began to speak vision into my life and treat me as if I was already at the point in my life that we were talking about for the future. One of the questions he asked me was, "Are you going to start your own ministry or YWAM campus someday?" I immediately responded with a big no, thinking that there was no way for someone like me, without any college education, to do something like that, and much less in a culture and language that weren't my own (and honestly, I couldn't imagine loving other people enough to work with them at that capacity).

As he presented me to some of his staff team, I began to feel very critical as I heard some of their stories, what types of families they had come out of, the things that they had done, the way that they looked, or even where I saw their personal character. I'll never forget, though, the way that he would then explain their stories to me and tell me how far they had walked on their journeys. He would say, "You don't just find leaders, but you believe in people and call out leaders by discipling them." I was very critical of this as I saw young Latin men who were young Marxist revolutionaries, South American artists, and local guys who were dads that had left their kids and wives—there was just so much brokenness. In my opinion, I saw no leadership.

Another reason that I remember these first couple of months with Giacomo was because my own parents had just been through a divorce, and I was still processing that reality. I had lived my whole life with a certain identity and belief about myself, my sister, my mom and dad, and yet I was beginning to question that reality. Who am I if my story isn't the story I had believed about myself my whole life? I was stuck between my past memories of my family and parents and the present reality. Who was I if the story of my parents wasn't the same as my grandparents' and great-grandparents'? They were the first generation to divorce, and it began to challenge everything that I had believed about myself, my family, and even my future. In the middle of this, I puffed up in my pride, believing I wasn't as bad off as all those other guys, and at least my story was a fairly good story. I had a solid foundation, a healthy story, basic character, and I knew that I could be used by God. He used people like me to work with people like them!

During the first four months with Giacomo, time and time again, I was amazed at the type of people he would grab on to and believe in. The next year, in 2007, I was back with him for another four months, and it was the same thing. A whole team of people that I would have never chosen. I don't think I realized that I was a part of that team and that Giacomo had also seen me with those same eyes of Christ, eyes of hope and faith, eyes of expectation. When I left in 2007, I knew that I wouldn't be going back to Costa Rica in a long time, and I was convinced that those other men would never be leaders, and I began to disconnect more and more from them just because of distance and time. Giacomo stayed close to me through the years, however; and every couple of years, I would go back and teach or see him at a conference.

In 2012, I was a part of a team doing a conference for leaders in discipleship in Costa Rica, and I was amazed to reencounter some of the same guys from years before. They were completely different people; they were leaders and were making some radical choices in their lives. Their worldviews had changed, and it was no longer a group of young Marxist rebels from Central and South America but a group of incredible, God-fearing, mature men. I had the privilege to speak to one of them one afternoon, and he began to open his heart with me. He said that no one had ever believed in him during his life like Giacomo had. He said that there was no one on earth inside or outside of ministry or Christianity where he could be accepted, but Giacomo had believed in him and had given him a platform in which to grow. I heard three different guys tell me a similar story, and it touched me in a way that I could have never imagined. His legacy was alive in those surrounding him.

Giacomo had also touched me in a personal way in how he had believed in me and encouraged me. Every time that we would talk, dream, and process, it was always an encouragement. To this day, he opens international doors for me, gives me an opportunity to be seen and encouraged, and has helped me to have the confidence to move forward. Throughout the years I've seen the fruit of the treasures that he has pulled out of these young men, and it has forever changed me and the way that I see the young people of this current generation around myself.

No one is useless in the hands of God. If humans have breath, then they have been given the breath of life from God, and His image and likeness is within them. They might not see it or believe it, but it's still there, their intrinsic value. Giacomo doesn't just teach this, but he has lived this since the first time I met him. He has stories of people from all walks of life, Latins and non-Westerners that would have never had a place in the church, in ministry, in YWAM, education, sports or business, but someone believed in them, and that was enough. Giacomo didn't just believe in them, but he took the time, the months, and years to walk with them until they were willing to look into the mirror and see exactly what he saw within them. He did this through forgiving over and over again and allowing failure today and still opening doors for greater successes and opportunities tomorrow. He has left an incredible legacy of strong Latin and non-Latin men alike following in his footsteps, and they are now multiplying this to the nations.

Several of these guys have now pioneered their own projects and are believing in another generation of young men and women that have never known their fathers, that have lived great brokenness and suffering, and have even caused great brokenness and suffering but are learning to walk with their heads held high. They are breaking the reality of generations past and preparing the way for future generations to run and dream. Every story has many chapters, but the final ending is defined by the sum of all the parts, and the climax is where change really takes place. These are men and women that give up everything and will never turn back, men and women who know that failure or falling is acceptable, as long as they fall forward running into the arms of their Heavenly Father. This is just a part of the journey of healing and success.

When I first shared this chapter with Giacomo, his response even further proves my point: "Thank you for being a part of my journey. I have also learned much more from each one of you, my friends, who have said *yes* and *amen* to Jesus! He is the Master Teacher! He is the spark that starts the fire in the heart of men and women, and His Spirit fans the flame! Our job is to see each person with the eyes of Jesus, to believe in them and call them forth into their God-given call and destiny. We do this by doing life with our friends. We do this by grabbing on to every teachable moment that comes our way and never missing them! As iron sharpens iron, so a man sharpens another!"

Having met Giacomo many years ago, to this day, he is one of the few people that will always seek me out, encourage me, believe in me, challenge me, and be willing to take time and words to help me become the man that God sees in me or that Giacomo sees that I can be. He is always quick to encourage, humbling me as he tries to step back so myself or others can be seen in our youth. Not many leaders would do this; not many friends would even do this. I have many people that I can count on and fall back on in the case of an emergency or if something were ever to happen, but I know that I would have to take the steps to open that door, to be the initiator. Giacomo showed me what it's like to keep that door open and actually pursue the treasures within others even when they aren't asking.

As we began pioneering a new ministry in 2016, the word that we felt in pioneering was "David and his mighty men." Jesus is the David, and we are just the thieves from the caves that were transformed in the presence of David and God by his trust and leadership in the one true God. We have staff with four or five different degrees and others that have never even finished high school. We have ex-cartel members or ex-prostitutes, and young men or women that have lived their whole lives for God with radical purity. We have the never-been-kissed or first-kiss-on-the-wedding-day stories, and those from the streets that felt that purity was unreachable for them who walked the heroic battle of same-sex attraction. We have individuals within our team that have suffered abuse and brokenness, who have lived for years staring at the ground and not into the eyes of anyone else. However, we've learned that no story is finished and that there is always another chapter. We are primarily non-Western and non-white, but we are the people of God, the people that someone has dared to believe in and help draw out the identity from the treasures of our heart—the eternity of God pulled out from within.

We've had the privilege of officiating at several of our young couples' weddings, of walking through some of the most difficult moments with some of our young singles and almost completely broken marriages, and then celebrating some of the greatest victories together with them after coming out of the valley of darkness. The most difficult moments are when the sin and brokenness affects those around them, and shame doesn't allow the individual to see a complete picture. It's in those moments that we continue to remember that the story isn't over, and today a choice can be made to begin walking in freedom.

For me, some of the hardest stories are those that begin with shame and silence. Almost every time a young man or woman just cuts me out of their life on social media and any form of communication, I hope I'm wrong, but I'm usually preparing myself for some difficult news and many times a difficult phone call sharing their shame, sin, and brokenness. Many times, this news is combined with some depression, which includes a type of eating disorder or cutting, only showing even more the depths of how much brokenness and pain can be within the heart. The shame and fear aren't just thoughts but usually the fruit of the reactions that everyone around them has verbalized, and their deepest fear and greatest shame are now their reality and identity.

When I've received those phone calls, it's a short process of me asking questions to quickly "discover" what has happened. The reason I'm sharing this part within this book isn't to highlight the shame or glorify sin but rather to highlight how deep the need is to be embraced with loving kindness and truth in these moments. I'm usually the last person that she or he would want to call, but when that moment comes, that moment of just wanting to hear some honest truth without emotion, trusting that there is still unchanging love, I get the phone call. Aside from the tears and listening to the sounds of a young lady devastated that she has become what she never imagined, it's these moments where you can still see that treasure. This undesired pregnancy leading to a baby will have a name and story, a future and dreams, and the choices that this young girl makes now will mark and determine not only the future of this baby but also to what degree God can now use this moment to create a redemptive story. Repentance, acceptance, and a willingness to now rise up with family, friends, and leaders will change the result of this story.

Multiple times, I've had the privilege to see how the long and difficult process of humility and repentance has developed years later into a ministry, a new marriage, or an incredible family from someone who believed she had reached her end in shame and brokenness. When she can't see the treasure within, we must still learn to fight for it, "the image and likeness of God." To my joy, I have now had the fruit of two different single moms that did our schools years ago, and now the kids have come back to do a discipleship training school with us, to love God, to change cycles, and to dream with Him, thanks to a redeemed story within their mother.

With young men, the hardest moments aren't the drugs and sex or even having a baby but the reality that a young man has allowed himself to cross a cultural line that the church has either said there is no forgiveness for or that it wasn't sin anyway: a same-sex relationship and same-sex attraction. After working with young men for almost sixteen years, I've come to realize that the percent of men that have been physically abused by another man is extremely high. Those that haven't been abused but have had an absent father, a dysfunctional family, or just a struggle with identity and crossed that line either physically or emotionally with the same sex brings them to a moment that few would dare be honest about.

When a young man shares with me that he has made a choice to go against his physical and God-ordained design for sex within covenantal marriage between one man and one woman, the thing that always impacts him the most is when I simply hug him and stare into his eyes without blinking, without fear, and without shame to physically draw close to him and tell him that I love him, and I'm not afraid to touch him or to be embraced by him. I'm looking for that treasure that seems to be so hidden that this young boy can't even imagine exists anymore. If he still has the breath of life in him, he has the Spirit of God working on him, and that treasure is there. The process of repentance, renewing the mind, and dominating the flesh aren't unique to this situation. All sin has roots in selfishness and lack of self-control. This moment needs to be filled with love and compassion and the truth that there is still a treasure within that just needs to be polished and rubbed free.

To my incredible joy, I've had the privilege of walking out these difficult processes with both young Christian men and women. Seeing single moms happily marry an incredible man and now having wonderful ministries, having prostitutes walk forward in life as incredible moms and women of God, and men from gangs and cartels become the leaders of today. Even what some think of as the impossible, men with same-sex attraction happily married with kids to an incredible woman, or walking in complete freedom having chosen God and purity in celibacy over selfishness. I'm always amazed seeing young men rise up and choose to reflect the father heart of God in an incredible way as they break all cycles of the past. The ability to see these treasures when everything appears to be ashes can only come with eyes that first see God. God isn't just stuck in this moment, but He is dreaming and seeing a bright and hopeful future for tomorrow. There must be a lot of character growth, self-control, accountability, and commitment. The power of the truth for tomorrow, combined with great depths of trust today, can pull the treasures out of the ashes today; and for many, we are that power in their lives. God never stops pursuing, and His Spirit never stops working. But in the most broken of moments, all too often, someone in the flesh needs to have the eyes of Christ, the words to explain it, and the actions to prove it!

Reflection

1. Who are the people that have helped you discover the hidden treasures within your own life?
2. Are you still discovering them, and who is helping you?
3. What treasures have you discovered, and what have you done with them?
4. Are you finding the treasures within the heart of those around you as well?
5. When working with difficult people, do you see the present reality or the past history leading to this moment? Do you see the action that has happened or the influences and choices that proceeded this action?
6. What does it mean for you to have the eyes of Christ?
7. How can you change to be better at discipling those around you based on this chapter?

Meditation

My team has begun to joke with me that I have a "taxi" or "Uber" ministry and that they want to buy me a shirt that says "Taxi Ministry." The reason is, in the past few years, I have had six incredible encounters in the car with men that were far from God, but He was still there present when I sat down in the car and was able to share His heart for them. One, in particular, is a young man that I love greatly. Our story began very unexpectedly. After spending all night processing with a friend at a leadership conference, we flew home and grabbed an Uber. In the next half hour, something huge happened. God gave me a word of knowledge for this young man. He showed me something that had happened when he was a little boy that no one knew about, and he wasn't sure how to respond because, obviously, God had revealed it to me. He had never met a Christian before and had never seen a Bible. He thought we were crazy, but he knew that God must be real. He turned control of his life over to God within the next week and decided to become a missionary to find out who the God of the Bible was.

A couple of years later, he is now one of our leaders with many of his own stories of seeing the treasures within someone else's life, and God uses him greatly all the time. He is a man of faith and miracles, and an amazing testimony to this generation. One day I walked outside angry because someone had parked in our driveway and had blocked the garage door, and then this young man, Felipe, came out to help. I was ready to make them leave, but Felipe wound up praying with them and ministering to them. I saw someone breaking the law, bothering me, and getting in the way, but Felipe saw a child of God!

One day just a couple of weeks after meeting us, he was praying with a team as they were going out to evangelize. They felt like God showed them to find an old woman wearing a black-and-white striped shirt sitting in front of a black door with flowers, with two kids, and whose husband had just been killed. This seemed like an impossible task, a needle in a haystack, to find a woman like this in the middle of a city, but they agreed that if it was from God, they would obey. Three hours later—you wouldn't believe me unless you saw the picture—they found her. An old woman, sitting on the ground in front of a black door with a flower painting, wearing a black-and-white striped shirt, who had two kids and whose husband was just killed.

When my Uber driver Felipe came to dinner that night, he ran up to me, shouting, "God is real! God is real!" Within only one month of becoming a Christian, God was teaching him to find the treasures in others. God is personal and close to everyone, and He wants to use us to pull out those treasures in others! Within one year, thanks to this incredible young man, now both of his parents are following Jesus, attending a church, and his family is all coming to the Lord. What an impact that one little talk in a car could have to an entire family and generation.

Just the other day, I was thinking about some of these stories of Felipe and talking to a young leader in Mexico City about evangelism and leadership development. I told her that our problem today is that we think both evangelism and leadership development are planned activities that fit into a class, structure, or set-apart formal time. I told her that I completely disagree. Evangelism, discipleship, and leadership development are simply having a lifestyle of seeing what God sees at all times and being willing to respond to what He sees in others with our time, with our words, and with our actions. For nonbelievers, this becomes evangelism with the power of the Spirit bringing healing, words of knowledge, wisdom and discernment, liberation, and faith that comes from seeing a real testimony within the messenger of the message. In discipleship and leadership development, it's seeing every real-life opportunity—car ride, bus ride, plane ride, night at the hotel, walk in the park, fun day, or work—to call out the treasures of the heart of someone else and helping them see their own capacity to do the same in others. Anyone can teach or preach, but evangelism, discipleship, and leadership development can only happen with the "eyes of Christ." May your vision become His vision, and may He reveal to you the diamonds hidden all around you!

The Bible and Compassion: The Eyes of Christ

- "And when she opened it, she saw the child, and behold, the baby wept. So she had compassion on him, and said, "This is one of the Hebrew's children" (Exodus 2:6).
- "Then He said, "I will make all my goodness pass before you, and I will proclaim the name of the Lord before you. I will be gracious to whom I will be gracious and have compassion on whom I will have compassion" (Exodus 33:19).
- "And the Lord passed before him and proclaimed, "The Lord, the Lord God, merciful and gracious, longsuffering, and abounding in goodness and truth, keeping mercy for thousands, forgiving the iniquity and transgression and sin" (Exodus 34:6–7).
- "And you return to the Lord your God and obey His voice, according to all that I command you today, you and your children, with all your heart and with all your soul, that the Lord your God will bring you back from captivity, and have compassion on you, and gather you again from all the nations where the Lord your God has scattered you" (Deuteronomy 30:2–3).
- "But the Lord was gracious to them, had compassion on them, and regarded them, because of His covenant with Abraham, Isaac, and Jacob, and would not yet destroy them or cast them from His presence" (2 Kings 13:23).
- "For if your return to the Lord, your brethren and your children will be treated with compassion by those who lead them captive, so that they may come back to this land; for the Lord your God is gracious, merciful, and will not turn His face from you if you return to Him" (2 Chronicles 30:9).
- "But He, being full of compassion forgave their iniquity, and did not destroy them. Yes, many a time He turned His anger away, and did not stir up all His wrath" (Psalms 78:38).

- "But You, o Lord, are a God full of compassion, and gracious, longsuffering and abundant in mercy and truth" (Psalms 86:15).
- "The works of the Lord are great, studied by all who have pleasure in them. His work is honorable and glorious, and His righteousness endures forever. He has made His wonderful works to be remembered; the Lord is gracious and full of compassion" (Psalm 111:2–4).
- "Then it shall be, after I have plucked them out, that I will return and have compassion on them and bring them back, everyone to his heritage and everyone to his land" (Jeremiah 12:15).
- "He will again have compassion on us, and will subdue our iniquities. You will cast all our sins into the depths of the sea" (Micah 7:19).
- "When the Lord saw her, he had compassion on her and said to her, 'Do not Weep'" (Luke 7:13).
- "Finally, all of you be of one mind, having compassion for one another; love as brothers, be tenderhearted, be courteous; not returning evil for evil or reviling for reviling, but on the contrary blessing, knowing that you were called to this, that you may inherit a blessing" (1 Peter 3:8–9).

CHAPTER 10

Testimony

Inspired by missionary and pastor Alfredo Guerrero

Testimony—a formal, written statement, spoken statement, or physical artifact of truth from a past event. The evidence or proof provided by the existence or appearance of something that has taken place. We are called to be living letters of the living God, as a lifestyle of living testimony from a redeemed past for the present witnesses in hope of a better future.

Special Introduction

> It is good that I would declare the signs and miracles that the Almighty God has done with me.
> —Daniel 4:2

In daily life, God presents many opportunities and privileges before me, but it depends on me to choose to either accept them or to reject them. One day, many years ago, I was sitting behind a little box for shining shoes on the streets in the town square of Monterrey, Mexico, and I decided that this wasn't what I wanted for the rest of my life. I discovered that within each one of us exists a desire to seek out something more. It isn't an easy path, but with the help of God and great determination, it can be achieved. God presented before me both blessing and curse (Deuteronomy 28). The greatest achievement in my life is to hear others say that I'm "unstable" because I'm always looking for opportunities, and I'm dreaming every day with even newer and greater things for God. Daniel Holmberg is a friend that has written a very simple narrative that provokes you to read through to the very end. God is very pleased with the men and women who turn this world upside down! May reading this chapter encourage you to form a story that makes your story one of those stories turning the world upside down!

Alfredo Guerrero
Missionary and Pastor
Founder of PUENTES
Global Public Speaker
Spearhead of the Tarahumaras Missions Movement
Loving Husband and Father
Mentor and Faithful Friend

* * * * *

Some of my earliest childhood memories are of sitting out on our wooden deck and watching my dad fix the boards that had been too weathered by the snow to make it through yet another year. We had a long front deck along the whole entrance of the house, and it was made of two inch by twelve-inch boards that were ten feet long. From my deck, not a single house was visible. Actually, there were no other houses to be seen as I lived one mile up from the highway and then another quarter mile up a small dirt road in the middle of the mountains in Colorado. Surrounded by trees and wildlife, those mountains and memories formed my life in unique ways. I can still close my eyes and a do a 360-degree picture in my mind of each tree, mountain, and every detail I could see from that deck. I can remember it in such a way that each image becomes a video of the changes from the 1980s to present day, throughout the different seasons, the death of certain trees, the planting of others, the widening of the road, different animals in the yard, and different plants in the garden.

An entire lifetime comes back to present with one simple memory of that deck.

On those roads, we would sometimes get such heavy snow that we would not only lose power for a few days, but we would literally be trapped without any way to get out for days. We could shovel the deck and driveway, keep the roof clean so it did not fall in; but at some point, there was nowhere else to put the snow, and we were just stuck in a beautiful white blanket in the middle of the mountains. As a young boy, I loved it. We would build big snowmen and long tunnels through the snow with our dogs, go sledding down the streets and mountains, and even snowboard down what used to be a dirt road.

During these heavy snowfalls, there was no access coming up to our house and no access going down. We had two woodburning stoves, so even if we did not have power, we could melt snow for drinking hot chocolate and coffee or soup. They would keep the house warm enough to enjoy the time we had isolated from the world, whether it was a day or a week. Preparing for these cold days was one of my chores in the summer. My dad would cut down trees, and we would gather the firewood. After cutting the tree with a chainsaw, we would use an ax to split the wood into smaller pieces, and then I would have to carry, stack, and move the wood so that we would have it during the winter. I was usually the one that would make the fires, and I loved the smell of that fresh pine that we would bring into the house. There was nothing like waking up early and seeing four feet of snow outside the window, knowing that the day was going to be a fun family time at home without any way to get to school or work.

Some of my favorite memories growing up are of those days in the snow. We would get up and call our friend who lived in town to see if school had been cancelled yet. Some days, we would not even have to call. We knew that no one could be out on the roads, and the day was free! We had an old six-foot-in-diameter satellite dish for watching TV, and the weight of the snow would build up on the dish so it could not move and receive a signal. I would bundle up, put on my boots and gloves, and make my way out to the dish with a shovel or broom, and knock off the snow so that we could watch some television until the power went out. A few hours later, I would go out and help my dad shovel all the snow from our deck and driveway, with the hope that maybe a plow would come in the next couple of days, and we would be free to get out again. As long as we kept our driveway shoveled, there still might be access if we had an emergency.

We would pile the snow up, and then we could jump from the upper deck down into the snow, and it would swallow us up without our getting hurt. Sometimes we would shovel off the roof if the snow was over three feet deep so that our roof did not cave in. The dogs would have tunnels everywhere under the snow to get to where they wanted. It seemed as if our horses were almost swimming in the deep snow. When I was little, we even had a miniature pig, Dudley, that lived in the house, and he would cry and grunt every time he had to go to the bathroom because his little belly would drag in the snow, and he did not like the cold. We would sled and ski or snowboard the road and just have lots of fun in the snow.

I could go on and on about everything we experienced growing up in the mountains of Colorado and everything I saw from that wooden deck. We had deer come down in the yard frequently, and we saw mountain lions. After a really big snow, we felt like the only people alive. The silence and the beauty of those huge snowflakes were unforgettable. I was always a bit sad when the sun would come out or the stars and moon would peek through. The temperature would drop very quickly, and I knew that soon our lives would be back to normal again.

When we shoveled off the deck, sometimes I would hit a nail with the metal shovel or see some of the wood come up with the snow, and I knew that next summer we would have to be fixing some boards again unless we wanted lots of slivers in our feet as we would run around barefoot all summer. Dad, like most dads, worked hard all day. Coming home, he would want to relax, and those boards would always last a couple of months through spring and into early summer, when we would have our last big May snowstorm. Usually, either my sister or I would be running around in the yard barefoot; and as we came running across the deck on one of those old boards, we would get a great big sliver of wood. Not long after, Dad would be on the deck replacing those boards again so we did not get hurt. After he was done, it would be a nice, clean board, and it did not fit in anymore. All the other boards that had been there for a couple of winters were dark brown, but the new one was green and much lighter. It was new, but it did not belong until after the following winter. It was not really a part of the deck until it had weathered its first winter.

Some of my earliest dreams came from thinking about how and what my life might be like in the future after a few storms and years, just like those wooden boards. I had great dreams of becoming a famous athlete. From the time I was little, I played baseball and basketball and, later on, football as well. I would think of the people that were "famous," and I would want to be one of them. At one of the churches we attended, one of the famous baseball players from Colorado was also a member. I remember one day he signed an autograph for me, and I thought for sure that I would be like that one day. I dreamt of being a doctor or fireman to save and help people. Doctors and firemen seemed to be so famous, and everyone loved them and talked about them. As I looked at those boards, I would dream and wonder about what I would turn into with time. I heard of the things people talked about and were impacted by, and little by little different dreams would come into my mind.

As I was good at math, people began to say that I could be an excellent engineer, and they would talk about how great engineers were. Or as I began to develop more of my personality, my mom used to joke and say that I should be a lawyer because I was a very quick thinker and could always argue my point and convince others that I was right even when I was wrong. From such a young age, I learned quickly that just like those boards, I would have most value for what I did and what others saw within me; that in some way, my self-worth would be defined by what I was preparing to do. The importance of school and studying, of good grades to get into a good college, to become "someone," to have the right titles or degrees, to "fit well" into society would be my ultimate value. Interestingly, I know that my parents loved me, and I had the best mother and father whom I could ever dream. However, this reality of being defined by what one does also seemed engraved within me from as far back as I can remember. Would I grow up to be one of those boards that has no use and just needs to be replaced? Would I become that board that was different and would be used to replace what no longer had value in someone else?

These questions, among others, at first seemed to merely be childlike dreams or fears. But with each year and each new experience, they were no longer just in my thoughts but became the forefront of what other people would speak into my life. If I did not do this or if I did decide to do this, if I spend time with these people or do not spend time with those people would all define who I would be one day. Each action or choice somehow became either the mask that someone else wanted to give me or the mask that I myself began to wear and hide beneath. Would I be defined by what I do? Or would I be defined by where I came from? Are either of these masks even real?

When I arrived in Mexico in 2004, I had so many different masks either given by others or created by myself that I do not think I even really knew the real person underneath all those expectations, images, and reputation. Aside from trying to prove that God did not exist during my journey of discipleship so that I could just move on with my life, another one of my major battles was to decide on what version of myself I wanted to share with those around me. I finally had a completely "new beginning" without any reputation or expectation of what I had to be, so who did I want people to see in me? What identity did I want to project, and what things was I planning to hide in this new reality around me?

Until that moment of arriving in Mexico, the whole idea of testimony, image, influence, and character had to do with charisma or power of appeal to achieve whatever I wanted depending upon whatever new group of people I interacted with. It was like the trip of manipulation for selfish gain, like many Hollywood stars who, before they have a new movie release or new record, change their hair, clothes, and even accent to become the person that others will follow and be drawn to. I had that same freedom entering a new country into a new community.

Upon arriving, though, I began to see something new: men and women who lived walking fully in the light without anything to hide, either from the past or present, the good or the bad. There was no fear, no shame, and full acceptance of reality. Testimonies of the redeeming power of God, that could only be experienced through raw truth and talent, were stories that had great appeal to me but also terrified me because in my story, that did not seem like an option to live.

As one of my Bible teachers began to share his story, I looked around the room to see if other people were reacting as I was. I was told that the man speaking this week was an incredible man of influence, the founder of different organizations, and the president of different national leadership groups, a well-known pastor, and a famous public speaker both nationally and internationally. His name is in encyclopedias for beginning the missions movement to the Tarahumaras people group. I had certain expectations of a man of "this profile," but from the moment he opened his mouth, every preconceived idea I had fallen through the floor.

In chapter 5, I mentioned this man, Alfredo Guerrero, and how my life had been forever marked from the time I first met him. It was not just his vivid testimony of growing up on the streets after his father kidnapped him and his brother. He had overcome what most people saw as impossible for a young boy that was "hopeless" and had never received any formal education of high school or college. He had every excuse possible to give up or to choose to live as a victim. This man had a story that I had never heard of or imagined for anyone that was successful. Every one of the cards of life that he was dealt appeared to be against him, like so many from the last chapter. Yet he still grew up to be an incredible son of God, a good husband, and father of four daughters.

When he began to share his story, he did not share with shame and fear of his past or with pride and joy as the identity of a victim but with hope and transparency. He shared his story from beginning to end as a story where the author of his present and future was God Himself. He was not determined by his past but by the hope of his future within the light of the Redeemer. There was an incredible humility and honesty that I had never experienced before. How did a man like this, from a background like his, become a man of great influence? His story had evidently been shifted and was now seen in the light of God Himself. Sin was not glorified, brokenness was not embraced as an identity, and freedom was not just a life-after-death dream. He had a story where the major character was no longer himself, but God Himself was the main character that redefined everything else. There was no fear or shame, no need for exaggeration or lies, but just the simplicity of God's perspective.

After that week, I had to reevaluate the story I had given to everyone around me. Was it the full truth? Was it a lie? Was I glorifying sin? Was I basking in the shadow of being a victim? Did anyone really know who I was, what I was doing in this place, and where I wanted to go with my life? I had been living a life where God was just another character in the story, but I was the author creating whatever I wanted depending on with whomever I was talking. It was not the truth in any sense of the word that I was showing people or sharing with them.

I've stayed in contact with Alfredo through the years. He has done some incredible things all over the world and left an incredible legacy. He has experienced and walked through some major losses as well. Through both ups and downs, his transparency, sincerity, and complete honesty have marked me to this day in a way that no other man ever has. He carries no shame or fear when I've talked to him, no desire for power or control, just leaving a mark of redemption as a living letter of God.

Through the years, this has been one of the greatest struggles to walk through in ministry for me: the power of testimony to glorify God. It is not about what I share and say but why and how I say it and even what words I use while understanding who my audience is. As I've tried my best to share my own testimony as a young man from the United States to a completely different culture and language that is not my own, I have begun to learn to see both my own story and how it can influence those around me in a different light. I can no longer be the focus, and the audience can't define my story. In the simplest details, there needs to be space for God to be seen and be glorified. The apostle Paul is who most challenges me in his ability to do this well in the New Testament. He really did become a Greek for the Greeks, a Gentile for the Gentiles, and a Jew for the Jews. When he said "to live is Christ and to die is gain," he really did mean it. Up to the point of death, God was going to be glorified within his story.

In life, we have an infinite mixture of emotions, options, perspectives, different words to describe the same story, even different tones of voice, but there is only one truth. When we can find the way to align who we are and what God says about our story, our testimony becomes one of power, for His glory, to heal others. Only when we align with His perspective, with His words, according to His emotions, taking into account what He is speaking about our present reality and walking toward what He declares for our unique future, can our story become one of inspiration and motivation. Our story, without fear and shame, and trusting when we have no control over today, can fully become His story, even as we share the journey from meeting Him as Lord and Savior through our current reality.

Thinking back to those boards that my dad replaced each summer on our deck, I realize that the whole process of the journey is important. From the strange new wood that does not seem to fit in with the others, to the weathering of the first few storms, and finally to the point of being removed to open space for a new board—they are all a part of that incredible memory. What made it special was having my father with me on that deck, cutting the wood with him, and seeing his heart through the whole process. The deck itself means nothing in the memory if my dad was not there with me. The impact of the story is from him being present, not what happened with those boards.

In the same way, my own story has no real power unless it is walking hand in hand with my Heavenly Father. The power of my story is never with the story itself or my being open and honest, but only within the great humility of showing the shift from when my story became His story. Only when He is seen as the Author and I shift from being the creator to being a main character that can be fully defined by His heart, by His dreams, and in His words is power really released. This becomes the power of testimony. As stated in Acts 1, "the power to be a witness."

I have met incredible Bible teachers throughout the years, men and women who know Greek and Hebrew, speak eight or nine different languages, have degrees like trophies, and are literally famous. I have been blessed to have charismatic public speakers come and be a part of certain seasons of my life. Through their witty humor, experience, and training, I will never forget them. The thing about Alfredo that has always marked me and always will is that his story came from the inside out, from the beginning to the end, the good and the bad, the shameful, fearful, and even raw reality that most people would hide. His influence from teaching did not come from what he knew or his abilities but from what he had lived and who he was. When I think of Jesus, He is the same way. His power of testimony came from having a message that was in complete alignment with what people saw. He was a man of great presence because He was entirely real, honest, and a truth speaker, never hiding in shame. He was born into a reality where he had to flee as a refugee to Egypt, and all the kids his age were literally slaughtered. He grew up with bullying from his brothers and sisters. He witnessed thousands of people being hung dead as criminals along the side of the road from Roman executions on the cross from the time he was a child. He lived through major segregation and division, major abuses of governmental power and corruption. However, His story, His testimony, was one where the Father was the author and guide of each step.

One of my deepest prayers is that as people see me, hear me teach, or listen to my story that it would be a testimony where Jesus is fully seen and I am not the one being glorified. His story is the one that transforms the nations. His Spirit is the one that touches the heart, and only He alone takes the place of King and the Master Teacher. My dream would be to show how His Spirit has radically transformed me and turned my story into His own, how His power came in such a way to my life that my redemptive story would now be self-evident. That His Spirit would be so alive within me that today, in the present moment, I could be a good witness. That my love of the Father would be so real and sincere that it would be contagious. That every relationship I have would be marked by my deep love of the Father. That my story would be so raw, honest, and real, without shame and fear, that others could rise and live the same, not trying to live as Jesus but trying to fully live an individual life—fully submitted, redeemed, and open for the world to see a testimony that is completely unique and different. The power of His story becoming our own!

As I have traveled more and more around the world, taught in many different settings and ministries, and begun to find my own influence in the lives of others, I've begun to see my own heart in a new way. Empathy and love, compassion and understanding, and even hope and faith seem to be born from understanding what has been done in my own life. He is so real and so good that it's actually become evident. Be it failures or successes, alone or in the public eye, within my marriage or with a complete stranger, what He has done in my life has not only marked me but is now marking others. As I travel and teach, I'm impacted to hear others now say that same statement about myself, "Thank you so much for sharing your story. Your testimony impacted me greatly, and I feel so connected to you. It gives me hope and expectation, and I want to have my own story now with God." In these moments, I often smile and just think of men and women like Alfredo who did the same thing in my own journey with God—imparting a contagious reality that shifted the course of my life.

Reflection

1. What is your real, raw, and honest life testimony?
2. Who is being glorified through the story that you share?
3. Are there roots of humanism where either you glorify yourself as a victim or you glorify yourself as the hero of this story?
4. Have you had that encounter with the Lord that has forever marked your own perspective of your past that now allows you to walk freely within it, or are you still hiding details that could glorify God?
5. Do your words, your emotions, and your details of your own story reflect truth and glorify God, or are you still

hiding beneath different masks, trying to be glorified for what you have done or where you come from?

6. Is sin and suffering being glorified, or is God and His transforming power being glorified?

Meditation

One of the stories that really impacts me from Genesis is when Jacob returns to encounter his brother, Esau, after so many years. Up to this moment, he serves "the God of his father Isaac and the God of his grandfather Abraham." He walks in fear, leading his family from behind. He is stuck in his past and willing to let all of them suffer or even die because of this. However, one night, he has an incredible encounter with "the Angel of the Lord" and wrestles with Him all night long. When the struggle is over, he is physically marked in such a way that everything changes. His story is the same story, and nothing from his past changes in that night. There is no magical touch that changes his memories, his fears, his failures or successes.

Even though he is physically touched by God, he still has to deal with his same story and current reality, yet when he arises, there is an evident shift, and he changes from walking behind everyone and hiding for his life while living in fear to face his future head-on, to walking in the very front and taking responsibility for whatever happened in the past and will happen in the future. Everything changes. He is no longer alone in his past and the story that he once had. Rather, he is able to rest in what God has now spoken over him, and he trusts the beautiful future that God promised him. This would now determine his past testimony in the light of reality and responsibility rather than hiding and making excuses.

Nothing has changed, but everything has changed. His past is no longer a story behind which he is hiding, but rather it becomes a story of his journey with God. He no longer needs to control it and fear it. Instead, he takes responsibility for it. His testimony now becomes a testimony of incredible power in the way that he meets his brother with great humility and with truth. To this day, Israel begins the story of God's redemptive plan for His people, not as a nation but as Jacob. Jacob becomes Israel not by becoming a nation but by having real testimony. Become the real story of today and don't be lost in the storm of the past or the fear of the unknown future.

The Bible and Testimony

- "You shall put the mercy seat on top of the ark, and in the ark you shall put the testimony which I will give to you" (Exodus 25:21).
- "And when He made an end of speaking with him on Mount Sinai, He gave Moses two tablets of Testimony, tablets of stone, written with the finger of God" (Exodus 31:18).
- "The law of the Lord is perfect, converting the soul; the testimony of the Lord is sure, making wise the simple; the statues of the Lord are right, rejoicing the heart; the commandment of the Lord is pure, enlightening the eyes" (Psalm 19:7–8).
- "We will not hide them from their children, telling to the generation to come to the praises of the Lord, and His strength and His wonderful works that he has done. For He established a testimony in Jacob, and appointed a law in Israel, which He commanded our fathers, that they should make them known to their children" (Psalm 78:4–5).
- "And Jesus said to him, 'See that you tell no one; but go your way, show yourself to the priest, and offer the gift that Moses commanded, as a testimony to them'" (Matthew 8:4).
- "You will be brought before governors and kings for My sake, as a testimony to them and to the Gentiles" (Matthew 10:18).
- "But watch out for yourselves, for they will deliver you up to the councils, and you will be beaten in the synagogues. You will be brought before rulers and kings for My sake, for a testimony to them" (Mark 13:9).
- "He who comes from above is above all; he who is of the earth is earthly and speaks of the earth. He who comes

from heaven is above all. And what He has seen and heard, that He testifies; and no one receives His testimony. He who has received His testimony has certified that God is true" (John 3:31–33).

- "I thank my God always concerning you for the grace of God which was given to you by Christ Jesus, that you were enriched in everything by Him in all utterance and all knowledge, even as the testimony of Christ was confirmed in you" (1 Corinthians 1:4–5).

- "For our boasting is this; the testimony of our conscience that we conducted ourselves in the world in simplicity and godly sincerity, not with fleshly wisdom by the grace of God, and more abundantly toward you" (2 Corinthians 1:12).

- "Moreover he must have a good testimony among those who are outside, lest he fall into reproach and the snare of the devil" (1 Timothy 3:7).

- "Therefore do not be ashamed of the testimony of our Lord, nor of me His prisoner, but share with me in the sufferings for the gospel according to the power of God" (2 Timothy 1:8).

- "And Moses indeed was faithful in all His house as a servant, for his testimony of those things which would be spoken afterward" (Hebrews 3:5).

- "Now faith is the substance of things hoped for, the evidence of things not seen. For by it the elders obtained a good testimony" (Hebrews 11:1–2).

- "Demetrius has a good testimony from all, and from the truth itself. And we also bear witness, and you know that our testimony is true" (3 John 1:12).

- "And they overcame him by the blood of the lamb and by the word of their testimony, and they did not love their lives, even to the point of death" (Revelation 12:11).

- "Therefore we also, since we are surrounded by so great a cloud of witnesses, let us lay aside every weight, and the sin which so easily ensnares us, and let us run with endurance the race that is set before us" (Hebrews 12:1).

CHAPTER 11

Accessible and Available

Inspired by beloved friend and mentor Darrow Miller

Accessible and available—the willingness to be at another's disposal, be able to be reached, and even when in a place of greater authority or influence than others, is friendly and easy to talk to, no matter what rank, capacity, age, gender, race, role, or experience the seeker might have. Someone that relates to others not out of a place of power and authority hidden behind human titles or worldly understanding, but rather someone who sees all humans on the same level, with equal value, worthy of time and investment.

Special Introduction

What an honor it is to have Daniel ask me to write the prelude to this chapter!

It was Francis Schaeffer, the evangelist and apologist of the faith, who modeled a life of accessibility and availableness.

Francis and his wife, Edith, had a home, Chalet Les Melezes, high in the Swiss Alps, in a small farming village, Huémoz, sur Ollon. Schaeffer was small in stature but great in heart and mammoth in his life and legacy. The Schaeffers defined accessibility. They opened their lives and home to the "world," to men and women, gay and straight, Christians and non-Christians—image bearers all—in a common journey in the pursuit of truth.

People came for many different reasons and motivations. They came with their questions, soft and hard questions. They often came in their loneliness and brokenness. They came looking for truth; they came to the families and homes of what is known as L'Abri Fellowship to find "honest answers to honest questions!" What they found was a space of "intellectual hospitality."

In today's world, which shuns the pursuit of truth and hard questions because the answers may be tough and offensive, we need spaces of intellectual hospitality, not "safe spaces" where people are protected from reality. For a generation of young people who are "fatherless" (absentee fathers) and "motherless" (inattentive mothers), we need "real" homes with mothers and fathers that are accessible and available to provide what only a family can provide.

In this chapter, Daniel provides a glimpse into his own journey of how he discovered the principles of being accessible and available, which he seeks to model in his own life.

Darrow Miller
Husband, Father, and Great-Grandfather
Author, Mentor, Vice President of Food for the Hungry
Founder of the Discipling Nations Alliance
Philosopher, Apologist

* * * * *

Time and time again, I have tried my best to remember my earliest memories in life. Whether it's a birthday, a special experience, or getting into trouble. My mom loves to bring up things from my childhood from a very early age and act extremely surprised by the fact that I don't remember all the complex details as a child that she can so easily remember as an adult. The conversation usually goes something like this, "Daniel, do you remember ——?" and I quickly respond, "Of course not, Mom. I was just a baby or a child." She would follow by saying, "How can you forget those things?

They were such important moments of our life." To which, I usually respond, "Children don't remember all those details, but only if it was positive or negative, and I have positive memories from my childhood." Then with tears, she usually responds, "Well, it was one of my favorite memories, and I can't believe you don't remember it. It was very special for me."

As I am now a father of my own three children, it is amazing the way in which a smell, an activity, or a given situation can remind me of something from a very early age that I thought would be impossible to remember. I would look at a face my son makes and remember the way my dad would look at me when I was his age. I would see him cry, and I didn't understand why, or I would remember a moment when I was little with an emotion that my own mom and dad didn't understand I was experiencing. I remember laughing and playing, wrestling, hugs and kisses, and so many memories that I had no idea were in my mind until I began to raise my own children. Now I can only imagine how I will feel one day when I reminisce about those "key" first years of life, and they will respond with, "Of course, I don't remember that." I know that my heart will say, "But they were so special for me!"

One special memory which really stands out to me was when my dad had a group of friends over at the house when I was little. They had just finished playing pool downstairs, went upstairs in the kitchen, and began to talk and laugh. What was happening was that ever since my dad had cancer, he began to eat spicy peppers because the doctors had told him that it was good for him and that it helped with preventing cancer. So he had been giving some of the spicy peppers to some of his friends. Obviously, they were hot to the taste, so they were all laughing at the reactions to how spicy it was. Some would cry, others would yell, and others would almost puke while trying to act tough. I remember I was sitting on my dad's lap, asking to eat one of those spicy peppers just like he did. The look on his face proved that he was not sure what to do and was probably worried about what my mom would say.

I'm sure that my dad didn't want me to eat it as he knew what would happen, but I must have been very convincing. I actually remember the look on my mom's face as he let me pull out a pepper and eat it in front of all of his friends. It was one of the worst experiences of my life! However, I did my best to hold back my tears, to not puke, and to my best ability, to not react and just drink some water (which didn't help at all). His friends were all laughing at me, but what I most remember is that he told his friends that I was just like him and that even though they couldn't do it, his little boy was tougher than they were, and he was proud of me.

For such a horrible experience as a young boy, I'm amazed to think about how many times I would eat those hot peppers when people were around—just to prove that I was like my father. His concept of me actually became more of a reality then the actual truth about me. I didn't need to like the peppers to be able to create such wonderful memories with spicy food, yet to this day, I love peppers and spicy food. Both my five-year-old and three-year-old now eat spicy food like me and love it, or do they? I'm sure a lot of it comes down to the joy of being like Dad and having affirmation from others.

If you've already read the previous ten chapters, you are starting to get the image of how influential and important my family was to me growing up. We are definitely not a perfect family, and we have many of our own skeletons in the closet—shame, fears, insecurities, and things that we just don't talk about with any random stranger.

I've tried my best to investigate my family tree on both sides as far back as I can. I'm primarily Swedish, Danish, Dutch, and German, so in summary—a good Scandinavian Viking. However, almost eight generations back on my mom's side, we discovered that I am also Ethiopian. The more I investigate and study my family history, the more I am amazed and value the legacy that has been left to me. We have an incredible anointing of leadership with colonels, captains, and leaders in the armed forces, many ministers, and amazingly strong marriages and families. There is almost a zero percent divorce rate in my family history; and for generations, whether they had a good education or not, there are incredible men and women who have been very successful with strong leadership skills, all starting with healthy families.

When I began ministry in Latin cultures in 2004, I was intrigued by their outward signs of love in their relationships. I was also confused about the lack of the depth within those same relationships. Everyone seemed to be a friend to laugh and play with, but no one seemed to have any deep relationships. I come from a culture where identity and responsibility, value and capability, are shaped first by family and secondly by government or business. Historically, in the Western world, education, business, church, and government are all fruits of what has happened in the family being formed by healthy individuals. However, within the culture where I now found myself ministering, it was a different story. Their roots in history began with government, defined by the Catholic church, bypassing the family and private business with little value of personal responsibility. This caused a push of less internal self-government, less responsibility at home within the family, and a less individual and independent mentality. Little by little, what I loved and was drawn to in the Latin culture also caused a major challenge in my search for a mentor and Christian leader who could be a role model as to what I should be as a father and husband.

Every missionary experiences culture shock and challenges in their journey to fully obey God. The roots of my culture shock and challenges came from these foundational differences in our cultural history that can be traced back to France, Spain, and Britain hundreds of years ago. The emphasis was either on the individual and family, followed by churches, hospitals, schools, and government, or government and churches first, followed by businesses, family, and the individual. There appeared to be two foundational differences: either deep family relationships built on love and trust as the foundation that determined every other sphere of society, or power and control through the government and church as the foundation of society that determined everything else.

I love the Latino culture, the language, and the people; *but* outside of the "work environment," I couldn't see the same values that I had cherished from my youth. The generations found within my family tree all the way back to Ethiopia, of marriage and family first, as "sufficient" with an identity in Christ alone. I know all of Latin

America is not like this, and every day I meet more and more pastors, leaders, businessmen, teachers, government officials, and friends who think just like me about the family. But in my "beginnings," this became my biggest challenge. How do I form community outside of my "ministry/work community" that reflects the roots of my core values when I'm living in a different country much different from my own? Family is the core of everything, and the foundational values seemed to be at major contrast between myself and those around me.

It really wasn't until I was living in Costa Rica for a season in 2006 that God responded to this need in a way that I would have never expected or imagined. I was blessed to be serving with my incredible friend and mentor Giacomo Coghi, and we had put together a conference for all Central American countries. There was a very famous man coming to share, a disciple of Francis Schaeffer, and in the words of Loren Cunningham, "the greatest authority on biblical worldview in this current generation"—Darrow Miller. He is self-described as "an author who has been influenced by the Reformation and the theology of the Reformers."

Darrow is very much a modern-day intellectual with whom no one could doubt the influence of Francis Schaeffer in his life, his passion for God, his family, and truth.

After the first day of conferences, I was curious to meet the man behind the pulpit. Despite being surrounded by many leaders and pastors much older than myself, I was amazed to see that no one had invited Darrow to lunch that first day. I was only twenty-one years old, and after hearing about this man for two years, I wasn't going to miss the opportunity to meet him. To my surprise, I invited him to lunch, and he said yes! My original intention was to figure out how to get him to come to Mexico to do a similar workshop. To my benefit, the conversation turned from a focus on ministry and workshops to family and day-to-day life. Within the first couple of minutes, we looked at our yearly calendars and set dates for him to come to Mexico the following year, which amazed me as I had been told that it was very difficult to get him to come and teach.

After business, which took only a couple of minutes, Darrow quickly began to "open up" about his life, his marriage and kids, his successes and failures, and so much more. His story is not mine to tell, but at that table, it was the first time in two years that I could see myself serving God with my whole heart while still having marriage and kids at the center of it all. With each story he shared from his past, I began to identify more and more with this man. As he shared his process of courtship, marriage, the in-laws, and his own children and grandchildren, I no longer saw the famous Darrow Miller but a man who was madly in love with his wife. Even though the journey had not been easy, he was a great father and a really fun-loving grandfather.

More than fourteen years later, I can still remember the stories about dates with his wife, raising their kids, the challenges of serving God when part of the family isn't Christian, and much more. This was one of my first talks in almost two years of ministry where it was evident that God was at the very center of it, even though our focus wasn't about projects or ministry at all. Doing things for Him or seeking to change the lives of others was a faraway thought. It was about living real life and being fully open before God—real life, real marriage, real family challenges, and genuine love being fulfilled in a real vocational "response to the voice of God," where everything is connected with no separation between secular and sacred, ministry and family, teaching and practice. It was a complete story.

A year passed, and I had some contact with Darrow through e-mail, but something about this man influenced me in all that I did. We all need mentors and models to follow in different seasons of life, and I didn't realize how long it had been since I had seen that in the domain of family. Many people who I met were amazed that Darrow was coming to Mexico and that I had a personal relationship with him. From that day at lunch, I never again saw him through the lenses of what he does or where he comes from but simply who he was in a complete sense, beginning with his marriage and family.

The conference we hosted in Mexico was great with many pastors and leaders in attendance, but the highlight of that week for me was another special dinner meal. For the next few years, Darrow would come once or twice a year and bring an incredible message, but what I cared much more about was sharing a special lunch or dinner with each visit. Before I was married, he became one of the men that I could most process some of my questions and doubts about marriage. In ministry, I was able to process my struggles and successes. When I became engaged and didn't know whom to seek out about options for family planning or contraceptives, I could freely write and communicate with Darrow to gain wisdom.

Some of you will read this chapter and be surprised at the way I see a man that many others see through strictly philosophical or intellectual lenses. Others will see these short paragraphs and know exactly what I'm saying and identity more with the man than the message that he has multiplied all over the world. For me, biblical worldview and understanding the dangers of Gnosticism became real over a lunch or a dinner, over a special meal that my wife would plan, and we would discuss real life and never focus primarily on ministry or what we were doing.

In Darrow's own words, looking back on our first encounters, I'm often encouraged. Even when I asked him about adding his name to this current book or doing the introduction, his quick response was very encouraging to me: "Daniel, I will never forget the first time we met, I think in Costa Rica at the Nurturing the Nations conference. I remember the young, enthusiastic man with the blond hair wrapped in a red bandana. I so remember the times in your home with Katie and the meals we shared at the YWAM base."

Many years later, even as I'm writing this, there are few people in the domain of church ministry or missions that I could feel so real and close to. It's been a few years since I've seen Darrow, since we've had a deep talk, but without a doubt, he has become one of the greatest influencers on me to live my whole life knowing I have to give an account to God for who I am in the privacy of my home, with my kids, and with my beautiful wife and not just what I do in ministry. It's not what I teach or write but how I look into my wife's beautiful eyes, the way I kiss my kids and tell them stories and songs every night, and the way I pray earnestly for my extended family who doesn't see the world as I do.

Darrow is the person who showed me that in the kingdom of God, Jesus was first just a good Son, an excellent carpenter, a good listener, and willing to let people around him fail without taking control. He reminded them that they weren't alone. He was honest about his struggles and fears but never submitted to what the culture or those around him expected. Jesus lived in an integral way in all that he did, without insecurities and as an incredible servant.

We had asked Darrow to marry us because of these reasons, but he wasn't able to travel in that season of his life due to health issues. As we shared our vows at the altar, we remembered the wedding of the Lamb with selfless love, complete surrender, and service. As we wrote our mission statement for our family that we use to this day, it all began with our marriage and our family: "To be a marriage and a family that reflects the relationship of Jesus to the church." I travel a lot as a teacher, and sadly, I have had to deny more invitations than I can accept. But even in those moments, Darrow's words stay close to me, and I remember the bigger picture.

I asked him once about how he chose where he traveled and whom he would accept an invitation from, and he responded, "I travel and respond to felt needs from those whom I trust and love and hope to support. I don't teach in places where I'm the one opening the doors and trying to create the platform. To continue returning, I need to see fruit and application and not just a dependency on my content and speaking from the outside." This impacted me in such a way that I try to pray before accepting any invitation now. I first consult with my wife, and quickly we consider how our three kids are doing and our local ministry. There is no dichotomy in the kingdom of God, but simple obedience to the faith in each season of life is what matters. The *what* has no special value, but the *how* changes everything.

I am a son of God. I am a husband of the woman of my dreams, Katherine, and I have three of the most beautiful and amazing children on earth: Caleb, Abigael, and Ezekiel. I'm no longer afraid of losing my family to serve God. I'm no longer afraid of my wife or kids rejecting God or being hurt because I'm a missionary. However, I am excited to understand that I'm called to glorify Him first as a husband and father, not as a leader, teacher, author, or anything else. There are seasons for everything, but it's never about what we do for value in the kingdom of God. It's about why we do it. May everything that we live and do be for Him, to glorify Him, and reflect Him without ever looking at any option before us as having greater value in the kingdom of God. God is all about relationships, and the family is the foundation of society. Marriage becomes the womb of blessings and curses for all future generations and cultures. Family is the foundation of society.

There was a season when we weren't sure what to do in ministry. Should we go home to the USA, continue in Mexico and accept a pastoral position within a local church, or go in a new direction? In that season, Darrow invited us to join the global movement that the Discipling Nations Alliance is a small part of—or to use the language they use today, "to engage with us to spread the 'virus' of the DNA messages." Despite saying no, in some way we keep that same heart.

After praying, God spoke clearly to us to continue in the ministry that we have, but his influence is so strong relationally in our hearts that everything within me wanted to say yes. Not for any reason in particular, to be seen or to have a new platform, but just for who he is outside of his books, not on the pulpit but sitting at the table drinking tea and meditating about day-to-day life. I fully desire to be a faithful servant with all my talents, to multiply and use all my gifts in the kingdom, and to increase in my capacity every year in what we do. Greater than this desire, however, is the desire that one day people all around the world whom I have impacted will have been more impacted by our casual conversation about marriage, family, and relationships. I hope and pray that my kids wouldn't refer to me as a good leader, a good teacher, a successful minister, author, or anything else. I would much rather them talk about a dad who is a good listener, fun to be with, and took them on family outings and trips. I want them to remember the *extraordinary* moments that marked their lives.

In one of those special dinners that Katie and I were eating with Darrow, besides some great sushi and laughing a bit, he said something that really challenged me. He began to share about how he and his wife had just begun to open their house to let young people come in, laugh, talk, and watch them live their marriage and family.

He said that after a few days, despite having some good moments of teaching and processing, all the guests began to share that what most impacted their lives was seeing a healthy marriage and family. He then looked into my eyes and said, "This generation needs more time of coffee and games, smiles and laughs, and opportunities to just watch and learn from a healthy marriage and family. They don't need more 'teachings.' They need more time to be close to real marriages and real families in real-life environments. They need healing, and it's a healing that doesn't come from an experience, special prayer, or good teaching. It's a healing that comes from redeeming the thought of marriage and family, and that will only happen by having a redemptive experience of what is real in your own marriage and family."

While finishing up this book, I have been on ten straight weeks of traveling and teaching a different topic in a different location every week. One of the weeks, I had the privilege to share the week after my wife had been teaching in a school. While she was teaching, I was also teaching in a different school with a different group of students. We had our daughter in school, our son was doing homeschool with a friend who helped us that week, and with our baby Ezekiel, we switched back and forth all day between Katie and me as we taught.

By the end of my week of teaching, the week after my wife had finished, the students took some time to pray for me and encourage me. Out of everything they said, there were multiple comments that really blessed me. They were all summarized in what one Mexican lady said: "You are a great teacher, but these last two weeks, what has changed my life is to watch you and your wife interact and to watch you both with your kids and to watch your kids' love for both of you. For me, my dreams of marriage and family have been redeemed because I've finally seen a family live a message that aligns with everything they teach. Your marriage, your kids, and your classes are all in order. Who you are as a family has transformed my life. I'm separated from my husband and have lost my kids, but I now desire and pray with all of my heart that we can restore our marriage and grow into a family like I've seen in you guys."

Despite having many of our own challenges and struggles in marriage and with our kids, this comment inspired me that we are taking great strides to walk into the consistency of the complete Gospel message.

What Darrow imparted to me over fourteen years ago has become a major value in my life. What do I have to show for my life if I have evangelized and discipled the world but have lost my wife and children? I've discovered that by loving my wife and kids with all that I can, naturally I am impacting and transforming everyone around me. Darrow was right: the healing that this generation needs is less teaching and experience and more real-life people who live a reality that can break the chains of lies, brokenness, and hopelessness. I hope that one day many will look back on our marriage and family and think of the healing and hope that came out of us learning to love God in all the simple little areas of life together.

Darrow shares often about the dangers of "Evangelical Gnosticism" or separating life into secular and sacred activities as a Christian, thinking that church activities are more valuable or spiritual than everyday, ordinary activities and relationships. There is an orphan generation in this world because many Christian leaders believed that loving God meant giving up the "nonspiritual" day-to-day activities. However, what most impacts humanity around the world are Christian leaders who live all aspects of an ordinary life in an *extraordinary* way!

Reflection

1. Do you have different mentors for the season of life that you are in, outside of just "ministry" models?
2. What has greater value in your mind and why? Having a healthy marriage, solid father/mother relationships with the kids, giving up everything and moving to a dangerous place for Jesus, or being a famous pastor/teacher/author?
3. Do you have any roots of Evangelical Gnosticism in the way that you approach ministry? If so, where and what are you doing about it?

4. Do you fight to guard your marriage and keep a hedge around it? Do you schedule date nights each week and special little things for each other? How are you continually renewing and developing quality time, romance, and intimacy?

5. How do your children see you? Are you the same man or woman at home that is standing on the pulpit or sharing on the microphone? Do your social media videos reflect what your children and spouse know to be true about you?

6. In ministry, there are many different models of families, of courtship, and marriage. Is there a model that you are seeking guidance from? If not, why? How can you change that?

Meditation

In this past season of life, I believe that God spoke clearly to me to focus my energy in several specific areas. The challenge has been that the direction I have felt from the previous season was to expand more and more in our local, regional, and global influence. Teaching and traveling has provided many wonderful opportunities in ministry. I began to teach online in a Bible school here in Mexico and was traveling one to two weeks a month to teach in different places in Mexico, the United States, the Caribbean, and Central America. Recently, however, our ministry has begun to have a lot of changes. We now have three kids, and God spoke clearly to me that for this next season, I am to focus the majority of my time and effort locally and to limit my travel.

Within a few days, my wife asked me, for the first time in many years, to stay home from an upcoming trip and another event. Within a week, multiple invitations and opportunities arose to expand our influence in leadership, and the temptations of my past crept up very quickly to just say yes and go. How can I say no to open doors? This is a great opportunity, and it's for God, I was reasoning! The old lies of finding my identity in doing came to the surface again. I remembered something that I heard Loren Cunningham once say, "Every time I get a new opportunity or something new enters my life, I lay it down at the feet of the cross and ask Jesus what to pick up. Just like God asked Moses to lay down his staff and then pick up a snake, I must lay down what I desire and pick up what He speaks." That's exactly what I had to do, lay the new opportunities at the feet of Jesus and pick up what He was saying for this new season.

The values I have learned through this journey of ministry need to be "applied principles," even when it's hard. There is a time for everything, and I don't want to gain the world and save the nations and lose my kids or my wife. I don't want to teach to the multitudes and leave my immediate ministry as orphans. It's not an "either or" but simply continuing to align with what God is saying for the current season of my journey. I've been working on this book for almost five years, and now I am actually going to finish it! There is always a new open door and even greater opportunities, but we must remember what God is saying. What He says and my first commitments are more important than any other need that I might perceive or what others might desire. God is God, and I am not! He is the Savior, and I am just a servant and an ambassador, and I can rest in that understanding within each new season.

The Bible and Being Accessible and Available

- "Moses was willing to dwell with the man, and he gave his daughter Zipporah to Moses" (Exodus 2:21).
- "Then one said, 'Please be willing to go with your servants.' And he answered, 'I shall go'" (2 Kings 6:3).
- "So David departed from there and escaped to the cave of Adulam; and when his brothers and all his father's household heard of it, they went down there to him. Everyone who was in distress, and everyone who was in debt, and everyone who was discontented gathered to him and he became captain over them. Now there were about four hundred men with him" (1 Samuel 22:1–2).
- "I have issued a decree that any of the people of Israel and their priests and the Levites in my kingdom who are willing to go to Jerusalem, may go with you" (Ezra 7:13).

- "And a leper came to Him and bowed down before Him, and said, 'Lord, if You are willing, You can make me clean.' Jesus stretched out His hand and touched him, saying, 'I am willing; be cleansed.' And immediately his leprosy was cleansed" (Matthew 8:2–3).
- "The Son of Man came eating and drinking, and they say, 'Behold, a gluttonous man and a drunkard, a friend of tax collectors and sinners!' Yet wisdom is vindicated by her deeds" (Matthew 11:19).
- "And large crowds came to Him, bringing with them those who were lame, crippled, blind, mute, and many others, and they laid them down at His fee; and He healed them" (Matthew 15:30).
- "When evening came, after the sun had set, they began bringing to Him all who were ill and those who were demon-possessed. And the whole city had gathered at the door" (Mark 1:32–33).
- "And they came, bringing to Him a paralytic, carried by four men. Being unable to get to Him because of the crowd, they removed the roof above Him; and when they had dug an opening, they let down the pallet on which the paralytic was lying. And Jesus, seeing their faith said to the paralytic, 'Son, your sins are forgiven'" (Mark 2:3–5).
- "And they were bringing children to Him so that He might touch them; but the disciples rebuked them. But when Jesus saw this, He was indignant and said to them, "permit the children to come to Me; do not hinder them; for the kingdom of God belongs to such as these" (Mark 10:13–4).
- "And standing behind Him at His feet, weeping, she began to wet His feet with her tears, and kept wiping them with the hair of her head, and kissing His feet and anointing the with perfume. Now when the Pharisee who had invited Him saw this, he said to himself, "If this man were a prophet He would know who and what sort of person this woman is who is touching Him, that she is a sinner" (Luke 7:38–39).

- "Then, when they had rowed about three or four miles, they saw Jesus walking on the sea and drawing near to the boat; and they were frightened. But He said to them, 'It is I; do not be afraid.' So they were willing to receive Him into the boat, and immediately the boat was at the land to which they were going" (John 6: 19–21).

- "When he came to Jerusalem, he was trying to associate with the disciples; but they were all afraid of him, not believing that he was a disciple. But Barnabas took hold of him and brought him to the apostles and described to them how he had seen the Lord on the road, and that He had talked to him, and how at Damascus he had spoken out boldly in the name of Jesus" (Acts 9:26–27).

CHAPTER 12

Humility

Inspired by scientist and missionary Wedrell Alman

Humility—to see the value of oneself, and the value of others, through the infinite lens, of absolute truth; all of humanity carries the same intrinsic value of being created in the image and likeness of God. All of humanity bears His Image. To not look down upon others feeling superior or to look up at others feeling inferior but to simply see oneself and others in the same light. Independent of gifts and talents, past decisions or present reality, age, race, sex, or experience, just embracing the truth of God in all places, at all times, about oneself and others.

Wedge passed away three years ago, March 5, 2017. His wife, author and missionary Shirley Alman has graciously offered some beautiful words to Introduce chapter 12.

Special Introduction

As I pondered this beautiful chapter on humility, I was reminded once again of how Wedge did life. He loved God and wanted to portray Him to others. I'd like to share some of the ways his daily life displayed humility.

Humility practices good manners, such as hold the chair for me to sit at the table, hold my coat as I put it on, and open the door for me to enter ahead of him.

Humility is being grateful. Wedge never left the table without thanking me for the meal. Even when he was very ill, he thanked me for every glass of water.

Humility encourages others. He bragged on my cooking even when I had no clue what I was doing. My first lemon meringue pie was impossible to negotiate with a fork, so we just picked it up with our fingers and devoured it, laughing our heads off.

Humility is being the first to ask forgiveness. Because of this quality in Wedge, our marriage overcame many crises and lasted 66 and a half wonderful years until he passed into his heavenly home.

Humility is loving unconditionally, and in marriage, there are countless opportunities for that.

Humility is kindness personified. Wedge never interrupted anyone. He waited to speak until the other person finished.

Humility is content with what one has. Wedge was six feet tall and handsome, and a sharp dresser, but it was I who urged him to shop for new clothes. He always felt he had enough.

Humility honors one's mate publicly. He generously praised me from the pulpit, whether I was in the audience or not. Can you imagine how that made me feel? I was being acknowledged publicly, and I loved him for that.

Humility is considerate. Once when teaching in Argentina, Wedge was invited to extend his meetings. He called me in Chile to ask if I would be too disappointed if he did so since he would arrive days late for our anniversary. Yes, I was disappointed, but I knew in my heart it was right for him to stay. God watched, was pleased, and gave us an incredibly awesome celebration.

So where does this humility come from? How do we acquire it? I believe it is a product of our intimacy with God. As we spend time with Him, we become more like Him. As we absorb His Word, we are cleansed, instructed, inspired, challenged, and transformed into His image.

Through the years, I watched my husband seek God early in the morning, late at night, even get out of bed in the middle of the night to spend time with his Heavenly Father. He was not perfect, but I have long forgotten any faults he had.

My prayer is that this chapter will help you recognize any shred of pride present in your life, hate it for the sin it is, and repent of it deeply. God longs to bring you into a more intimate relationship that only comes as you walk in true humility.

Shirley Alman
Cofounder of YWAM, Latin America
Missionary, Wife, Mother, Grandmother
Teacher, Author, and Inspiration

* * * * *

In day-to-day life, finding the right balance, the proper response not out of emotion and reaction but in truth and therefore choosing to be intentional in relationship is more difficult than most of us like to admit. From birth, we have an innate desire to be a part of a family, to belong, and to be accepted. This develops into a real desire to be loved and affirmed that who we are is okay and to be told that what is most hidden within our hearts and desires are normal and that we are normal. It's good to be who we are, even if we are different from others around us.

In an ideal world, where everyone had full application of intentional relationships at all levels, things would be different than they are today. Every child would be born into a family with two loving parents, a mom and dad who have a healthy marriage relationship, and both would invest greatly in their maternal and paternal relationship with the child. They would both be very confident in identity, living in love and trust relationships through mutual accountability with each other and carry a desire to be attentive in all ways with every need of every child. Wisdom and empathy would be normal, and a clear understanding of unity and diversity would guide both mom and dad to love each child on an equal plane, never comparing and never trying to impart dreams of their own but being sensitive to the reality within each child's heart, helping to guide and nurture but never control. Parents would seek the right balance of justice and mercy, tender and genuine love, doing what is right all that time without wavering. Unfortunately, this just isn't real life. With all the different areas of intimacy through marriage, having kids, grandchildren, friends, mentors, extended family, church, coworkers, and more. Sadly, none of us will ever really find complete community and intimacy.

Many parents of today are young men and women without conviction about marriage. Young men and women that haven't understood the responsibility serve one-another , and often both are struggling in their own identities and confidence. All too often, they are still just like big kids and still have a lot of brokenness and selfishness continually fighting within their hearts and minds. The way that this affects children within this type of home environment is far beyond what we can imagine. Add to this challenge the reality that no parent can read a child's thoughts or fully understand the secrets of the heart, which makes it even harder. These unspoken absolute desires within a child at some point will have to cross paths with a world, a sibling, a parent, a friend, or a culture that just doesn't understand the complexities of all the things needed for a unique individual in a postmodern world. It is a world that has a different story and therefore reacts in judgment by saying that something is wrong in being an individual and different. It is a world that fights more about what we don't believe or agree with, than even what we do. More often than not, this creates an environment of hurt, causing great desires of acceptance that just can't be fully communicated or met by the two young adults dealing with their own identity challenges, which creates the perfect storm for raising a young family.

Now that I'm thirty-four years old, I feel that I am beginning to fully accept and embrace the reality of the way that I am, which has been a huge battle most of my life. To learn to just rest in the way that God has created me has been very freeing, but it's still a daily battle. In many ways, I'm like many before me from generations past but at the same time an individual and, therefore, like no one within either side of my family. I'm completely different. I'm finally understanding that belonging to a nation, to a tribe, to a clan or family doesn't take away the individual identity. I am just different, and it's okay. It is, in fact, a good thing, embracing and accepting myself and embracing and accepting those around me.

As I watch each of my children grow and develop day to day, passing through the different stages of development, forming their own worldviews, understanding how they fit into the community but also continue to be an individual, it makes me remember my own life journey. I remember both the times of seeking God and times of fleeing from Him and only seeking my own desires. This causes a certain fear within me as a father because I'm forced to remember the fact that I'm not enough for my own children! No one ever has, ever could, or ever will fully know my heart intentions or deepest thoughts. Only God can do that. On a similar level, I can't do that for my children, and they can't do it for me. They will always see the external that I say or do, even if there is a major disconnect between the two for whatever reason. I might see the *why*, but they will see the *what*. I might judge what happened, but they try to explain to me why it happened. Identity, truth, and humility all go hand in hand. Humility is just the ability to accept the truth and live within its identity without trying to hide behind a mask.

The first reason in my life that I found to hide my own identity was fear that I wouldn't be enough. I had no real reason to believe this, but I allowed the doubts of my mind to internalize a new reality about myself. I loved hunting, fishing, sports, and many other things. They were sincere joys in life, but I also enjoyed music and art. I remember from a young age being captivated by the sound of a stringed instrument, a brass or percussion, and the incredible tones of a beautiful voice while watching someone dance, the ballet, and opera. At the same time, I've had a hearing problem with one of my ears since I was a child, which has limited my ability to sing or recognize certain tones. As a result, I've learned to hide that secret passion within my heart.

I learned to read music on the piano from the time I was a child, and I have some experience in piano, guitar, drums, and the trumpet, but have never developed any of these into anything more than a casual hobby. I'm sure that I could have, but within my own mind, these hobbies were not affirmed as much as others. I would say the same thing about art and poetry, drawing and painting, dance, and pottery. I have had a fascination in each of these areas from the time I was a child, and although it wasn't verbalized in a negative sense, I fell into the cultural fear of having to fit into a box that wasn't big enough to hold all of my design, dreams, and passions and still just be me. To live truth, to accept identity, and really embrace true humility is a tough journey for all of us. At least it has been for me.

A second reason that I remember hiding my thoughts and passions was my own insecurities. From the time I was a child, I was affirmed by my family and teachers that I had the ability to be a leader. Many could see the *what* I could do as leadership. I had so many insecurities, though, and I never learned to express the *why* of the way that I was beyond what was easy to see. Consequently, it wasn't until these last nine years, after being married, having kids, and studying more in depth about human psychology, and developing deeper within my own personal relationship with God that I've been able to accept and embrace who I am, learning to embrace my own weaknesses and strengths.

On one side, it helps me to naturally be a good leader in some areas; but on the other side, I struggle to connect with others in many cases, to express my heart thoughts and feelings most of the time, or to be understood fully by others. Being different can have strengths, and I've begun to see those strengths. But for most of my life, I've accepted roles of leadership naturally without being fully comfortable with myself about who I am and the way that I process information or think, especially when working with others. It can be hard for me to understand why others do what they do and how I can best relate to them. I can easily see the *what* but have no way of seeing the *why* and within the heart. Just like me, every person is different and unique, with much more than what I can see.

The first challenge to see truth comes out of being affirmed in a very positive way in certain areas but never giving myself an opportunity to be affirmed in others for fear, which was totally my fault.

The second is because somewhere along the way, I was discouraged for being different and not being like someone else or the cultural "norm," which became an excuse to hide—therefore, also missing the truth. The third reason is even harder. Even when I knew the truth about who I was, what I desired, and what God was speaking and asking of me, I hid the truth. I can't blame anyone else for not knowing the full intentions of my heart, for having affirmed or discouraged me, but it's simply my pride when I choose to not walk in the truth. To this day, this pride is the biggest battle that I have had to fight daily in all that I do. To measure myself by any standard, my own or others,' as a standard that isn't the truth from God. There is no one to blame, no one to claim as the cause, but just my own reality that the truth wasn't enough, and I must become something more or do something different to be complete or to please others by rejecting the truth.

In 2005, I had just finished my discipleship training school in Youth with a Mission. I had been working more on my ability to understand Spanish vocabulary at a deeper level, and I took my first class without an English translation. It was a course we did for staff development called "The King and His Kingdom by Wedge Alman." I'm sure that I missed many things throughout the classes because of my Spanish limitations, but for me, it was a huge accomplishment to take a full course only in Spanish. Not only was it in Spanish, but the teacher was a leader that used to be "an electronics technician who worked in guided missile R and D [research and development] at White Sands Proving Grounds." He was using science and laws of nature to prove the existence of God. His name was Wedrell Alman, and I'll never forget that first video series with him.

It was a name that I had heard of before from some books and from being quoted by different leaders for different reasons. I knew he was some American guy that basically pioneered all of YWAM Latin America and was now in his '80s. I felt superprivileged that I could at least watch his videos, knowing that I would never meet him; but the following year, I was given the opportunity to lead a school, and I decided that I wanted to try to get this man to come and teach. I was studying the roots and major influences of the ministry I was working in, and I wanted to have him come and teach in person. Why would he accept my invitation, though, and he would get nothing out of investing time with us? To my surprise, he didn't just come, but he came with his wife and responded quickly without having any reference of who I was or any reason to trust a young twenty-year-old American living in Mexico! I had sought out different "famous speakers" like him, and most of them either completely ignored me, gave a long list of requirements to walk through before they would consider coming because of their "very busy schedules," or I had to prove that it was worth their time. Wedge and Shirley Alman, however, just prayed and said *yes*!

They came for two weeks in 2005, and their classes were amazing. I remember so many things from this man and his incredible wife, but what I most remember wasn't what was taught in the classroom but the man and woman outside of the classroom. He was so open about both his failures and successes, his strengths and weaknesses, his great victories and his moments of shame. He talked about everything he would do differently as a young man if he would have known all that he knew now. His vast knowledge and experience didn't create any sense of pride but rather brought forth an incredible sensation of humility: an eighty-year-old man that shared all his failures on courtship, in marriage, as a father, as a missionary, as a scientist, as a soldier in the war with his family and so much more, but without shame. At the same time, he would share about his passions and dreams in the area of music and science, education, and the church; his love for his wife; global missions; and an incredible heart for Latin America as a whole. The first Spanish book I read was called *Él Es Tu Dios*. (By the way, the 2019 update is *¡Él Es Tu Dios También!* In English, *He's Your God Too!*)

I was sitting before this incredible man with an amazing legacy, and all I could do was think about how I came to Mexico as a missionary without any type of college degree, without anything to open doors for me, but somehow I still felt superior to an entire culture and language group because of my unfounded pride. "The others were the people that needed to be reached and transformed in my mind," and "I was the one being used to come and save them." Now

I found myself face-to-face with a man who literally had everything, or could have had everything, and in any culture could hold that over their heads to have influence or authority, but he didn't. He could have charged large amounts of money for conferences, have requirements of certain types of leaders to be there, and reject anyone that didn't meet what he wanted, but he didn't. Rather than "rising up" over people, he taught out of his weaknesses and humility and met the nations on a heart level where he was just another face that loved them. He was quick to show his humanity and complete reality, having an open door for anyone to walk in. He would identity and embrace the reality of those secret desires of the heart of the child within everyone he met, to be valued and honored, just for carrying the image of God. He took a responsibility for his life in a way that I had never seen before, without excuses, and he was rawly honest. He had global influence, but it came out of truth, honesty, identity, and humility, not out of insecurities, power and control, or fake authority. He obviously taught out of many successes throughout the years, miracles and stories that would leave you in awe; but even in those stories, there was something so clear about the fact that he and his wife weren't the center of the story but just another character being used by God like so many others. The biggest strengths and successes weren't enough, and their biggest failures weren't either, but God and His Truth were; and in both successes and failures, God was glorified. He would leave a sense that, *I can do this too.*

Sadly, Brother Wedge passed away a few years back on March 5, 2017. When I think of hospitality, honoring in-laws in courtship, living by faith, etiquette, radical obedience to God, teachings like "Being a Soldier of Christ," "The Little Foxes," "The King and His Kingdom," and so many other incredible teachings that I carry with me daily that have challenged me to be responsible in the kingdom of God. All I can do is remember Wedge. For several years, I would have him come to teach with us, to laugh with us, and to be encouraged by him. Now there's something in ministry that feels a bit different knowing that he can't come down next year to speak wisdom into my life, and he never will again. It's not his degrees, being a scientist from working in the space program in guided missile research, being an author or a pioneer in a Global Missions Project with testimonies from all over Latin America that speak of his good fruit; it's his soft heart of humble truth. His willingness to just ask God and say yes. He never saw greater numbers as better or more important, certain locations or ministries as superior, but rather just saw people with God's eyes and allowed himself to be used.

The following is a short story that I have probably never told before about a very personal encounter with Wedge and Shirley, but it's something that I think about often. The last time I had Wedge teaching with me, I was in a very difficult moment with my own personal finances and really fighting as a young missionary to take steps of obedience to God and live by faith. I was leading a discipleship school in Mexico and needed to bring him and his wonderful wife to the airport. I never told him what was going on, but all morning, I was filled with worry because I didn't have enough gas to get to the airport and back, and I had no money left. I gave them their offering for the time they had been teaching with us, prayed with them, gave them big hugs, and told them how I looked forward to the next trip, not knowing there would never be another trip for me to see him again. I took them to the airport. Again we hugged and prayed together, and they left. At that moment, I walked back to my car, knowing I didn't have enough money to get home. I looked at the seat where Wedge had been sitting, and there was a little white envelope. I opened it, and there was a note that read, "Danny, you always thank us and bless us when we come to Mexico, but you are the real hero. We wouldn't be here if it wasn't for you, and the students wouldn't be here if it wasn't for you, and we don't deserve this money, but you do." This was one of those moments that, as I drove off, overwhelmed me with emotion in a way that wasn't normal for me. But as I held that little envelope and counted the money, I began to shed some tears. Who was I for a couple like this to be honoring me and investing in me while struggling with their own health, upcoming surgeries, and travel? Who were these people to love me and honor me even when, in comparison to them, I was just a nobody?

This is a man that touched the depths of my heart and deepest thoughts on more than one occasion. I remember driving home, not knowing that I would never see Wedge again, but all I could do is say a little prayer in my heart through soft tears, "I want to leave this type of fingerprint behind me anywhere I can go into the world. I don't want to rise up and force things with the authority of man, but I want to embrace the truth of who I am and learn to meet people through the most open door that exists—the door of humility and truth, of honesty from the heart without hidden agendas. I want to plant seeds of hope and truth anywhere that God allows me to go. I want to see people the way that God sees them, and I want to see myself through His eyes."

As I mentioned earlier, this is one of the biggest challenges for me daily in my marriage, with my kids, while I travel and teach, counseling, or simply in casual conversation and walking down the street. I want to let the truth from within flow to those who are around me—the good, the bad, and the ugly. Within all of it, there is no space to be loved if what people love about me isn't the truth. My desire has grown more and more to simply walk in the light as He is in the light and that at the end of the conversation, a week of teaching or the journey together, God would be glorified by His truth in my sincere story.

That first series of videos that I watched in Spanish, "The King and His Kingdom" by Wedge Alman became one of my biggest tools in my first few years of ministry. I was a young foreigner living in Mexico. Who was going to listen to me? So I would offer a fifteen-hour seminar, and we would go through his videos, and I would just facilitate a process of discussion groups and application. This was how I started our first youth group. The pastor didn't know me or did not yet trust me to teach, so I offered the seminar. By the time we were done, they allowed me to teach freely within the church. I used them in another Bible study I started years later in a spa as well and a few other places. I wound up baptizing a group of people from that spa and from the youth group within just a year of beginning those videos about the King and His Kingdom. Even through a video, his personality and words, his truth and honesty, his conviction and testimony came through in a way that his humility would begin to transform our lives. He left a great space for God to move, for the Spirit to have His way, and for Jesus to be glorified. He wasn't trying to raise up a generation to follow himself or to glorify his own ministry but rather to learn from his own failures and successes and to go to the Source and do even greater things. He would talk about it, and he lived in a way that made us believe it!

Most years, I get to baptize different people at different moments, to marry different young couples, and I often think of Wedge. Will my words point to me independent of God and others, or guide people to the source of God and His example, learning through my failures and successes within my testimony, being seen in the here and now? As soon as the young couple says "I do," then they are on their own, and I'm no longer a part of it, so it had better be based on His Truth. When that person comes up from the water, he or she had better remember that I was just another witness to this incredible step and not the one to be followed or sought out first. I'm a fellow brother of the faith, a fellow lover of Christ, a coheir of the kingdom, but the King must be glorified.

Recently, in the beginning of 2019, I had the privilege of baptizing a young lady whom we had been discipling closely for several years. We have walked through some major life moments with her, and she has become a part of our family. When my wife and I baptized her, I realized that three of the other guys standing with us praying for her had also been baptized in the last few years. They were just married, and they had asked us to marry them. We were unable to be there to marry them due to previous commitments, but I am so proud of Jacob and Pam, and I in turn have learned so much from them as well. It's an incredible privilege, but it's extremely humbling because the truth is that every day we are in our own battle to align our lives with God, to submit to Him, and to allow both our failures and successes to come into the light. I don't know what's best for someone else, but I do know Who does and Who is, and I'm able to point them to Him. I would hope that these young men and women whom we disciple today, in twenty, forty, or sixty years into the future, could be fully honest about my family, my marriage, or my own life and that it would be as real and truthful, stable in identity, humble, and honest as this man, Wedge Alman, had done in my life! May we be a legacy to his name, and others a legacy to mine, as each of us becomes more of the legacy of Jesus Christ here on earth.

May He be glorified in our victories and successes, and may He be glorified in our brokenness and repentance. In the end, may we simply be "walking in the Light as He is in the Light."

I was just recently with Shirley Alman in December of 2019 for a couple of days. At eighty-nine years old, she keeps pushing forward. I asked her about her grieving process with Wedge, who died in 2017, and she smiled and said, "Why would I be sad? We've lived our whole lives to spend eternity with Jesus. Don't get me wrong, I miss his arms around me every night. We were lovers. We were madly and romantically in love, and I miss him holding me tight every night. But I'm not sad that he has been released to be with Jesus." When she found out that I had been teaching in Tyler, Texas, in those days, her response was something I'll never forget: "Why didn't the leaders invite me? I want to go and learn from you!"

We looked at pictures of Wedge. I listened to many of her stories, and in great humility, she would look at me and ask questions and listen to me. She cared about my opinions and sincerely believed that she could learn from me, someone just one-third her age. As I left and kissed her on the cheek, again I was challenged to bring mountains low and valleys high and never lose the humility to learn and love anyone and everyone that God brings into my life. Wedrell may have passed away from this earth in 2017, the rich legacy that he and Shirley began so many years ago continues to inspire and challenge me. Again I find great gratitude in knowing that I have been blessed to cross their journey of life.

Reflection

1. How do you define humility?
2. Do you struggle more with "superior" or "inferior" pride?
3. Is your true story what is being seen in the light by others in what you say and do?

4. Are you willing to look at your own life in the light of Truth from God's perspective?

5. What mentors or examples of leaders in your life have most challenged you with their humility? What did they do, and why does that impact you?

6. How would you define the truth of your heart and meditation of your thoughts today? Who knows this reality about you other than yourself and God?

Meditation

For years, a little white lie, a small exaggeration, a change of a number, or an extra detail or removal of a detail within a story were far too easy to say within everything that I would think and do. We were sitting at a lunch one day, and a friend of mine was making a little joke, and the little girl next to him looked at him in the eyes and said, "Son of Satan." We were all shocked and had no words to respond to her, but this little girl looked at us and said the Bible says that liars are sons of Satan! It was quite funny in the moment, and my friend was telling her that it was just a joke, but I'll never forget the voice of that little girl speaking to us.

The reason that her comment was so strong in my heart was because it reminded me of Wedge and his story. If the truth isn't enough, then there isn't anything else to share. Why can't the truth be enough? Do I not have a true-enough story with God? Is my life and my experiences not true enough to tell what really happened? Are my passions and dreams not enough to be honest about them? Are my failures and brokenness somehow less if I hide them? Why isn't the truth enough? Why hide the past, and why create a fake present?

While processing this one day, I felt like God asked me the question, *Why do you go where you go to teach or preach? Do you go because of the money, because of the quantity of people, because of how well known the location is or isn't?* I think for years I couldn't really answer that question, and part of why I went was probably just because I was invited. And as a young man, I would say yes and go without asking any questions. As I began to get invited more and more, however, and I began to have to commit my year out far in advance, I began to have to rethink why I go where I go and why I do what I do. The question arose about whom do I say yes to, certain locations, and how to accept an invitation if I was going to share? I talked about this and processed it with my wife and came to the conclusion that whenever possible, half of my travel and teaching opportunities I wanted to do in places that were well known, that could afford to fly me in and cover my costs, but that I wanted at least half of the people that I invested in to be the people that many other speakers or teachers would probably say no to. Places that would have no money to get me there, no honorariums, and I would even have to pay for my own travel sometimes. Places that might be as small as two or three students or with leaders that no one had ever heard about before. I felt a strong conviction about what Jesus did with His disciples, and I wanted to do the same and to invest where God could move freely and be glorified!

Many times, I've done the same thing that Wedge has done for me, and I try to ask God how to bless the young leaders around me. I've had to choose between two invitations when I have an invitation to go and teach with a large school or church that can cover all of my expenses somewhere or a young leader that only has a few students or church members. God has told me to say yes to the young leader many times and not the other opportunity. I feel badly, but I've said no far more often than yes to traveling and teaching invites recently as I'm just in a season of life where I can't right now, so we've even offered to cover the costs of our staff to go and teach in other places. When I do go, it's been one of two reasons: it's a place that others might not want to go and God tells me to go, or I believe in the leader and want to bless them because of our relationship. This is a legacy that Wedge left me, and I hope to leave it to others who have a gift of teaching, that they would go to the nations not for what they can receive but to serve with great humility and allow the King to be glorified through what we can give.

Too often, humility is compared to personality or external demeanor. Someone that doesn't speak much or walks with his head down is seen as meek or humble. The man or woman that walks with his or her head held high with a lot of confidence, strong words, and great honesty is often judged as overconfident or even arrogant. It's interesting, though: Jesus was the essence of humility and meekness. Paul was a man of meekness and humility. To be humble is to walk in truth. To listen and obey. To be completely honest at the right time in the right way for the right reason. Humility is not a personality trait but rather an issue of the heart. Wedge left an incredible teaching in my life to be able to rise up in confidence with who God has created me to be while at the same time falling to my knees in worship as I understand who He is and how to most glorify Him.

The Bible and Humility

- "The fear of the Lord is the instruction for wisdom, and before honor comes humility" (Proverbs 16:6).
- "Before destruction, the heart of man is haughty, but humility goes before honor" (Proverbs 18:12).
- "He leads the humble in justice, and He teaches the humble His way. All the paths of the Lord are lovingkindness and truth to those who keep His covenant and His testimonies" (Psalms 25:9–10).
- "Seek the Lord, all you humble of the earth who have carried out His ordinances; seek righteousness, seek humility. Perhaps you will be hidden in the day of the Lord's anger" (Zephaniah 2:3).
- "Therefore I, the prisoner of the Lord, implore you to walk in a manner worthy of the calling with which you have been called, with all humility and gentleness, with patience, showing tolerance for one another in love, being diligent to preserve the unity of the Spirit in the bond of peace" (Ephesians 4:1–3).
- "Do nothing from selfishness or empty conceit, but with humility of mind regard one another as more important than yourselves; do not merely look out for your own personal interests, but also for the interests of others.

Have this attitude in yourselves which was also in Christ Jesus" (Philippians 2:3–5).

- "So, as those who have been chosen of God, holy and beloved, put on a heart of compassion, kindness, humility, gentleness and patience; bearing with one another, and forgiving each other, whoever has a complaint against anyone just as the Lord forgave you, so also should you. Beyond all these things put on love, which is the perfect bond of unity" (Colossians 3:12–14).

- "You younger men likewise, be subject to your elders; and all of you, clothes yourselves with humility toward one another, for God is opposed to the proud, but gives grace to the humble" (1 Peter 5:5).

- "When you are invited by someone to a wedding feast, do not take the place of honor, for someone more distinguished than you may have been invited by him, and he who invited you both will come and say to you, 'Give your place to this man,' and then in disgrace you proceed to occupy the last place. But when you are invited, go and recline at the last place, so that when the one who has invited you comes, he may say to you, 'Friend, move up higher; then you will have honor in the sight of all who hare at the table with you.' For everyone who exalts himself will be humbled, and he who humbles himself will be exalted" (Luke 14:8–11).

CHAPTER 13

Leadership

Inspired by missionaries Don and Barb Johnson in Nicaragua

> *Leadership*—the skill and ability to walk in plurality and see ahead of others, walking forward and paving the way, by setting an example, and making the journey easier for everyone else that will be coming with you. An ability to do the right thing at the right time, saying the right words at the right moment, and staying quiet for the right reasons, always seeing God and others first, desiring to serve others to go further, be more successful, and have an easier journey than your own. Inspiration seen through vision, direction, guidance, and passion all uniting others in expectation of success both along the journey and also in the final destination.

Special Introduction

We have learned so much from so many humble leaders in our long ministry experience. As young people, our concept of leaders was the guy in charge to blindly obey out of fear and obligation. As we began to study in a YWAM Bible School, School of the Bible, the Lord brought us around 180 degrees. The Bible actually teaches from the ground up servant leadership. The government will be upon His shoulders. As we were transformed by these truths, we wanted to take these truths to the nations and see them multiplied.

When we first came to Nicaragua, we began teaching servant leadership and biblical government. Some people told us that no one would respect a leader who serves. He would be seen as weak. Even pastors were seen as those who ruled in the singular and made all the decisions. Understandably, the nation suffered through one dictator after another, and it was seen all around us, even in the church.

It's common to think of leadership as the person in power who rules over others with a strong hand. But Jesus said the servant of all is truly the greatest. He is meek and lowly of heart, and in His yoke, we find rest for our souls. His power was love and truth. Our job as leaders is not to just tell people what to do but help them discover God's ways and lovingly serve Him. Even God doesn't want to control us externally. Biblical leadership builds people of character who willingly and diligently serve from the heart. This kind of leadership produces freedom and responsibility. One way we build God's kingdom on earth is to model this type of sacrificial leadership He taught us in all that we do. As you read through this chapter, may you be challenged to self-examine your own leadership and dare align it with the message of a servant-leader.

Don and Barb Johnson
Missionaries, Founding Leaders of YWAM Nicaragua
Co-Team Founders of the Bible School for the Nations
Founders of This Little Light of Mine Community School
Incredible Teachers, Parents of Two Children, Grandparents
Wonderful Mentors and Dear Friends

* * * * *

There are two things that, to this day, my mother did that still doesn't make sense to me. The humor in this next story about my mom is that my wife does the same thing. As a three-year-old, it made no sense to me as I watched my mother with confusion, and now it just makes me laugh with my wife as I just bite my tongue and walk away.

There are two details that come together in many of these stories with my mom. To understand her a bit more, she was raised in a house with two older sisters and a father who was a colonel in the Air Force. This created a system of living that was a bit militant, and my mother as the youngest child was raised as the favorite "son" who liked to do everything with her dad. It's funny, though, because to this day, one of the things she most hates is any type of rigid lifestyle due to the fact she felt it was so hard for her as a child—always being on time, having to respond in the right way at the right time, even to the point of the type of haircut and the clothes she wore. After leaving her home, she really pushed to create a different home environment that was much more relational and relaxed. On one side, she still carried a lot of her childhood values and therefore never wanted to be late; but from my earliest memories, everywhere we went, the last fifteen minutes at home felt like chaos as we ran all over the place, only to be late. The day before any trip was always when I witnessed the biggest fights in my family as stress would be high, and we'd always be late, no matter how much my mother would try to plan to arrive on time.

I think that this is probably a pretty normal story for an American family with two small children, but what made it unique is what she thought was a good answer: set every clock in our house fifteen minutes fast. I would see her look at her watch and then move the clock fifteen minutes forward. It wasn't for my father, it wasn't for my sister, and it wasn't for me—it was for her. The part that really confused me as a child was that as the three of us would be getting ready to leave on time, she would always tell us, "Don't worry, we still have fifteen minutes." The one person that changed the clocks to never be late would be the one that most reminded us that the clock was wrong and not to worry about being late. The result was just as you can imagine: we would be late. I never understood my mom's reasoning as a child, and it never seemed to work; and to this day in my own home, I don't understand it with my wife, and it still doesn't work. I can have all three kids in the car, in their car seats, be sitting in the driver's seat with the car started, drinking my coffee while watching the minutes pass away, and my wife is somewhere doing something, and it brings me back to my childhood when I would just smile and watch my mom running around the house while we were waiting for her.

A typical morning event that required all of us to wind up at the same place would usually end with my sister slowly coming out of the bathroom, my mom running all over the house, my dad grabbing a quick coffee, and me sitting on the steps in front of the fireplace in the kitchen. This happened hundreds or even thousands of times, but there was one morning that was going to be a morning that would mark me for the rest of my life. It's kind of funny because to this day, when I share this story with my family, my mom doesn't like it. I remember details that don't seem possible for a three-year-old, yet I've never forgotten what took place that day. I think she sees this story as if it were negative, but you will see why this story is so key in my own life journey.

On a normal morning, I would expect my mom to be running around and checking on my sister and me, blow-drying her freshly frosted hair, and doing her makeup while changing. And then she would remember that she needed to feed the horses and give them water at the last minute and begin to stress a bit. She would then run down the stairs, through the basement, and pass me sitting by the fireplace trying to tie my little black boots. She would open the garage, run out to feed and water the horses, run back up the stairs, grab my sister and me, look at the clock over and over, and complain that we were late again. She'd give Dad a quick kiss, if he hadn't left yet, get us in the car, back out of the garage, and shut the garage door as we speed off down the mountain roads.

My dad also had his morning routine of shaving, putting on his aftershave, getting a cup of coffee, walking past me to go out the front door and down the deck to start his car and let it warm up because he didn't park in the garage, and then come back for another quick refill of coffee. He would kiss me on my head, kiss my mom and sister, and head back out to his car. I can still remember the sound of his car pulling out of the driveway. On family days, we would do something together in the morning and then separate afterward. Therefore, we would always take both cars, and there was a fifty-fifty chance that I would go with Dad or that I would go with Mom.

This particular morning in 1988, I can remember my dad having grabbed his coffee. I was sitting by the fireplace trying to tie my black boots at three years old, and I vividly remember being frustrated that one lace was too short to do the loop in my little black boots. I remember my mom running around because she felt like we were going to be late and remembered that she needed to feed the horses still. She ran past me and went down the stairs. I heard the garage open, and she ran out to the horses. I still remember even which car my dad was driving that day; it was his old Hyundai that he drove for work. I remember he walked out the door, walked down the deck, and went to start his car. These are the details that align with any other day, except for what happened next. I heard my dad pull out of the driveway, which let me know that I wasn't going with him; and then to my surprise, I also heard the garage door begin to close. That had never happened before: two of the most familiar noises that I knew but in a chronology that I had never heard. Fear began to come over me.

For a couple of minutes, which seemed like forever, I just froze and listened as I waited in expectation for something else to come in that strange sequence of all too common events. I was waiting to hear Dad's car pull back into the driveway and hear him run across the deck to come and get me, or to hear the garage open and my mom running up the stairs, but there was nothing. The garage had closed, my dad's car had left the driveway, and there I was—all alone, in front of the fireplace, still trying to tie my shoe. I had been left behind.

This was a moment in my life where everything to the last detail was normal except for one thing: I was all alone. It couldn't have been for more than a few minutes, but slowly tears began to fall down my cheeks. I walked to the front and expected to see a car coming back up the road, but there was no one. I went and sat back down by the fireplace and remember staring at the door that went from the stairs to the garage where I had last seen my mother and back at the door that went to the deck where I had last seen my dad, and they were both closed. No sound. I was all alone. I'm sure that the reason my parents don't like this story and have even chosen to forget it is because they remember it through a lens of what happened and my tears, which no parent enjoys, but that is not what I most remember from this story. Up until now is just the context, but the climax comes a few minutes later, when Mom and Dad both came home.

I'll never forget the sound of the garage door opening and hearing my mom's feet coming up the stairs and the sound of my dad's car pulling into the driveway and hearing him come across the deck, but it must have been at almost the exact same time. I tried my best to pretend like I hadn't been crying, but my mom just reached down and embraced me. I remember her big hoop earrings by my head, the color of her recently frosted brown hair, and her smell while she stared into my eyes and held me.

I'll never forget seeing my dad's black shoes and smelling his cologne with his black-and-white sports coat as he leaned down and kissed my hair like always and asked, "Did you think we left you?" Of course I said no, smiled, and just hugged him and let him hold me.

It was an unforgettable moment of love. Only Mom and Dad together could give me what I needed. Only they could provide me with this type of love and protection. Neither of them were angry. My dad didn't say a single word to my mom or question her heart or attack her. My mom didn't try to blame my dad or accuse him of anything. Neither of them were mad at me, and it was a moment that their love for me was more important than being on time. Their love for me was more important than a quick defense or attack toward the other in blame, and we just smiled together. It was a moment that will forever mark my life. I didn't have my shoes tied, we didn't leave on time, I had been left behind, but everything was still somehow okay!

Throughout these past sixteen years in ministry, I continue to come across friends, leaders, pastors, teachers, and parents alike that have somehow combined a couple of these principles in a way that has hurt many people. The reason I have always laughed at my mom and still laugh about seeing the clock fifteen minutes fast is because the problem was never my dad, my sister, or myself—it was my mom. To this day, the clock doesn't affect my kids or myself, but it's for my wife. However, in the same way that my mom knew it wasn't the right time (so does my wife), so those minutes don't change anything in their own lives. If I was the one that did it for her and she didn't know about it, it would only work for a day; but as soon as the truth of the deception was discovered, then it would not only not work, but I would no longer be trusted because every human knows that forced external control and deception is never real change and can't be trusted again tomorrow.

Sadly, over and over again in ministry, I hear these same phrases of "spiritual authority," "covering," and "headship" in terms of control and oppression instead of in terms of influence and choice. The fifteen minutes on a clock won't do anything for a family of four or even for the individual that sets it, and just like with my story when I was three, the "what happened" isn't the biggest part of people's testimonies; it's actually the response to what had happened in those difficult moments that matters.

In leadership, from some of the good ones, I've heard a lot of people quote a few phrases: "It doesn't matter how much you know until people know how much you care," or "The biggest issue isn't the sin or action that took place but rather the amount of time it takes after that act to repent and put things 100 percent in the light that shows the heart and level of pride," or even "It's not what you say, it's when you say it; or not just when you say it but how you say it; and not just how you say things but how you listen; and not just that you listen but how you respond; and not what you say with your words but what your facial expressions and eyes tell about your heart in the way in which you respond." These are all functioning out of the same principle: that the heart can't be touched from the outside in, but only from the inside out can transformation be achieved.

Despite many negative experiences with leaders in my life, I've also been very blessed to encounter many incredible men and women in leadership. These have been the leaders that have redeemed my hope and trust. These are leaders that have incredible families, inspiring marriages, and have amazing gifts and talents in leadership in all that they do.

In 2005, I began to hear story after story and testimony after testimony about the love and guidance of an American couple. Many shared the same inspiration from having experienced their leadership. They seemed to be crazy in the eyes of many in both Nicaragua and the United States. This couple had made the radical choice to move to Nicaragua in the middle of the Marxist revolution in 1989 with two little kids after having spent three years in Guatemala. This was a moment when the majority of foreigners, many businesses, the educated, and some of the wealthy of Nicaragua had chosen to leave. Don and Barb Johnson were doing the opposite; they were coming in to one of the most dangerous countries in Central America with two little kids, no team, few resources, and believing that the people still within Nicaragua were also the people of God and that He was worthy of all of them.

Through the years, this couple entered my life; and just like with many others, I was left greatly inspired. My first encounter with them was in 2006 in Montego Bay, Jamaica. They quickly became one of the greater influences in my life about ministry, biblical studies, history, missions, marriage, and family. I would see them once or twice a year, and they acted as if we were friends or even family. I was amazed at how generous they were with their time, knowing that they had nothing to gain from me. I lived in a different country, with a commitment to another ministry, but they never stopped investing in me and communicating with me. To this day, when I hear them share their story, I sit in awe as I look at their community school with over three hundred students, but I am also amazed knowing the roots and the journey they had to walk through to get there. I'm in shock to see everything they have achieved but very aware at the cost they have paid, the blood they have shed, the tears they have cried for the people of Nicaragua—and the many people that have followed them for the same reasons.

During the Marxist revolution, the government began to control the country by reeducating the children. The kids sang a song from the government that literally said, "Keep your kids away from the Yankees because they will still them and kill them." The United States and democracy were turned into the enemy and the cause of all suffering. Just like with the fifteen minutes that never worked to make my family be on time, a revolution from the outside within a whole country brought lots of blood, brokenness, a lack of trust, abuse of power, and great anarchy. Anarchy takes away responsibility or need for internal-self-government, so the strongest group within the anarchy will always choose tyranny and need a dictator to take control for them. The people will willingly give away their freedom and rights in the name of being a victim, and now the tyranny will control the family, marriage, government, and much of society. Country after country, decade after decade, the same result happens by just doing an external change, with the same fruit of great destruction, and in the end, everyone is just a victim of someone else.

Sadly, I see this most relevant around me in the name of God and the Bible within the church of today from many regions of the world. Great friends but with great confusion about the different domains of authority. As I've watched Don and Barb Johnson achieve everything they have achieved, it's enlightened me greatly with biblical principles of the individual, of marriage and the family, covenants, church, and government. The understanding of the five domains of authority has radically changed the way I see the world, leadership, and service. It's been a life lesson of Don and Barb to me and many others that those external shifts alone can't touch the heart. There is no cause and effect within humanity, externally forcing someone else to do something without conviction. There is only influence and choice, love and trust, and winning people's hearts to make the right choices.

The Five Domains of Authority

1. Individual
2. Family
3. Covenantal relationships
4. Church
5. Civil government

Looking at history and watching Don and Barb, I've seen how important it is to understand the domains of authority. There are really only two ways historically:

1. The church and the government are basically one domain that tries to control individuals, families, and all decisions in the name of God by whoever has authority, through power or control, hope and fear.

2. The individual is enlightened through a process of discovery within Scripture and the Holy Spirit within the domain of a healthy family. The fruit becomes internal self-government and individual restriction by choice. This gives freedom to be responsible. This forms incredible families that don't have a hierarchy but rather mutually submit in love/trust relationships, and therefore covenants between individuals aren't broken. The church is full of healthy individuals and families, and the government reflects its people, which does transform a nation by serving and protecting them.

Change must always come from the inside out. From both the heart and mind of the individual because of love and trust, not because of force and control. Having watched Don and Barb Johnson throughout the years, I have heard many testimonies of others but also had many experiences of my own with them. One of my favorite stories actually comes from Giacomo Coghi from when he was working in Nicaragua with Don and Barb.

He was working in maintenance with Don at a missionary training campus, and the previous night, someone had turned on the water in the middle of the property and forgotten to turn it off. In the morning, there was no longer water, and Giacomo was frustrated. He said Don went down with him to fix things, and Giacomo said, "Let's go and get a lock so this doesn't happen again!" Don looked over at him and simply responded, 'Why don't we spend some time with these guys and play baseball with them? Maybe we can teach them why we need to be careful with the water. We don't need more locks and rules. We need some more understanding and truth, and truth birthed from deep relationship and healthy conversation, not just rules from a heart of power and control."

I remember that it wasn't even a few days after I had that talk with Giacomo that something happened at the ministry in Costa Rica that he was leading and where I was staying. The next day, I saw signs up all over the kitchen, the bathrooms, and other areas with big letters saying "DON'T" do different things. The kitchen was locked, and no one was allowed in the office. Giacomo sat down and talked to the guys and gave them the same response that Don had given him. They took down all the signs and began the difficult process of winning the hearts of people and the very complicated task of biblical leadership and discipleship.

Just recently, something similar happened in our ministry here in Mexico, and one of our young leaders told me that she was going to add locks and that people no longer had permission to do certain things. I smiled and told her that, instead, she should go and have a talk with everyone, and she needed to win their hearts. I also told her that by being a more responsible leader, she would teach them by serving even when it wasn't her responsibility. "If you want to be great, serve!" I'm amazed at how often I find myself using those words, remembering Don and Barb and how to serve. "Win his/her heart, understand his/her story, develop trust, use your influence and not control. Set the example. Be willing to suffer for others, be patient, show self-control. First give up your own rights. Don't take away the rights of others."

Don and Barb have dedicated their lives to serve and work in a place where there was no benefit to be responsible and that by being a victim, you would actually gain more. They didn't get mad at the kids that stole things and broke things. They didn't hate the people that were mean to them, but they just began to serve in great love and humility. They gave their lives to people that just needed love and trust, a hug and a smile, safety and protection. Everything that I needed when I was three was exactly what these young leaders needed in Nicaragua. All around the world. it's the same thing: less excuses, emotional reactions, control and power, and more love, right relationship, teaching of truth, and a model of leadership that takes away excuses through example, not authority.

They have taught me the importance to study history and culture, to understand economics and business, to dig deeply into education and the family, and how to understand the differences between reformation, awakening, and revival. Just like many before them who had a great influence of Francis Schaefer, they have given that same passion to me.

1. Either man will be responsible and accountable to God in all things because Truth is Absolute, and man is able to respond in relationship, both thought and action: *choosing to be responsible.*
2. Man will be oppressed by his fellow man in his own ignorance and insecurities, giving over responsibility to someone else and expecting the government and church to do things that they never should do, becoming a victim that looks to everyone else and every other institution to fix things: *choosing to be a victim, dependent on someone or something else.*

In the words of Hugo Grotius, who was a Dutch lawyer, theologian, and writer who lived from 1583 to 1645,

> He knows not how to rule a kingdom that cannot manage a province; nor can he wield a province that cannot order a city; nor he order a city that knows not how to regulate a village; nor he a village that cannot guide a family; nor can that man govern well a family that knows not how to govern himself; neither can any govern himself unless his reason be lord, will and appetite her vassals; nor can reason rule unless herself be ruled by God, and be obedient to Him.

Or in the words of Robert Winthrop from MA Bible Society in 1849,

> All societies of men must be governed in some way or other. The less they may have of stringent State Government, the more they have of individual self-government. The less they rely on public law or physical force, the more they rely on private moral restraint. Men, in a word, must necessarily be controlled, either by a power within them, or by a power without them; either by the Word of God, or by the strong arm of man; either by the Bible or the bayonet.

Either we are teaching responsibility and accountability through love and service, giving understanding and ownership of the future to others accountable to God, or we are taking away their freedoms and doing things for them that will only bring chaos and failure in the future. We are not called to be God for others. We are not called to be the head of anyone else but rather shoulders that carry the burden and weight. There is no place within the domain of church to overstep the domain of family, the individual, and covenantal relationships. The church is not within the domain of civil government or the family and must be very careful to not try to take control of individuals.

Don and Barb used to talk about what they lived upon arriving in Nicaragua many years ago. They would tell me stories about how there was complete disorder, no cleanliness, and no concept of responsibility within an entire country. Rather than creating rules, complaining, judging, or looking down upon the locals, they discovered what the kids loved in Nicaragua and began to build relationships. The kids loved baseball, so baseball became the doorway to the heart. One day, Don and Barb bought a bunch of baseballs, gloves, and bats and gave them to each of the kids. They then had the kids write their own names on the ball, bat, and glove. This changed everything. It was now their own private property, and there was initiative to be responsible. There was great teaching on generosity, compassion, and love, but also stewardship. The future of the baseball game depended on the kids, not the government, not the parents, not the church, and not Don and Barb. Through failure, there would be a process of building love and trust, of failing forward, and learning to live as a steward of God's creation from the inside out.

If you want to be great, serve! So often today we are quick to judge and even quicker to control when we feel insecure. In our insecurities, we want to control others; and in our own wounds of identity, we want to rule over others rather than to trust and serve. Terminology of "over" and "under" will always go against kingdom truth of *with* and *together*. Don loves to teach how the priests carried the names of the tribes on their shoulders. The leaders carried the weight and responsibility to serve, but not to be the head and control other humans. God is the Head of every believer. In marriage, women came from the side, not the head to be over man or the feet to be under but from the side to be *equally accountable* to God and equally able to serve as humanity. As humans, we are called to rule over creation but never over each other. We are all image bearers of God, and therefore there is no space for power and control to be used over other humans. We can administer things, but we work together with other people.

I have often heard, even in my own team, "But it's my responsibility," or "But it's *not* my responsibility," Or "I'm responsible for them," "It's my department," "I'm the leader of this," or "They are my immediate leader," "It's my school [or my ministry, my vision, etc.]" This is all vocabulary found within the domain of government or business models of today, but not in the Bible for the church or individuals. There is no "over" and "under" but rather *together* and *with*. The principles of conscience appeals to the stronger believer to change for love, not to use "freedom" for offense in power and control. We serve at our own cost and actually gain nothing. We love and serve out of fullness, not for a reward. Service is the goal, not the means to a way to control a multitude or for personal gain. It's for His glory, not our own!

Leaders all over the world teach about these ideas, and I'm sure that Don and Barb have failed many times within their own insecurities or in difficult moments; but for over sixteen years, Don and Barb have modeled this type of leadership far beyond just their words for me. They have fruit all over the world that speak about their leadership. In one of the most difficult moments of my life, Don and Barb were there to walk with my wife and me. They were there to counsel us and encourage us. Don would often tell me, "Always be sure you aren't an Absalom even if your leader is a Saul, and be sure that you don't become a Saul even when you encounter an Absalom in your team." As the cofounder of YWAM Global, Darlene Cunningham says, "You must always be in a posture to never be offended because no one intentionally offends."

I feel like daily, weekly, and monthly this becomes my challenge, not who am I leading but who is walking with me? I can't lead if I I'm alone and I will always be alone if I think I am the head, authority, or truth for someone else. I am accountable to people, not for them. I walk with them, not away from them. I need to continually take time to build the relationship, to listen, to lean forward when others step away, to extend my hand when others turn their backs, and to just serve because it's for God's glory. I can't change anyone else, but I definitely can take away their excuses toward me. I can show them love with my actions, and I can be responsible when no one else wants to. The truth will always be what's seen in the aftermath, not in the vision. The biggest teaching I can give someone else in this stage of my life with three kids, my wife, and a pioneering ministry is to take my time to serve and be responsible where someone else wasn't and hasn't—to do this without condemnation or judgment even when I've seen time and again how the person has not completed their responsibility or been faithful. Many times, the response is the same: the individual quickly comes, apologizes, and tries to get me to stop. They feel bad because they love me and know how hard it is for me to invest in someone else's task with my limited time, not because I was mad at them.

Love through service will do more than any revolution in anarchy or tyranny. We need to push down the responsibility from a posture of love and service in every detail of life with deep trust. The *what* can't change; but with each new person, with every new generation, and within every new season of life, the *how* will look very different. Love and trust isn't how I want someone to receive it, but it really does depend upon how they interpret it. The truth of leadership many times will be within the eye of the interpreter around the leader and not the leader himself. Leadership and being alone go completely against each other. Leadership implies being surrounded by other people and walking in humility with teams. You can't be a good team leader if no one wants to be on your team and be close to you.

The more we have learned and begun to understand a biblical model of servant leadership, the more we have had to look at our values and practices. Just a few years ago, our mission signed a covenant called the Singapore Covenant. The heart of this had to do with a model of Christian leadership that had been contaminated by business and governmental models. We shifted away from titles of *director, national director*, and *regional director*, which were all terminology within the singular since and began to use more biblical terminology of eldership and teams within a plural understanding. The heart of this document was the three Cs: *circles, cylinders, and cycles*. Circles of leadership, cylinders of common passions, and cycles of rotating leaders.

As of December 2018, we were super excited to see our first functioning eldership circle of six people falling into place and see the fruit here in Morelia, Mexico. The heart is to have a team style leadership as biblical leadership should be more and more plural and less and less singular. Christ is the head, but even He lives in a team (Father, Son, Holy Spirit, and body of Christ), and we build teams within the body. Our team was made up of three guys and three girls representing three languages and five different countries, and our meetings were not in English, even though both my wife and I speak English as our first language. This has really helped bring stability into our ministry.

In 2019, we had to adjust our teams a bit, and now we currently have an eldership circle of six people and a leadership circle of four more. Within the two teams, we have six different cultures and four different languages. They are nine very strong leaders working with me who can keep me accountable as a leader, and we always make better decisions together. They have no fear to be open and honest with me or to challenge me, nor do I with them. Some of the requirements to be on this team are solid Christian character, a healthy capacity for leadership, and good chemistry. I can't work with a leadership team that won't be open and honest with me and with whom I can't fully be who I am while being open and honest with them. The idea is to always expand out and push down more responsibility as opposed to try to climb up a ladder of authority and hide alone. It's been having great models of other leaders who has helped us to begin to walk into this type of stability within our own ministry, which in turn attracts other strong leaders but also allows us to be more successful.

Throughout the years, I've had to really battle the tendency to want to control, be "final authority" for others, or to be an independent. The kingdom of God really is *upside down*, and it takes great effort to not do what is normal and natural in the flesh as a leader, especially within my own insecurities. A couple of years ago, I was invited to join a group called the Counsel of Michoacán, which is a group of key pastors from our state representing each denomination and key ministry. These men and women are quick to listen, slow to react, and slow to speak. They carry a lot of wisdom and are all almost twice as old as me. They always give me a place to speak, and they always take my ideas into account even if they are different. They have taught me more about living leadership in just a couple of years. It was with these individuals that I was able to go to Congress in Mexico and be a part of putting a Bible in the hands of every new member of Congress. They've inspired me greatly, and often I wonder how my own team sees me compared to how I see these incredible men and women, challenging all that I do.

In both our recent staff retreat in 2019, and then on my thirty-fourth birthday just a few weeks ago in May, I was humbled more than I have been in a long time. All leaders have insecurities, and we are very aware of our own failures and weaknesses (usually). A friend of mine told me years ago, "If you want to be affirmed and encouraged, then don't be a leader. Leaders need to encourage and affirm everyone else, but everyone will judge and criticize a leader. You must have a lot of confidence from God's affirmation in what you do to be a leader and learn to have really thick skin." This is very true and has been my experience and journey through the last sixteen years. In my own insecurities, it is often easy to doubt or to question my own leadership. As each of our staff opened their hearts, however, they affirmed and encouraged me, some even through tears. I was reminded that I might not have made it to my ultimate capacity and calling in leadership, but I'm far beyond where I was sixteen years ago, ten years ago, five years ago, or even two years ago. I'm both proud and greatly humbled to look at my team, the people that have surrounded my wife and I, and chosen to follow us in one way or another. For God's glory, I think I'm getting closer to becoming the depth of what would most glorify Him and leave a mark on others in the same way that Jesus did, that Paul did, that so many throughout history have done, and the same way that Don and Barb have done for me.

As I looked at the different young men and women surrounding me at our staff retreat, I began to think of their stories. We've married two of the couples and will be marrying two more in this next year. We've baptized a handful of them, evangelized some of them, and I began to remember their stories one by one. So many incredible stories that show how incredible God really is. One in particular that we talk about a lot is Pablo from Honduras. He has grown into a dear friend and young leader that I have learned to trust. I have had to ask him to leave our ministry twice, and throughout the years, I have had many difficult talks with him when he was at the lowest moments of his life. He has come and gone, and he said that outside of myself, he had no one to reach out to. We have cried together, prayed together, and just tried to figure out how he could make a step forward and no longer be alone. He is one of the most talented men that I have met, and despite coming to Mexico illegally many years ago on the train, he has figured out how to do things right and be quite successful as an actor and artist.

One day, however, a couple of years ago, he began to flee from God, to flee from our ministry, and to flee from his relationship with me. He had flown across the country to Cancun rather than coming to our staff retreat, and after a really bad day and night, he had been chased by the police, and his friend had almost been beaten to death. The next day, to try to get out of his own mind, he decided to go on a run until he was exhausted. At that same moment, I was in Cancun for a conference and had been meditating on how it was probably good that Pablo had left and that it was now easier for me. At that exact moment, he stopped the next bus and paid the driver. To his surprise, and my own, he turned to sit down, and I was riding on that exact bus. He began to laugh and said that he felt like Jonah, and I was his whale from which he couldn't escape.

He spent the day with me but decided to go back that night and continue partying with his friends. I didn't hear from him again, and after my conference, I moved to a new location in the city where I was helping to lead a leadership conference for discipleship. I was so tired of being with people and traveling that I decided to get a hotel room to renew some of my energy. At 10:00 p.m., my phone died, and so did my charger, so I went for a walk on the streets in Cancun to buy a new charger. As I came out of the store, there was a group of young men drinking and being pretty crazy walking right toward me. All I could do was laugh as I saw a huge afro in a bright-pink shirt. Pablo saw me, and I saw him. I could tell he wanted to run away, but there was nothing he could do, and so he walked up to me and introduced his drunk friends to me and me to them as his Christian leader. I gave him a big hug, whispered something in his ear, and I walked back to my hotel room. I messaged him a bit later that night and didn't hear from him for a couple of months. Sure enough, though, he came back home with us. When he had nowhere to go and no one to trust, he came back with great humility to us. He had closed doors all over the world, but for some reason, he knew that he could come back to our family, to our ministry, and to our leaders.

It's been a tough last year for Pablo, but he's done it well, and I'm so proud of him. He jokes a lot with others about his two encounters with me in Cancun and how God is so personal; that there is no way to flee from His presence—or mine, he always adds. Good leaders are able to do that, to actually bring the living presence of God in a tangible way to others that need to experience it. Don and Barb Johnson have definitely done that for me. With nothing to gain, they have continued to love and invest. As I look at Pablo and many of our guys, I'm very grateful, even in my weaknesses, that I've been able to multiply this same servant leadership to others. I'm seeing them now, doing it for others, and I'm so privileged to have so many incredible men and women in my life. May His story continue to be more and more visible within my story and those that surround me!

Reflection

1. Define your concept of leadership and service.
2. Who carries the biggest burden to need to change, others or you?
3. On the day that we give account to God, will you give account for what others did and believed first, or for what you did and believed and how that affected others?
4. Do you reflect a cause-and-effect external government or influence and choose internal government in difficult moments while working with others?
5. Do you have a healthy model of leadership, marriage, and family that reflect love/trust relationships to follow and be inspired by? Why do you respect these people, and in what ways can you apply those principles to your own life?
6. Is it easier for you to be a victim or to be responsible before accusation and failure? Why?
7. Are other people following you and why?
8. What does the fruit of the character of the people following you say about you as a leader? Who is being glorified, you or God?
9. In your struggles as a leader, do you tend to be more like Saul or Absalom?

Meditation

There was a difficult season in the history of our global mission that I serve with. We really are in almost every country on earth, every language on earth, most major cities, and our greatest strength seems to also be our greatest weakness. We give a lot of freedom to love, to serve, and to be responsible before God and man. This freedom brought forth in order by the Spirit working with the truth that we have discovered is incredible. However, this same freedom can turn into tyranny or anarchy if there is no order birthed out of the truth guided by the Spirit. In these moments, people get hurt, and the truth becomes distorted due to a bad testimony.

During this season, a few leaders moving out of their insecurities, as opposed to the order that aligns with truth guided by the Spirit, developed into some communities and ministries with a very governmental and business way of doing things. There were some extreme over/under concepts of leading others. There was actually a little book written that had this phrase, "You must please man first [human leadership] in order to please God." This point was to say that you follow your leaders no matter what because they will be held accountable to God. Even if they are wrong, you just submit and follow. This is wrong!

Our founding leader of YWAM made this comment: "There are two ways to vote: with your mouth and with your feet. If you have been honest with your mouth with your leaders from a place of love and humility and nothing changes, then you vote with your feet and walk away. Don't tell anyone else and don't take anyone with you. Simply walk forward in obedience to God." I've thought of this advice throughout the years in difficult moments. Have I first shared with my heart and mouth in love? If so, what keeps me from obeying and following God? I hope that I can give that same freedom to those that choose to walk with me in the future in difficult moments, and I'm sure we will have them, we have had them, and there will be many more.

As a servant-leader, we are accountable to God and accountable to anyone that interacts with us. They become our living letters to the world, so we had better be a living letter of Jesus, the Truth of the Bible, and His Holy Spirit for those that are surrounding us. Failure is normal, and we will all do it. But how we respond toward others, how we humble ourselves and repent, or ask for forgiveness will make the difference. Either we will isolate ourselves and draw away in pride, or we will draw close to others with openness and humility. Either we will be a bad leader or a good leader, pointing people closer to God or pushing people further away. We choose!

The Bible and Leadership

- "When a leader sins unintentionally and does any one of all the things which the Lord his God has commanded not be done, and he becomes guilty" (Leviticus 4:22).
- "Send out for yourself men so that they may spy out the land of Canaan, which I am going to give to the sons of Israel; you shall send a man from each of their fathers' tribes, everyone a leader among them" (Numbers 13:2).
- "These are the journeys of the sons of Israel, by which they came out from the land of Egypt by their armies under the leadership of Moses and Aaron" (Numbers 33:1).
- "So Moses the servant of the Lord died there in the land of Moab, according to the word of the Lord!" (Deuteronomy 34:5).
- "Just as the Lord had commanded Moses His servant, so Moses commanded Joshua, and so Joshua did; he left nothing undone of all that the Lord had commanded Moses" (Joshua 11:15).
- "Now, therefore, thus shall you say to My servant David, 'Thus says the Lord of hosts, "I took you from the pasture, from following the sheep, to be leader over My people. I have been with you wherever you have gone, and have cut off all your enemies from before you; and I will make you a name like the name of the great ones who are in the earth'" (1 Chronicles 17:7–8).

- "A servant who acts wisely will rule over a son who acts shamefully" (Proverbs 17:2).
- "A leader who is a great oppressor lacks understanding" (Proverbs 28:16).
- "Do not be called leaders; for One is your Leader, that is, Christ. But the greatest among you shall be your servant. Whoever exalts himself shall be humbled; and whoever humbles himself shall be exalted" (Matthew 23:10–11).
- "And He said to them, 'The kings of the Gentiles lord it over them; and those who have authority over them are called "Benefactors." But it is not this way with you, but the one who is the greatest among you must become like the youngest, and the leader like the servant. For who is greater, the one who reclines at the table or the one who serves? Is it not the one who reclines at the table? But I am among you as the one who serves'" (Luke 22:25–27).
- "He who loves his life loses it, and he who hates his life in this world will keep it to life eternal. If anyone serve Me, he must follow Me; and where I am will be also; if anyone serve Me, the Father will honor him" (John 12:25–26).
- "Obey your leaders and submit to them, for they keep watch over your souls as those who will give an account. Let them do this with joy and not with grief, for this would be unprofitable for you. Pray for us, for we are sure that we have a good conscience, desiring to conduct ourselves honorably in all things" (Hebrews 13:17–18).

CHAPTER 14

Character

Inspired by my best friend and wife, Katie Holmberg, from the USA

> *Character*—the mark that is left behind in the world, seen by others, from the life of an individual based on his or her external actions in continuity or faithfulness. Christian character is usually connecting internal moral excellence and firmness to the external faithfulness of actions. Reputation, position, and capacity are all in accord with an individual's normal qualities and traits. Character is often connected to the individual's disposition, temperaments, attributes, internal properties, and personality.

Special Introduction

As I reflect on my journey with the Lord, my greatest desire is to be more like Jesus. Growing up, I was not raised in a Christian house. We did not go to church except when we would visit the grandparents. We did not pray before meals or give thanks to God together really for anything, and my understanding of Jesus and God was very limited. At sixteen, when I came to really understand and had a real encounter with the Lord, I did not decide to follow and begin a journey of getting to know Him deeper out of fear of hell, but I was drawn to the Person of Jesus: His heart, His compassion, His unfailing love, His mercy, His justice, and His patience. As I read through the Bible, cover to cover, in three months, I began to see who this man was, and I wanted to be transformed into being more like Him for others.

When I think of Christian character and being like Jesus, I am convinced it is for others. Yes, it is for my well-being, but to be like Jesus is to look outward at others and live for their well-being as well.

I pray that as you discover more of Him, you will become more like Him for the world around you and that your life would bring healing, love, justice, and mercy into the lives of others. I pray that His truth will transform all you are and all you will become.

Katie Holmberg
Missionary

* * * * *

An excellent wife who can find her? For her worth
is far above jewels and treasures.
—Proverbs 31:10

One of the habits I formed on my first trip to Mexico in 2004, which I continue to practice to this day, is reading a proverb every morning. Proverbs is a book of wisdom, and wisdom is applied knowledge in the fear of the Lord. There are thirty-one proverbs in total. I was given advice to read the proverb of the day every day so that every month for the rest of my life, I could read the book of Proverbs and grow in wisdom. This exercise has helped me learn what it means to be either a fool or wise, to walk in truth or lies, and to process through implications of my actions before making any choices. I've missed many days throughout the last sixteen years, but I have tried my best to read a proverb a day, and it's totally transformed my life.

There was a season in particular, in 2006, when I was living in Jamaica, and I tried my best to apply Proverbs to my life every day. I decided to study the power of the tongue, the fool and the wise. I made a conscience effort for three months to just listen and bite my tongue as much as possible. It was amazing how waiting and listening, not speaking, and giving space for others changed not only my life but their life as well. There are so many testimonies from those ninety days and what the book of Proverbs did in my life. The most ironic testimony occurred on my graduation day from my Community Development School. A young lady came up to me and said that I was so wise, and she could just tell by watching me; and even though I didn't speak much, I must carry a lot of wisdom. If you know me at all, you know this is the opposite of my personality! However, it does say in Proverbs, "Even the fool is wise if he doesn't speak." In my early years of ministry, it became these little things that really began to transform my life.

Being married now and having a greater depth of study, I look at every aspect of the Bible and leadership differently. Proverbs has completely new meanings as I further understand the historical background, cultural reality, and general context. The proverb that has maybe most changed through the years is Proverbs 31. For years, I read it through the understanding that it was about the "virtuous wife" of a good Jew serving God. This change in my understanding came primarily for two reasons: one being that it's one of the only proverbs written by a non-Jew from a pagan nation, and two, because it's not about a wife but actually the role that a wise and virtuous queen played in preparing her son to be a wise king. Proverbs 31 is about the wise queen who prepared her son in all ways to be a wise king through educating and imparting how to fully live.

From the time I was a child, my mother was the one that would pray with me every night. She was the one that would pray with me about my future wife from as long as I can remember. She was the one that shared her dreams for me in the future, what it would be like to be a good husband and father, and asked me the profound and personal questions about life. She talked about all the possibilities of my future, practiced my numbers with me at the table, helped me with my science projects and my letters as I learned to write, and processed with me how I felt after a victory or loss in a sports game. For so many reasons that could never be fully understood in a book,

I have become the man I am today thanks to my mom, thanks to her long-suffering, protection, and faithfulness to love in spite of past or future circumstances. I've been on my own for almost sixteen years now, but she still has guided much of what I know about budgeting and finances, credit and debt, insurance and legal requirements, and so much more. Just like Proverbs 31, if I can become wise today in my life or in my future as a leader, then a good sum is owed to wisdom imparted by my mother.

From the time that I had my first crush to when I was a bit older and had some more serious dating relationships, I was always afraid of getting married and having kids. I felt like I was too selfish to be with the same person every day of my life. How could I love the same person for the rest of my life? I was extremely afraid to have kids and felt superselfish. How could I love a baby and sacrifice my sleep? How could I ever be a father and fully impart love when it's often very difficult? I dealt with those questions a lot in relationships, and a part of it is due to my way of processing information. I am quick in my mind and often slower in my heart. Relationships require a lot of empathy, quality time, commitment, communication, and suffering. Thanks to my mom and sister, I learned some of these skills very naturally. When it came to the thought of having a wife and kids, I wasn't convinced that I could ever do it and give all that is required to do it well.

If you know the story of Katie and me, then you know that the little bit of what is found in this book is just the tip of the iceberg regarding the depth of our relationship and crazy history. How do you share the reality of seventeen years in a relationship in just a few paragraphs? I turned thirty-four on May 22, 2019, and from that moment, I've known Katie, my wife and mother to our three children, since I was eighteen years old in high school. I remember the first time that I saw her, this beautiful little mulatto girl, beautiful dark skin with bright-green eyes and full of attitude. She didn't appear to have a care in the world, and to this day, I'm still baffled about what took place to get someone like her to be with someone like me. God was faithful! In my entire life, I had never spent time with someone younger than me, but from the first moment that I saw her, I wanted to meet her. I'm so thankful that Katie's single mother took a risk to allow me to draw close to their family, despite what some of the other parents might have said or thought about me.

A lot of people had opinions about me at eighteen, including many parents, and they weren't all good. Katie, on the other hand, was adorable. Everyone loved her. At that time, she was the beautiful mulatto girl, she and her sister being raised by their young white mom in a town that doesn't have a lot of cultural diversity. As we began to have a more formal dating relationship, I had many open and honest talks with my family and extended family about Katie, yet I never imagined we would be where we are today. I was doing my best to honor her family and respect them while also getting to know her, but she was a fireball that kept me very interested in trying to understand her and always kept me on my toes. To this day, it hasn't changed.

We have gone through our tough times, and in multiple seasons, I was convinced that there was no way that we would stay together or get back together after we broke up multiple times. We actually dated for over seven years, with me living in Mexico and her living in the United States. I would see her once or twice a year, and outside of that, it was MySpace, AOL, Messenger, or letters sent through snail mail. Later our communication turned into text messaging and eventually Skype. I don't know how we made it, but she finished college, and she taught me more than she will ever know throughout those seven years. She became one of my greatest inspirations, the one who would most encourage me to just believe and have faith, to trust and dream, and to tear down the barriers. Those were seven of the hardest years of my life, but they were also seven unforgettable years.

One of my biggest fears was a few years into our relationship when I had been convicted by God to never kiss another woman that wasn't my wife. I don't believe kissing is bad or sinful, yet I simply felt that given my past, I needed to guard that area for my future now. I wrote a covenant that several leaders and friends signed, and my end goal was to have her sign it. I was superworried. I believed that I would lose her, but God greatly convicted me that if obeying Him meant losing her, then she definitely wasn't the right one for me. That night before flying to the United States, I wrote up the covenant, had some friends and leaders sign it, and prepared myself to show her.

God,

Through all that has happened in my life, my family, friends, or external circumstances, You have never failed to be faithful with me. I've grown to understand how deep Your love truly is for me and see that my own heart has a desire to live a life of intimacy and love with You. I commit myself to please You and daily live a life that gratifies You, reflecting the love that is within me for You. I want to have a devotion of all that I have daily to You and put nothing before You. Aside from all that I have and ever will have with You, my Father, I don't want to rob anything from You. I choose to give You my right of love, God. I believe that You are calling me to walk alongside an amazing woman one day to serve You in all that we do, but I commit and surrender that right of marriage to You in Your perfect wisdom. I don't want to just do my will but truly please You! For anyone to come to me, they must first come through You, my God.

For any woman to break through this, Lord, I commit that I will go through the judgment of my parents and sister in Your never-ending love and wisdom. If and when someone passes into my heart through You, God, *I commit my body as Your temple alone until my new covenant with You.* Until the day my *new testimony is made before both You and the world*, I commit my body to You alone, my hands to serve You, my feet to follow You, my heart to abide in You, my eyes to follow You, and my tongue to worship You. As I walk before You, I commit to walk hand in hand with whomever You put in my life but still focus my eyes on You, my God! *My mouth I seal* to You, my Father, until I open it to speak my vow to the world before You. *Eye upon eye* will I seek Your love and await for Your glory to shine beyond what I may see within view of the world. For You are my perfect love, my Lord. I will not sway to the right or the left but will walk in the light of the path You have set before me, God—alone or in company. But I will follow You alone. And when *You unite the path* of love, God, I will keep my eyes upon You and continue straight to where Your light may lead. Whether I come into Your heavenly kingdom or You return first to claim me, God, my commitment will always be You above all!

This covenant I make with you, Father, this 14th day of April 2007. I commit to *fulfill without cease* every and all obligations of my love unto You until the day my vow is made before You and the world for a *new covenant*, giving my gift of love to the *woman worthy of ALL* of me.

Sealed with my love, much more than an emotion but commitment of every breath within me, Daddy!

Daniel N. Holmberg III

I was convinced that by showing this to Katie, I would lose her, and it would be the end of our relationship. To my amazement, she told me she had already made a special covenant to God, a covenant to not kiss another man until her wedding day, and she didn't know how to tell me because for years that wasn't our reality. What I most thought would make me lose her wound up being one of the things that kept us together. To my shame but to her credit, she was being more radical than me, more obedient to God, and challenging everything within me. We have many other stories about key moments like this, but that is not the point of this chapter, and neither are relationships or biblical courtship. But because of who Katie chose to be and live, on my wedding day, I tore this covenant and made a new one to my wife!

In August of 2010, I went to Colorado with another fear: either we were going to finish our relationship, or we were going to get engaged. She had just finished college, and we had some serious talks to do. My heart was to take a day to bless her and to do a special date with God and her. I had already talked to her mom and stepdad, and they had given me their blessing, and I had spoken to her biological father on the phone, and he had also given me his blessing.

I woke up early, nervous, and with a special diamond in my pocket, I picked her up, and we went out to breakfast. We then went to a park to read our Bibles and had a short devotional together, followed by a day trip to the zoo, which has been one of our favorite things to do since we were kids. She loves the elephants, and I love the tigers and reptiles. After the zoo, we had lunch, and I took her up to the mountains to a special lake. I made a special plan to take her out on a canoe and to give her a few of the poems I wrote about her. I gave her a woman's Bible I highlighted and where I had written special notes. I wrote blessings and encouragements for her as if they were from a husband and God. At the end, we just shared our dreams together.

After, I took her to my mom's house, where I cooked what used to be her favorite meal, fettuccini alfredo with white wine. I left many little notes on the table, which she still loves to receive to this day. After dinner, I washed her feet and prayed for her and asked her to marry me, and she said yes! That day shows just how incredible and special this woman is for me. Katie has been a dream come true and many times the greatest stability of my life. On our wedding day, I broke my old covenant. We made a new one together, and I made a new one with God.

These were our wedding vows:

Daniel

> I, Daniel Noble Holmberg III, have saved my heart for you and you alone. I have no way but forward to go with you, and I vow to love you not just with an emotion but a daily exercise of my will to seek first God and then your highest well-being before my own; to serve you and love you; to fulfill your highest calling, sharpen your strengths, support your weaknesses; and to acknowledge that Christ is our success by His Holy Spirit. You are the greatest treasure that I could ever be trusted with, and I vow to serve you and love you, above and before all others—friends or family, ministry, or anything else this world has to offer. I take my dreams and desires, plans and visions, and lay them at the cross. I vow from this day forward to be your best friend, supporter, lover, and godly leader as a husband, in sickness and in health, good times and bad, unto death do us part, wherever and whenever that may be. I love you and you alone, baby! May God use us to daily heal each other and filter His perfect love and patience so the world may know, by seeing our selfless, enduring love, that He is Lord!

> I have been praying for you since I was five years old:
> You are the greatest answer to prayer I have ever had.
> You are not mine but God's.

> I commit my eyes to affirm you and watch over you.
> I commit my ears to listen and to support you in patience.

I commit my mouth to bless you, confront you, and build you up daily.

I commit my hands to hold you, to love you, and to protect you.

I commit my feet to lead you and to point you to God daily, to help carry your burdens, and to walk by your side daily as a best friend.

You are my best friend.

Today I lay down everything, and with empty hands together with you, I take up this new life as *one* together with you, with love, humility, and service. I am now yours and trust the rest of my life to your heart, soul, and spirit, together with God.

This is my commitment of love!

Katie

I praise God for you. I know He has placed us in each other's lives to help us grow in His love. As I look back and think of our pasts so far together, you have already helped me. You are an amazing man of God and wonderful example of God's love.

Daniel, you have inspired, encouraged, challenged, and loved me in such a unique and fun way. I know I am not always expressive, but I have loved every gift, flower, and letter you have given me. You really do know me and have a genuine way of expressing it, and making me feel so unique and special.

As Paul says, "love never fails."

As we start this new chapter in our lives that our Lord has set before us,

I desire to be not only your helpmate but also your best friend!

I vow to love you and cherish you, seeking nothing but the best for you.

I vow to be by your side, regardless of any obstacles or challenges, and to respect you in all we do, supporting your decisions and trusting your judgments.

Daniel, you are an awesome man of God and have been a man of integrity.

I vow to be faithful to you and will always pray and seek God for you and our love.

You can always count on my support.

In God's support and guidance by His grace, I desire to love you and to spend the rest of our days growing with you and doing "life" together.

I love you, Daniel, and you are my blessing from God. I will spend the rest of my life sharing our joy in the Lord and wanting nothing but to make you happy.

I vow to spend the rest of our lives together, and I say,

"What God has joined together, let no man separate.

I love you!

After breaking my old covenant to God on our wedding day, I wrote a new covenant to God for this new season of life with Katie:

God,

Through the years, You have continued to prove faithful and eager to take my hand daily to guide and lead me. I have seen how Your way is the only way that brings me to the goal. Through many things I haven't understood, through brokenness, hurt, rejection, or even my own selfishness, You have always been faithful. You never cease to be selfless and supporting while wooing me closer to You daily. In obedience and submission to You, I have never lost anything but rather gained the world and the love of my life in my wife. Thank You for protecting my heart, mind, soul, and spirit through this first phase of my life of singleness. I gave You my right of love, and You blessed me with much more than I deserved in a wife and life mate.

Again I come before You looking into the eye of my heart. What seemed like the end was just the beginning, and I can see how I need You more now than ever before. I cannot give what I do not have. I know that You have called me to be the Christ of my marriage, dying daily and reflecting Your unselfish and understanding love daily. You always see the heart and not just the external, but how do I do the same? Created in Your image, I feel, I hurt, I break, I suffer, and I question. I need You to be my strength. Seeing that You have never left me or failed me, I fall on my knees again and proclaim my need for You first.

I commit my hands to hold, care for, and create life in Your image. I commit my mouth to proclaim truth in love. I commit my ears to hear, to listen to the heart, and to find the hidden meaning that my emotions don't want to see in You, in my wife, and then those around me. I commit to listen to Your guidance and Your voice before mine, my wife or family, or the world around me. I acknowledge that my need is in You and You alone. Life flows out of this relationship with You, and I commit to hear from You first. I give you my eyes. Please mold them into the reflection of my soul where people can see Your light and hope. I don't want to be my own. I want to be Yours. Help me to take my desires that I have in my wife and to live them before You daily. I commit to fight for, protect, and guide my time with You first, followed by my wife, and then whomever You call us to work with, serve with, or to invest in. I am Yours! Take me and mold me into the husband, father, friend, leader, and most importantly, the lover of You that You desire.

This is a love beyond any emotion but engulfed in the memories of me in Your presence. A love beyond experience but proven by what You have done and continue to do. This is a love that goes beyond my life through my death into Your resurrection. You are my Lord and First Love.

Daniel N. Holmberg III

This is one of the many poems and notes that I had written about Katie in that previous year and gave her the day I proposed:

Your Eyes

Your eyes: I've dared before to wonder at this beauty,
Looking within and being lost,
The moment my fingers begin to move, I'm frozen and
lose all that controls me,
A maze so deep that I can't begin to say, the only thing I
can do is to look away,
I take the pen and simply give it a toss,

So many questions and thoughts all lurking within,
But then you smile and it's broken,
Who could have given this beauty, every doubt is broken
and all I can do is grin,
This is Katie, no word to describe thee or any way to hide me,
I turn around and dare to stare at this beauty and I freeze
once again,

This is much more than what I can see,
Much deeper and stronger that keeps controlling me,
A reflection of my God with this Body, Soul, and Spirit
Beyond the eyes now I close and can just feel it,
God's beauty can never be hidden, it can never be given, it
can never be forgiven
Through these perfect green eyes once again I feel driven

What could it be to be alone?
Two blind steps and still wondering, looking around, and
having nothing,
But with you I've seen this love that they say can never be
shown,
The Christ within is what your eyes continue to bring,
Don't close your eyes and don't turn away, the more you
hide what is there...
All I can do is stare!

God has placed this perfection that I see,
We both can agree that this is just the reflection of His
intimacy,
This is the place I can see you set free, where we can
fully agree,
Not what's been spoken, but the light in the dark, it's
your eyes
I come back to the beginning and see that you are much
beyond what say just hides,
This is the real you planted in Him,

Not falling or screaming or looking to anyone else,
Just close your eyes and you will see what I see, it is yourself!

Now set yourself free and be all you can be,
Don't blink but agree that you're all I can see,
The beauty within is simply this, it's you, KATIE!
A reflection of Him is your permanent identity…

These are by far some of the most intimate details of my life or Katie's within this book, but Katie is by far the greatest thing that has come into my life, and it's impossible to talk about character, the mark left behind, without seeing a bit of her mark first in my life. I never imagined when I was a young child praying with my mom what faithfulness God would manifest in my life. When I think of Katie, I think of so many things, but Proverbs 31 and 2 Peter 1 are two passages that always come to mind. Just as my mother did, she now prays with two young men to be princes within the nations and with a young girl to be a princess. She is equipping them in all ways, and they are far beyond any child that I interact with in many areas. She is also the highlight of what I understand to be character and virtue. She is what she is, without shame or fear of what others will say or think. She leaves that same mark with anyone she meets, anywhere she goes, in all that she does.

I have traveled throughout different parts of the world, but she is the one that holds everything together. She unites the ministry; she brings His wisdom and creativity into all that we do. Many people think of our ministry and think of me, but the reality is that day to day, a lot of the vision and life all come more from her than myself. Her dreams often seem bigger than mine, but her faithfulness and desire to fight for our family gives me the ability to believe there's still more, and we are just beginning. Most people meet her and don't know how to react and feel superintimidated by this natural confidence and evident mark left by just one look, reaction, or word.

Most people change when they meet people and try to please them, but Katie never has and probably never will. She is who she is. She is stable and real with nothing to prove, and it inspires me every day to become all that God desires from me. When I give up on myself, she restores my hope, and I can take another step forward. Most people say the same thing, "Katie, when I first met you, I was either afraid or thought you were superintimidating. Now I like you a lot more than Daniel. You are fun and loving, faithful and sweet, and I was just really intimidated by how sincere and quiet you were."

Too many people in the world seek knowledge and truth before virtue and character. Moral excellence or applied understanding is where character and transformation are found. Katie carries everything that we see in other chapters throughout this book and so much more. It would be wrong for anyone to see me and not see her. Her conviction, stability, belief, and dreams have held us together and on track so many times. So many times through the Scripture, God will speak to me, but then I will see it in her actions. We get in a fight or big misunderstanding. She might cry or yell, but then she has her Bible out on the bed, her notebooks out, and she's looking to apply anything that God speaks to her with great humility. She's educated, a natural learner, equipped in business, administration and finances, grammar and language, leadership, and so much more, but knowledge comes after faith and virtue for her, and especially fear of the Lord.

This past year, we had to deal with some major relational challenges in leadership, and in an emotional moment, myself and other leaders were ready to make a drastic choice. She stood up, with tears in her eyes, and said, "I'm too hurt and sad right now to make any decisions. All of us are. I need time to process and to seek God. We can't decide anything right now!" Her character and wisdom brought us to make the right choices with the right people in the right timing, and we saved relationships, leaders, and most importantly, fell in the fear of the Lord. The same emotional moment for all of us, but she took a step back and drew us all closer to God.

We are in a season of life where I'm exhausted many times and feel like I can never catch up on energy and sleep. She sleeps less than me, nurses our newborn day and night, wakes up throughout the night, and appears to have more energy than I do on any given day. She is more patient and encouraging with our kids than I ever could dream of being. I can come home exhausted on our date night, and she has been sick all day and working with the baby (or possibly, all three of them), and I would consider doing nothing, but she already has a babysitter. I might wake up on a Saturday and want to do nothing, and she has the kids running around excited because we are going to the park or the zoo. We go camping, or they want to go on a bike ride—not because she is superwoman or has more energy (even though in my eyes she is superwoman), but every day she counts the cost of being a leader who is also married with kids, married to me, and having our three kids and measures it with our future and God. It's worth it for her. She gives me the strength and conviction every day, and I wish I could write her a book every day to remind her how much I need her in my life and how important she is to me. For me, she defines everything that I know about character in 2 Peter 1. She exemplifies Proverbs 31 with our kids. Every time I compare what I do for my family to what another mother or wife does with theirs, I am without excuses.

For years, this struggle of virtue and character has been a struggle for me. Character comes from proven hope in suffering and consistency. We all want hope, but none of us want to suffer. We all want to claim faith, but few want to walk 24-7 in a posture of clean conscience in virtue. We all want someone else to change, but few are willing to live that change even when we have great excuses. Katie Holmberg takes away all of my excuses, and I desire that in the same way that I see her and admire her, love her and value her, one day God will look at me and say in the wedding of the Lamb, "Wow, you have been a faithful bride, my good and faithful servant. I love you, and I'm proud of you."

As a ministry, we spent a season doing what I started doing myself many years ago: reading the proverb of the day together to begin each day and then sharing and praying together. We did this for almost five months straight. One of our staff said, "Daniel's going to make us read proverbs until we choose to stop living as fools and finally begin to live in wisdom!" He said it as a joke, but now all of our staff and students take some time to just read a proverb and pray, asking the question, "What is my character? Am I living a virtuous life? Am I a fool or the wise man/woman?" Don't be stupid! I've tried to multiply this task all over the world when I travel and teach.

A young man had heard me teach on this in the past and wound up living with my family and me for over a year in Mazatlán, Mexico. One day while walking to work, I heard him run up behind me, laughing. He could hear me listening to the audio Bible, and I didn't know it, but he had been following me each day. He said, "You really do listen to or read a proverb a day." Years later, this young man now does the same thing and has multiplied it to others. He is a man of virtue, a man of character, and he had his first kiss with his bride the day we married them because both he and his wife decided that character and the fear of the Lord must come first. Both Nayeli and Jose Luis have become another mark of Christian character and virtue for a broken world without stability.

As I've had more and more opportunities to meet incredible Christian leaders from all over the world, I've realized more and more how their charisma, ministries, vision, or gifting no longer impress me very much. We don't really do anything to get capacity and charisma. Gifts are by grace and don't speak at all about someone's character or morality, and good visions come from God Himself, so again it doesn't really speak about the quality of a leader. More and more, I want to know the man or woman behind the public light. I want to know what the kids have to say about mom or dad's consistency and faithfulness. I desire to sit with the spouse and hear about the reality of self-control and good communication. I want to hear from the ones that know everything hidden in the darkness, shame, weaknesses, fears, and suffering. In this light, I can see what is truth about this leader, the real depths of self-control, of being quick to listen and slow to speak, reflecting the character of God in being slow to anger, quick to forgive, and quick to extend mercy.

I want to hear the kids share about how they see mom or dad reading the Bible, doing devotionals, praying and fasting with an understanding of why. I want to hear the spouse share about the character of the other in moments of tension, suffering, doubt, and anger because it is in this place of raw and honest reality that I can hear about the character of the leader. As we teach in one of the

Bible schools we have helped pioneer in Mexico and lead in three different locations, the Bible School for the Nations, "The character of the messenger must be consistent with the message being carried." Character is the one thing that is real in the eyes of others. When I die, I can't give an apology for what I lived, said, and did. The mark I leave behind will just be what others perceived, heard, and saw of my real character.

This is why Katie is the only person that I could really use to write about character. I know her strengths and weaknesses, her failures and successes, but she has never given up. The founders of the Global Missions Movement that I am privileged to be a part of say two things: "Self-control is the number one quality of a leader," and "A YWAMer is someone who loves God, listens to Him and obeys Him in a team, and never ever gives up." The dream they have for our Global Missions Movement, in essence, is a group of Christians that have good character—and because God is faithful, so are we!

Reflection

1. What impacts you most about this chapter and why?
2. How do you define character and virtue?
3. Does your character reflect your heart motives? If not, what can you do to become more faithful as an individual created in the image and likeness of God?
4. If you aren't yet married, what needs to take place to have this type of faithful relationship with your future spouse? If you are married, is this the type of virtue and character that you are seeing? How can you grow in this area?
5. Create a general daily, weekly, monthly, and yearly schedule of your life. If character has to do with consistency, how consistent is your life daily, weekly, monthly, and yearly life in relationship to God, yourself, and others? What needs to take place to see better fruit in your virtue and character?
6. Is your character as a Christian consistent with the message that you carry?

Meditation

A big moment in life, I often ponder is this: What will my wife, children, and those that really know me say about me at my funeral? What will they really think even if they don't say it? I'm not worried about the critics from afar, and I know that God will receive me with open arms and be proud, but what character did I really live? At the end of my story, what will my in-laws really think even if they never told me? What will my enemies really believe about my life even if they never let me know it? What will those that were most marked by my life, my wife and kids and my immediate team, really think? These are not bad or negative thoughts, and I know that I will never know this, but this is what I think about when I think about my own Christian character.

Character is not what we defend to others about our heart intentions. Character is not what we try to convince someone else they should have understood or perceived, but it is actually what people saw. In real life, heart motives aren't enough in humanity; heart motives are not enough in marriage or with family. Character and actions are what is real. Reality is what was, not what could have been. Reality is what was actually spoken, not what we desired to speak. Reality is what was seen, done, perceived, and understood by all and nothing less. At the end of the day, we do not get to give an apology for our lives, but others will. What will that look like for your life when you give account for every word, thought, and deed?

The Bible and Character

- "For I proclaim the name of the Lord; ascribe greatness to our God! The Rock! His work is perfect, for all His ways are just; a God of faithfulness without injustice, Righteous and upright is He" (Deuteronomy 32:3–4).
- "But I will not break off My lovingkindness from him, nor deal falsely in My faithfulness. My covenant I will not violate, nor will I alter the utterance of My lips. Once

I have sworn by My holiness; I will not lie to David"
(Psalm 89:33–35).

- "Either make the tree good and its fruit good, or make
the tree bad and its fruit bad; for the tree is known by its
fruit" (Matthew 12:33).

- "Woe to you, scribes and Pharisees, hypocrites! For you
tithe mint and dill and cumin, and have neglected the
weightier provisions of the law; justice and mercy and
faithfulness; but these are the things you should have
done without neglecting the others. You blind guides,
who strain out a gnat and swallow a camel! Woe to you,
scribes and Pharisee, hypocrites! For you clean the outside of the cup and of the dish, but inside they are full
of robbery and self-indulgence. You blind Pharisee, first
clean the inside of the cup and of the dish, so that outside
of it may become clean also" (Matthew 23:23–26).

- "And not only this, but we also exult in our tribulations,
knowing that tribulation brings about perseverance; and
perseverance, proven character; and proven character,
hope; and hope does not disappoint, because the love of
God has been poured out within our hearts through the
Holy Spirit who was given to us" (Romans 5:3–5).

- "Love is patient, love is kind and is not jealous; love
does not brag and is not arrogant, does not act unbe-
comingly; it does not seek its own, is not provoked, does
not take into account a wrong suffered, does not rejoice
in unrighteousness, but rejoices with the truth; bears all
things, believes all things, hopes all things, endures all
things. Love never fails" (1 Corinthians 13:4–8).

- "Now the deeds of the flesh are evident, which are:
immorality, impurity, sensuality idolatry, sorcery, enmi-
ties, strive, jealousy, outburst of anger, disputes, dissen-
sions, factions, envying, drunkenness, carousing, and
things like these, of which I forewarn you, just as I have
forewarned you, that those who practice such things will
not inherit the kingdom of God" (Galatians 5:19–21).

- "Now for this very reason also, applying all diligence, in your faith supply moral excellence, and in your moral excellence, knowledge, and in your knowledge, self-control, and in your self-control, perseverance, and in your perseverance, godliness, and in your godliness, brotherly kindness, and in your brotherly kindness, love. For if these qualities are yours and are increasing, they render you neither useless nor unfruitful in the true knowledge of our Lord Jesus Christ" (2 Peter 1:5–8).
- "Make sure that your character is free from the love of money, being content with what you have; for He Himself has said, "I will never desert you nor will I ever forsake you" (Hebrews 13:5).

CHAPTER 15

Individuality within Community

Inspired by my own life journey as a missionary in Mexico

Individuality—the quality or character of a particular person that distinguishes them from others of the same kind, making them different from others. Seen in character, identity, personality, and the reflection of being created in the image and likeness of God. The quality of being the only one of its kind and the ability to celebrate the uniqueness of each individual. The state or condition wherein someone or something is unlike anything else in comparison.

Community—a social unit with commonality in norms, needs, religion, values, customs, language, culture, or identity. When united, it creates an environment for durable relationships that extend beyond immediate genealogical ties or personal needs, creating a public spirit of shared communion, mutual benefit, and expansion of individual identity within a family, clan, tribe, and nation of human beings, all being created in the image and likeness of God.

Special Introduction

For me, the journey of discovering the truth about myself and others has been very challenging. For me, for many years, poetry was my outlet of expressing emotions. There was a poem that I wrote years ago, and I'd like to share it for my introduction to this chapter.

> A maze of ideas, a matrix of thoughts, the truth of a life lost but learned with great cost. A web of truth that spins away, still focused, caught, and flowing out, a fall of ideas. Men, nations, the philosophy well bought, each idea well thought and taught, but the foundation of truth has been shifted, shadowed, and blurred to a simple notion of life, my truth, my absolute, a past forsaken but your God is taken, just adapt.
> Don't think, don't wonder, don't plunder in heart, the law within is just an image of a lost bridge that has no connection. We look, we seek, a Greek a Jew; the ideas of a past once lost and taught, now re-bought and twisted, relived and shifted; no absolute, look around and listen, each sound, each vision, all chance, just one God, one quick view, a nice deep look; only you!
> A great fall, a gap, a broken spirit, a disease within, are we born that twisted? White or black, it was the WORD of the day, but look around and ask, whose foundation, nothing clear, a consistent gray.
> Yes, we can see it, all man has known it, the hate is not portrayed where we feel it, but we've lost control and can no longer seal it. We look away and point out, not me must be you, the consequences we shout and still foundation without, we're lurking and grasping with nothing to give, one to bring five but this finger alive, one, two three, a twisted circle, no end no beginning, we've adapted a world, taught, developed, and moving away, but nothing to show, who am I anyway?

Gay, I'm sorry, politically correct, a gender and choice, but look the effect; we ponder and plummet and continue to fall, my rights my truth, the faith of the youth, the leaders of life, the future of a nation, spirals going down, who needs pro-creation?

Matter, nothing more, I see my lost cousin, an ape, fish, snail, a bird in the air, one in all and from one…a cell, there, it comes from the core, no gender, no truth, who needs absolutes? A repented heart, not God to me, He's waited and watched, hoped and taught, a world of truth in existence, just lacking one thing…who am I? Not all based in a lie, the only thing that sees me; just one question, what right in my life?

I don't know you, can't owe you, can't give you a thing, YOU say YOU know me, and want me, and call me by name; wait, a glimpse of light, nothing left to achieve, I've fallen and shaken, not right being me; a train of thought just flowing, and moving so free, but where can I be without knowing just one thing, one small step, a change of heart, change the mind, my will just comes next, such a small part, but wait, who still feels vexed?

Identity in creation, the walk with my EESH. A Father and truth, this lie just can't be, repent and be saved, the light in the gray, what keeps me to stay, just see, it's me, my creator holds my identity…always waiting, watching, an open arm, extended, receiving, last chance, it's always been waiting and now I can see. It's perfect, undaunted, without blemish, a baptism gone under, but awake and I see…oh what can this be? My God and my Lord, it's my IDENTITY.

Always existing and predestined to pass, only lacking one part to make it come fast, one choice, one step, renouncing the me, how crazy it seems, this is ME, walking again, but wait, it's liberty. Absolute, black and white, it takes heart to bring fight; founded in truth, no lie, no pass by, no deep spiral, no broken truth but just clear, pure, me and YOU, intimacy of heart, nothing more and nothing less, it's the ABSOLUTE PART.

October 2007

* * * * *

As long as I can remember, I have felt partially at tension with both myself and the world around me. There was a side of me that has just wanted to be alone and do what I wanted while I watched, analyzed, and read the people around me from a safe distance. There was another side of me, however, that was constantly curious about people and enjoyed the company of others and desired to be close to them. From a young age, I felt trapped in this split reality. Was it better to be completely alone, in the safety and comfort of my own mind and thoughts, or to dare to draw near others, whose emotional needs, actions, and words seemed almost illogical and untouchable?

I had three close friends as a child: Ryan, Zach, and Austin. I even had a best friend in elementary school named Matthew for about a year, and somewhere between elementary school and high school, another Ryan from church came into my life, who to this day is a close friend. Within each of those friendships, we had some good memories, but I was always just a bit different from most of the people around me, and there was something about being alone that enticed me and which I actually preferred. Each of the people I met growing up had a "singular" lifestyle, hobbies or things to do, and I didn't fit into any of those categories. I liked animals, but I also enjoyed hunting. I liked team sports, but I also enjoyed skateboarding and snowboarding by myself. I owned and rode a motorcycle, but I was never really into motors and engines. I had fun being a guys' guy, but I also enjoyed music, art, and dance. There were benefits of being wired a bit different, but at the same time, each of my close friends chose a specific group of friends. Little by little, I felt like I didn't fit into their groups anymore and would struggle to keep close friends that I could be deep and honest with without hurting or offending them.

I always had friends, but never really large groups of close friends. I learned to have fun with everyone, but I was just as happy being at home with my family or to have my dad or sister as my best friend. Throughout my life, I've been most drawn to the strange people, the unapproachable people, the people whom others are intimidated by, and those that people seem to stay away from or even reject. I enjoyed the group that actually seemed to enjoy being alone and didn't follow social norms or just didn't seem to care like everyone else did around them. This is likely something that greatly influenced my life but also something that I never fully understood about myself until more recent years.

This principle of being unique, individualism within community, isn't discussed as much as others, but I feel this topic merits including when examining leadership development or discipleship. I am, I always have been, and I always will be just a little bit different than a lot of people around me. People that have known me for years still tell me that they are just trying to figure me out and understand me; I still feel the same about myself. I often hear, "I've known you for however many years, and I didn't know that or had no idea you felt that way or thought that way."

In 2004, when I first left my culture, my country, my family, and my language, I began a journey that I would have never expected. I wrote a blog a few years back in 2014 in an attempt to explain my process of being trapped between two different cultures, two different worlds, and two different realities, but words just couldn't fully explain my reality. In the beginning chapters of this book, I expressed my desire to have my story become His story, and a large part of my journey these last sixteen years has been learning to embrace my own identity that God has given me. A large part of that process has turned into me discovering who I really am and the way that God has created me. This has been a long journey, and I have a long way to go; but more and more, I'm finding myself confident in who I am and accepting the reality of who God created me to be, even when others aren't able to feel the same about me. God made me this way, and if I don't embrace and understand it, I will live without joy in my life and never be able to fully be used by Him.

Somewhere between our teenage years and late '20s, this acceptance must take place to live real life in community. For most people, this transition from adolescence comes after college, after having studied for a specific degree and then discovering years later that they don't really want to work in that field or what they thought was a passion was actually planted by someone else, and they don't even like it anymore. I love hearing young adults talk about how something they once hated is now what they enjoy most, or the things they said they would never do have now blossomed into their daily life and passion. It's the beautiful yet very difficult journey of embracing reality of identity and individuality.

A reason I enjoy Acts 9 so much is that it chronicles the story of a young man who must experience great conviction and understanding of what his true identity really is in God, despite everything that he had believed about his own past. He has received the Holy Spirit, which began to fully redefine being a Jew and the importance of the temple. He is a new creation living in the kingdom of God. He is willing to be the temple of the Holy Spirit and to serve the purposes of the Father while listening to and obeying Jesus as the resurrected King. Just to be who he was, a God fearer outside of the Temple, implies rejecting most of his past and also standing against most of the present and future where Jews didn't believe non-Jews could follow Jesus, the Jewish Messiah—and much less outside of the Temple laws. This was an incredible victory for a man like him, but it wasn't enough. If you continue the story, this man Ananias had no doubt he was talking to Jesus, no doubt about being in the kingdom and having the Spirit, and no doubt about the message of the Old Testament.

So what's the problem? He had a great doubt about the person whom Jesus wanted Him to interact with and serve with in community: Saul of Tarsus. God had just asked him to go and serve the one man that everyone knew was killing people like him, the one man that people like him didn't go to, didn't trust, and definitely didn't pray for healing. Not only was Jesus going to send him to Saul; He was actually going to tell him that Saul, the sworn enemy, was also now a part of the family and intimate community of believers in the Resurrected King!

For Ananias to accept his own individuality as a follower of Jesus, being a God fearer, is a miracle in itself. Now Jesus Himself asked Ananias to be united in community with a man who seemed impossible to unite with. He must go against all social norms, his own past story and conviction, all because his present reality as an individual and how he saw others was being defined by Jesus Himself! God didn't ask him to stop being who he was, but God didn't accept it as an excuse either.

Understanding the way that God has created us to be, to live in our uniqueness and to embrace that we don't need to follow social patterns (like what others like), or even value a lot of what others value is so key in this life and essential for any leader. Without a deep conviction of how unique we are as individuals, I don't think it's really possible to love others the way that God commands us to. Only when we accept how truly strange, different, and unique we are do we actually stop comparing ourselves to others and can begin to embrace our individual reality. Comparing is always about superior and inferior, better and worse, and hoping to be on the better side of the comparison. The challenge is that this doesn't really exist in humanity. There is no superior, better, or higher value; all humans are created in the image and likeness of God on earth. Absolutely no one truly thinks alike, values everything the same, has the same story, and has the same dreams. Understanding and embracing our unique identity is where we can finally begin to love others in the same way that Jesus does, especially when they aren't like us, have a different capacity, and many times are just difficult. But we can still find unity through diversity.

This journey through childhood, through adolescence, young adulthood, and beyond is hard. For those of us from the Western world, it seems to be much more complicated on the journey to understand our individuality within community. We tend to err on the side of "uniqueness" being defined by "what I feel or think" as opposed to "what I actually do or what others need." It's so ego-centric within our Western culture that there is little shift from childhood to adulthood like the rest of the Global South. We have created a unique developmental stage of extended adolescence that seems to expand into mid- to late-twenties or even thirties. This stage has become the stage of "finding myself." We value individuality so much, that we sacrifice family, community, and nation in the name of personal responsibility and freedom.

The majority world, on the other hand, has the opposite struggle. From a young age, the tribe and community are understood, but few people really get to discover individuality. The Global South goes from being a child to manhood or a child to womanhood at a young age, usually between twelve to fifteen years old. This identity defined by marriage, kids, and quickly learning the community aspect of real life leads to the extreme ideas within the Global South, leaving little to no concept of thinking or doing anything as an individual. There is a major strength and value of "us" but little understanding of the weight in "I" and *personal responsibility.*

We see two very distinct realities: there is complete dependence on others and "us," or there is a reaction in absolute emotional independence, lacking deep thought and action because all we see is "I need" or "I want." One side doesn't allow for independence from the community, and the other becomes an independence that is always changing and shifting, undefined and just a fractured emotional drift in postmodernism.

After coming from one reality for half of my life and then living another for the other half of my life, it has become clear that we need a wake-up moment like Ananias had. We must fully accept and grasp the message of the kingdom of heaven, the person of Jesus as the resurrected Christ, and obedience to the Father by the Holy Spirit—all without becoming a Jew externally—learning to live as an image bearer here on earth. Ananias found an identity that wasn't within the community of the Jews, of the Christians at that time, the Romans, the Greeks, the Herodians, or even the Barbarians. He was simply unique as a Son of God. That was a huge step to find and understand, but it wasn't enough. He had to see others in the same way. He had to see that what united him to the community of others was God Himself and, therefore, his own obedience to the faith. In the kingdom of God, we are not united in conformity or separation but rather in God Himself. Unity through diversity, self-acceptance, and sacrificial love.

For me, personally, I am not naturally an overly empathetic person toward others. I don't hide well in a crowd, being unseen and quiet where I'm not noticed. I am not in any way the person who can walk around without being noticed or having a hidden opinion, vision, or conviction. Sometimes I hate this part of myself! Sometimes I want to tape my mouth closed, to close my ears, and to hide under the table and act like I don't care about what is happening around me as I feel like life would be a lot easier to just not care or to have no opinion. It would be a lie, though, to act as if I didn't care because it's not true. I do care and have strong opinions about what I think and why. It's not usually an issue of self-control but rather an issue of deep conviction and desire to always see things grow and develop and to never lose hope or become stagnant. I can't pretend I don't have an opinion because I do. I can't pretend I have no idea about something because in the depths of my soul, I'm a student of history, and anything that I don't understand, I begin to investigate and study. I need answers for myself to survive my own mind, and there's no way to pretend it's not true. I don't have all the answers or know anything in totality, but I'm always reading multiple books at the same time. Every day I feel the need to search and discover something new, and when I hear an interesting question from someone else and I don't have the answer, I have to find it before I go to bed. Is this a curse or a blessing? When I'm alone, I love it; but when I'm with people, I hate it!

I can be my biggest self-critic but also my own greatest encourager. I seem to have no way to turn off my mind, to stop thinking, to stop dreaming, to stop planning, and to stop stepping out in faith while thinking through strategies to make it more successful. It's like having a hamster running one hundred miles per hour all the time in my mind, and what makes it worse is that I'm never happy with just the idea. I have to actually try to implement it and do it, to activate it and see the change become reality. Good or bad in the eyes of others or my own, God made me this way. He designed me and called me by name, and He wants to use me the way I am and not the way that someone else is or wants me to be. This isn't just true for me but also for every individual around me; and within our distinct individuality, I'm learning that I can still find community.

So how do we discover our independent identity beyond desires and emotions or an external community? We must start with God. We must start with the renewing of our minds. We must start with a deep understanding of biblical truth so that the Holy Spirit has something to work with within us. We have to embrace the truth of our individuality in identity while learning to honor those that aren't like us. We can also do some practical things. I'm going to recommend a few tests for you to take to begin to study some of what makes you unique.

- Meyers Briggs (I was a strong INTJ and now have almost developed into an ENTJ after sixteen years of ministry in Latin America.)
- Strength Finders (I am Command, Strategic, Context, Activator, Ideation as my top five.)
- DISC Test (I am a strong D [68 percent] followed by I [15 percent].)
- Enneagram (I am an 8.)
- Spiritual Gifts Test (Teacher, Exhorter, Leader, Giving, Evangelist as my strongest five.)
- Sacred Pathways Test (Intellectual, Naturalist, Ascetic are my highest three.)

Today there are so many creative and unique ways to understand more about the way you are created to be. These tests are by no means absolute, but they can be useful in helping you understand some of the ways you think and act as an individual and how to fit into the greater community of others. I am proud to say that it's true about me most of the time in any of these categories that I have discovered because God has made me this way. However, none of these are boxes that I can put myself into. There are attics and basements, and our greatest strengths can be our biggest weaknesses. Only when we are submitted to God in our thoughts and deeds can our thoughts and actions really reflect what He has created us to be.

Again, for me, discovering my individuality in each of these areas has brought great freedom. For most of my life, I have thought I must be crazy because I'm different than most people around me. I don't see what others see, feel what others feel, or see the world like most of the people around me. I'm not crazy, though. I'm just different and have my own individuality. Some of these tests were like staring into a mirror and finally saying, *Yes*, I understand who I am, I agree, and it makes sense. There are strengths and weakness involved in each area of my individuality, but I've been learning to embrace what is naturally good and strong and to celebrate it. It has made life a lot easier to embrace my own reality as an individual. It's also helped me create my community of people who are different from me, who can offset my weaknesses and also support my strengths. It's helped me to find leaders that can be successful with someone like me rather than fail.

One day, the founder of Youth with a Mission International, Loren Cunnigham, said to me, "You must have Command as your top strength!" I was caught off guard and replied with, "Yes, and some people like to actually prefer to call it domineering." He didn't laugh but just looked into my eyes and said, "So do I. Surround yourself with leaders just as strong as you or even stronger to keep you accountable. And just keep running, don't stop running."

I think that he was the first person to so quickly pick up something about me that can make others very uncomfortable and to encourage me to just be who I am. In one quick phrase, he both fully affirmed a part of my individuality and exhorted me on what type of community I needed to be successful within my individuality. He was the first person to address both my role as an individual and my future team with such clarity, and it was so good for me to hear! Who I am is good, but it's not enough, it's not complete, it needs a community.

Once you know who you are, you begin to also see what you're not. You can begin to see why you need others, why your perspective isn't always right, and why you are a very important piece of the puzzle but why you are incomplete without the other pieces. It starts with God. He helps us see the truth about ourselves. In this process, His heart within us should begin to help us see others through His eyes and not our own. In the same way He helps us to accept our own individuality, He should create within us a heart to do the same with others around us.

To now fit into the bigger puzzle, you need to ask for God's heart. You need to have empathy. Empathy is not agreeing or having experienced the same thing as others, but it is accepting that what has happened to someone else and what they think and feel is relevant and 100 percent true for that person in that particular moment. What people feel is always legitimate; even if it isn't true, it's true for them in that moment, so we must have some empathy. It doesn't mean it aligns with God's truth. If we aren't careful, though, it is very possible to change and align with God's truth externally and to not align with what you have lived or experienced up to this moment in your life internally—to create a fracture in identity and to lose individuality.

Transformation happens at an individual level, but love, mercy, and compassion occur at a community level. Repentance and renewing of the mind happens first from the secrets of the heart and mind revealed by the Holy Spirit, but unity comes with accepting that the journey for others won't look like your own. We are united around the Godhead, not around ourselves—unity through diversity. As iron sharpens iron, so one man strengthens another.

This is necessary for all sons and daughters of God. Different cultures, different families, and different individuals have different lies that must be dealt with on a heart level, repented of, and truth then applied. Marriage and the family becomes the fruits of this reality, and leadership and discipleship is the essence of this reality. I am first a son of God being renewed by His Spirit and Truth as I obey and follow Jesus here on earth. I am also a husband, but that never takes away my responsibility of obedience in being a son of God who must give account for what my wife feels, thinks, and understands throughout our marriage with me. I am a father of three, but my relationship with my kids is independent of my relationship with

God and with my wife. My wife's relationship with my kids can't be imputed to me just like Jesus's relationship with the Father can't be imputed to me. What I say, what I do, and how I respond is what will define that relationship. The burden is on me as a husband and not my wife in our marriage as I obey God. It is on me as a father and not on my kids as I obey God, and it is on me as a leader and not on those that have chosen to walk with me as I obey God. I am responsible to them, not for them. I am responsible for myself, in my obedience first to God in all relationships.

Learn to embrace what God has to say about you. God desires with all of His heart that you would have the mind of Christ and to fully embrace your individuality. He desires that you would repent and begin to think like He thinks. This repentance should extend outward, and you should begin to do what He does, to dream what He dreams, and to desire what He desires. He was responsible to show His love even when you didn't want it. Every time you have rejected Him, He still reacted in confidence and mercy. He continues to love and extend His hand toward you even when you don't deserve it because He is good, and He has hope in who He created you to be.

Let God's story become your story. Let the history of mankind become *His story* in your life. God doesn't have grandchildren; He only has sons and daughters. Learn to be a son or daughter and learn to partner with Him to heal the nations. Learn to heal a broken world and an orphan generation that needs a real story, not a fake gospel story—a story that is so real that you have actually become a living letter of the Good News.

The King is alive! He is Jesus, He is King! His Kingdom has come, and I am submitting to that kingdom now—for Jesus, by Jesus, and through Jesus. He gave everything so I can be free. Begin to live free! Begin to accept the truth beyond what you feel in a postmodern culture where absolutes no longer exist. Don't get lost in your individuality but don't hide within a community. Embrace what makes you unique, understand who God created you to be, and then learn to glorify Him within an incredible community of people that are nothing like you.

Learn to live in redemption in both individuality and community. Be redeemed and learn to redeem those who are around you, even when they are nothing like you. A word I love to meditate upon is *theomorphis*. *Theo* means "God," and *morphis* means "to transform." Be transformed into the image and likeness of God as a human. Learn to love God with all your heart, all your soul, all your strength, and all your mind.

Some of these ideas have been my biggest challenges throughout the years. I have to daily find my identity in Christ and let what He says define me and be enough. I have to give up the right to please others and meet their expectations from me but strive to meet God's expectations of me, even when others don't like it. For me, to accept my calling in ministry and leadership is also to recognize my need to surround myself with many other strong leaders. I don't do it alone, and community is the fruit of my need of other image bearers to fulfill the task of God, multiplying beauty, order, and abundance throughout the world. I've had to grow greatly in self-control, recognizing that I can't give up any of my responsibilities; and in my biggest weaknesses and personal need, only God can fill me. Extended times of fasting and prayer, meditation and worship, and seeking out good counsel keeps my emotions in check and limits me from making decisions based on the fear of what others might think and want, living in the fear of the Lord and not the fear of man.

For me, to be an individual means that I have to daily accept that being different is good. My capacity, calling, gifts and talents, relationships, and ministries shouldn't be compared to anyone else's. I must give account to God for everything He has given me. I must be a good steward, and therefore, it's okay to say no to others if it means saying yes to Him. It's okay to not meet others' expectations if I am meeting His. No one else can fill me, but I can't be full of His Spirit and ignore others. No team or ministry can give me identity, but it's not possible to fully love Jesus and work alone independent of a community. It might not be easy, but in most cases, my desert has become my promised land, and I've come to feel comfortable in my own skin. I can do my best to help others understand me, but at the same time, I must embrace what God has called me to be and not only accept it but fully develop it and multiply it for the glory of God in the nations.

As I have been learning to understand who God has called me to be, I've had to redefine my life vision, calling, and purpose. One day as I was praying for guidance on what God wanted of me, he brought me to the book of Ezekiel. As I read Ezekiel 2 and 3, I felt like God began to speak straight to my heart:

> And He said to me, "Son of man (Daniel), stand on your feet, and I will speak to you." Then the Spirit entered me when He spoke to me, and set me on my feet; and I heard Him who spoke to me. And He said to me: "Son of man (Daniel), I am sending you to the children of Israel (the church and Christian leaders), to a rebellious nation that has rebelled against Me; they and their fathers have transgressed against Me to this very day. For they are impudent and stubborn children. I am sending you to them, and you shall say to them, 'Thus says the Lord God.' As for them, whether they hear or whether they refuse—for they are a rebellious house—yet they will know that a prophet has been among them.
>
> "And you, son of man, do not be afraid of them nor be afraid of their words, though briers and thorns are with you and you dwell among scorpions; do not be afraid of their words or dismayed by their looks, though they are a rebellious house. You shall speak My words to them, whether they hear or whether they refuse, for they are rebellious. But you, son of man, hear what I say to you. Do not be rebellious like that rebellious house; open your mouth and eat what I give you."
>
> Now when I looked, there was a hand stretched out to me; and behold, a scroll of a

book was in it. Then He spread it before me; and there was writing on the inside and on the outside, and written on it were lamentations and mourning and woe.

Moreover, He said to me, "Son of man (Daniel), eat what you find; eat this scroll (Bible, Word of God), and go, speak to the house of Israel." So I opened my mouth, and He caused me to eat that scroll.

And He said to me, "Son of man (Daniel), feed your belly, and fill your stomach with this scroll that I give you." So I ate, and it was in my mouth like honey in sweetness.

Then He said to me: "Son of man (Daniel), go to the house of Israel and speak with My words to them. For you are not sent to a people of unfamiliar speech and of hard language, but to the house of Israel, not to many people of unfamiliar speech and of hard language, whose words you cannot understand. Surely, had I sent you to them, they would have listened to you. But the house of Israel will not listen to you, because they will not listen to Me; for all the house of Israel are impudent and hard-hearted. Behold, I have made your face strong against their faces, and your forehead strong against their foreheads. Like adamant stone, harder than flint, I have made your forehead; do not be afraid of them, nor be dismayed at their looks, though they are a rebellious house."

Moreover, He said to me: "Son of man, receive into your heart all My words that I speak to you, and hear with your ears. And go, get to the captives, to the children of your people, and speak to them and tell them, 'Thus says the Lord God,' whether they hear, or whether they refuse."

Then the Spirit lifted me up, and I heard behind me a great thunderous voice: "Blessed is the glory of the Lord from His place!" I also heard the noise of the wings of the living creatures that touched one another, and the noise of the wheels beside them, and a great thunderous noise. So the Spirit lifted me up and took me away, and I went in bitterness, in the heat of my spirit; but the hand of the Lord was strong upon me. Then I came to the captives at Tel Abib, who dwelt by the River Chebar; and I sat where they sat, and remained there astonished among them seven days.

Now it came to pass at the end of seven days that the word of the Lord came to me, saying, "Son of man, I have made you a watchman for the house of Israel; therefore hear a word from My mouth, and give them warning from Me: When I say to the wicked, 'You shall surely die,' and you give him no warning, nor speak to warn the wicked from his wicked way, to save his life, that same wicked man shall die in his iniquity; but his blood I will require at your hand. Yet, if you warn the wicked, and he does not turn from his wickedness, nor from his wicked way, he shall die in his iniquity; but you have delivered your soul.

"Again, when a righteous man turns from his righteousness and commits iniquity, and I lay a stumbling block before him, he shall die; because you did not give him warning, he shall die in his sin, and his righteousness which he has done shall not be remembered; but his blood I will require at your hand. Nevertheless, if you warn the righteous man that the righteous should not sin, and he does not sin, he shall surely live because he took warning; also you will have delivered your soul."

Then the hand of the Lord was upon me there, and He said to me, "Arise, go out into the plain, and there I shall talk with you."

So I arose and went out into the plain, and behold, the glory of the Lord stood there, like the glory which I saw by the River Chebar; and I fell on my face. Then the Spirit entered me and set me on my feet, and spoke with me and said to me: "Go, shut yourself inside your house. And you, O son of man, surely they will put ropes on you and bind you with them, so that you cannot go out among them. I will make your tongue cling to the roof of your mouth, so that you shall be mute and not be one to rebuke them, for they are a rebellious house. But when I speak with you, I will open your mouth, and you shall say to them, 'Thus says the Lord God.' He who hears, let him hear; and he who refuses, let him refuse; for they are a rebellious house."

God used these two chapters to shape the call of my life as a teacher and as a student of the Bible to affirm my personality and strong character, and with a call to have influence within the spheres of church and government, with raw and honest truth. He began to show me that my region was primarily the Americas: English, Spanish, and Portuguese speakers. Just like Ezekiel, I was called to a specific community of people, and my personality and individual reality is perfect for the calling that God has placed on my life. As He clarified more and more my personality as a part of His design, I've been able to understand more of my life calling. This has allowed me to listen to Him and begin to let Him define and speak clearly about my marriage and family calling as well.

General purpose. To be a marriage and family that models God's love and transformation through our love for each other and relationship with

Him. To see individuals, communities, and nations transformed through holistic development as models for multiplication.

Vision. Be a marriage and family that reflects Christ's relationship with the church, having established long-term missionary families and individuals throughout Mexico and overseas to the nations.

Mission. Serve, educate, and bestow.

God has been showing me more the way He has created me to interact with others has a divine purpose and calling. In both my strengths and weaknesses, He is actively working and moving in my life. My role is to believe what He says and embrace it, even when my personal insecurities or criticism by others don't want to. In embracing my own individuality, I've been challenged that I must also embrace anyone that He calls to be a part of my community and team, finding the way to be successful together in our greater strengths and allowing them to offset my weaknesses. I need them, and they need me as well. I know that I have much to learn, to grow, and to continue to mature and change, but I'm blessed beyond words to see how my story, year by year, really has become more like *His* story.

Reflection

1. How do you live as an individual within community?
2. Who are you as an individual? What makes you unique? What is unique about the way you think and what you do? What do those results from the above tests teach you about yourself?
3. What community do you have to share those results with? Whom would you like to know and understand more on an individual level about others and what makes them unique? What will you do to make that happen?

4. What needs to take place in your life for your story to become His story?

5. Take some time to meditate and ask God, "What are some goals or dreams that you have in the next two, five, ten, fifteen, or twenty years?" If you were to write a book about some of your own victories in the years to come, where would you be, and what could you do?

6. What are some action steps that you need to do to begin to become the person that God is saying He sees in you today?

Meditation

I began this book over five years ago, with a lot of fear that it would be a total failure and rejected, that I would be laughed at, or even have it outright rejected for publishing. Five years later, I still have some of those same thoughts. I made a choice to be open and honest, to tell my story, to try to give Him glory in the best of my ability. I'm believing Him for what He has shown me and promised me in my calling to be a writer and author among other things I have been called to do. I am currently beginning my second book at this time: *Extra-Ordinary Church: "what on earth have I gotten myself into?"*. I really hope it doesn't take me another five years, but even if it does, it's okay. To hear and obey, and *never, ever, give up* should mark each and every one of us as children of God.

I am thirty-four years old, and there is nothing special that has equipped me to write this book or do what I do in life. I have no formal college education or degree. I have a degree within the University of the Nations, but I have never formally filled out the paperwork to receive my diploma. I love God with all of my heart, and I desire to help be an answer to this world more than being another problem or burden. I desire to see people's lives change. Sixteen years ago, I would have told you that you were crazy if you told me that at thirty-four years old, I would be married with three kids, finishing a book, having a ministry, traveling and teaching, and calling Spanish my primary language during the day as I build a life in a country not of my own while also being a part of seeing the Bible being translated into every indigenous language in Mexico.

Where will I be in another sixteen years? What will I be doing? Whom will I be with, and what will my community look like? I have no idea, but my desire is that if I told the story at fifty years old, it would be evident that it's God's story within me; that I'm changing the world through the day-to-day reality, and it's no longer I who live but Christ who lives in me. I can't imagine learning another language, living in a different country, starting another ministry, or even having more kids, but I know what God desires out of my life is far greater, far deeper, and just so much more that His grace and love will keep Him from scaring me away from His story by speaking too much too soon! One step at a time, one step of faith to live in obedience to the faith for all nations.

May future generations look back on my day-to-day life and see the *extraordinary*. May they remember His written letter within my life. May those that surround us tell His story over our own, and may He be glorified through whatever we do or don't do for His glory. My dream would be that this book has inspired you to take one step further, one step deeper, and make one more radical choice today that will transform everything for tomorrow for you and everyone around you. You will never be someone tomorrow that you don't decide to actively become today. Don't wait. Become the *extraordinary* and turn the world upside down!

The Bible and Individuality within Community

> Then God said, "Let Us make man in Our image, according to Our likeness; and let them rule over the fish of the sea and over the birds of the sky and over the cattle and over all the earth, and over every creeping thing that creeps on the earth." God created man in His own image, in the image of God He created him; male and female He created them. (Genesis 1:26–27)

Now there was a disciple at Damascus named Ananias; and the Lord said to him in a vision, "Ananias." And he said, "Here I am, Lord." And the Lord said to him, "Get up and go to the street call Straight, and inquire at the house of Judas for a man from Tarsus named Saul, for he is praying, and he has seen in a vision a man named Ananias come in and lay his hands on him, so that he might regain his sight." But Ananias answered, "Lord, I have heard from many about this man, how much harm he did to Your saints at Jerusalem; and here he has authority from the chief priests to bind all who call on Your name." But the Lord said to him, "Go, for he is a chosen instrument of Mine, to bear My name before the Gentiles and kings and sons of Israel; for I will show him how much he must suffer for My name's sake." So Ananias departed and entered the house, and after laying his hands on him said, Brother Saul, the Lord Jesus, who appeared to you on the road by which you were coming, has sent me so that you may regain your sight and be filled with the Holy Spirit." And immediately there fell from his eyes something like scales, and he regained his sight, and he got up and was baptized; and he took food and was strengthened. (Acts 9:10–19)

As a result, we are no longer to be children, tossed here and there by waves and carried about by every wind of doctrine, by the trickery of men, by craftiness in deceitful scheming; but speaking truth in love, we are to grow up in all aspects into Him who is the head, even Christ, from who the whole body, being fitted and held together by what every joint supplies, according to the proper working of each individual part, causes the growth of the body for the building up of itself in love. (Ephesians 4:14–16)

ABOUT THE AUTHOR

Daniel, born in the mountains of Colorado, and having lived the last sixteen years of his life internationally, has a passion for discipleship and teaching whenever and wherever possible. Aside from traveling and teaching in different ministries, churches, and organizations, Daniel serves as a part of the Global Eldership Team for Bible Education and Leadership Training (BELT) representing the non-English-speaking Americas. He is a part of the Discipleship Training School Resources Team for Mexico and Central America, the Bible school for the Nations Regional Team, and serves with other responsibilities both within YWAM and outside of YWAM.

Daniel is a member of the Evangelical State Alliance for pastors and leaders of Michoacán and has a heart for seeing individuals transformed by both the spoken and written Word of God. His heart of leadership development and discipleship has opened doors to minister in many different nations; and together with his wife, Katie, and three children—Caleb, Abigael, and Ezekiel—they are currently the founding leaders of YWAM Morelia, Mexico, an international and interdenominational missions movement.

Daniel and Katie often speak of family as the first passion and ministry but love to invest in those around them as well. Whether it's putting a Bible in every home in Mexico, pushing forth Bible translation for every people group in Mexico, equipping and training other leaders, or just teaching and preaching, Daniel's heart for truth and radical transformation is evident in all that he does. This has morphed from traveling and teaching to daily devotionals and online resources through extraordinary training, to conferences, and now writing.

CPSIA information can be obtained
at www.ICGtesting.com
Printed in the USA
LVHW040459220721
693352LV00001B/1

9 781098 040475